An Outline History of Western Music

Ninth Edition

An Outline History of Western Music
Ninth Edition

Milo Wold
Linfield College, Emeritus

Gary Martin
University of Oregon

James Miller
University of Oregon

Edmund Cykler

WCB
McGraw-Hill

Boston, Massachusetts   Burr Ridge, Illinois   Dubuque, Iowa
Madison, Wisconsin   New York, New York   San Francisco, California   St. Louis, Missouri

McGraw-Hill

*A Division of The **McGraw·Hill** Companies*

OUTLINE HISTORY OF WESTERN MUSIC

Recycled/acid free paper

This book is printed on recycled, acid-free paper containing 10% postconsumer waste.

 4 5 6 7 8 9 0 DOC/DOC 8 7 6 5 4 3 2

ISBN 0–697–34056–2

Publisher: *Phil Butcher*
Sponsoring editor: *Chris Freitag*
Project manager: *Marilyn Rothenberger*
Production supervisor: *Laura Fuller*
Designer: *Mary Christianson*
Compositor: *Shepherd, Inc.*
Typeface: *Times Roman*
Printer: *R.R. Donnelley & Sons Company, Crawfordsville, IN*
Cover design by Lesiak/Crampton Design, Inc.
Cover image © Peter Harholdt/SuperStock

Library of Congress Catalog No. 96–79545

http://www.mhcollege.com

Contents

List of Illustrations

List of Figures

Preface

Narrative music histories are often long, scholarly works containing detailed accounts of Western musical development. The authors think that there is a need for a succinct account that will provide students and lay readers with an introduction to the history of Western music. This book is a brief overview of the development of Western music that will help students gain a clear understanding of the evolution of musical styles.

Because chapter divisions are arbitrary, some composers whose careers overlap style periods are discussed in more than one chapter. For example, twentieth-century composers may be discussed in chapter 8: Early Twentieth Century, and chapter 9: Music Since World War II.

A chronology of historical events relating to music and composers has been expanded in this edition. Frequent references are made to musical scores in current anthologies and corollary recordings. Because performers in recent years have become increasingly important as an influence in compositional style, some of the more prominent performers are now included in chapters 8, 9, and 10. Chapter 10, on popular music, has also been expanded and updated.

The authors appreciate the suggestions for changes offered by users of previous editions of this book. We extend special thanks to our colleague, Dr. Stephen Valdez, and to the readers of the manuscript, for their generous help. The reviewers include:

Michael J. Budds
University of Missouri

JoAn Kunselman
California State University, Los Angeles

Robert Prowse
University of North Alabama

None of these people are accountable for errors in the book. We hope our decisions regarding what to include and exclude accurately represent music in history.

Introduction

An Outline History of Western Music has been planned and organized to be used in a variety of ways.

1. It can be used as a textbook in music history, along with collateral readings in the many authoritative, specialized studies that are readily available to students. In this manner it will serve as a practical source from which students can expand their studies to include the vast amount of material that has been edited and published in recent years.
2. It is designed to be used as a source for the review of music history. Its format is based on a consistent outline among the chapters. Students can utilize its plan and material to focus attention on the most important musical developments and forms.
3. The present edition will prove valuable to students who wish to embark on a study of the literature and history of music without the guidance of an instructor. Its information on scores, recordings, and collateral readings can be a guide to further reading and to a selected list of musical examples that will serve as a basis for understanding musical styles.

It is the authors' experience that the best source material for teaching music history is the music itself. Consequently, the book is designed as a guide to musical examples that illustrate the historical developments relating to music. To facilitate the study of the music of the first five chapters, the authors have included in appendix 2 references to recorded examples of music and their scores contained in *The Development of Western Music: An Anthology,* 3rd ed., by K Marie Stolba, *The European Musical Heritage: 800–1750,* by Sarah Fuller, and the *Norton Anthology of Western Music,* edited by Claude Palisca. References to these recorded examples are included in the text as: (Ex. 1.1), and so forth. This facilitates the use of actual music as source material. In chapter 6 and thereafter, because of their greater availability, specific scores and recordings are not identified. Other music that the instructor might suggest, or the student might seek out, will serve to broaden the student's acquaintance with forms and styles.

In many periods of history, the names of composers were translated into various languages. The authors have followed the preferred spellings of *Baker's*

Biographical Dictionary of Musicians, 8th ed., which is the most common desk reference source for English speaking scholars. It is recognized that this is not always in agreement with the spelling in *The New Grove Dictionary of Music and Musicians.* Most often, the titles of compositions are given in the original language, and English titles are often included in cases where they have become a part of our common musical vocabulary.

The authors have avoided the temptation to divide music history into a series of short, specialized periods. Rather, the generally accepted historical periods and their dates (Medieval, Renaissance, Baroque, and so forth) are specified. Although the music of every composer is unique in specific details, and the earliest music in a style period differs from the later music in the same period, it is the opinion of the authors that a consistent stylistic pattern is often identifiable throughout such a style period. For example, the principal characteristics, patronage, function, performance practice, and musical style in the Renaissance are fairly uniform.

In the chronologies at the beginning of each chapter, musically significant entries are presented in italics. Other entries are presented in regular typeface.

The authors analyze each major period of music history with respect to important movements that influenced the patronage and function of music, musical devices, forms, and composers. No claim is made to exhaustiveness of the categories or of the details in each category. Only those facts that the authors believe to be pertinent to an understanding of the development of music have been included. No doubt teachers and others who use this book will wish to supplement it with additional material.

The following is a brief survey of the plan of each chapter. The authors have attempted to avoid repeating information among the various subdivisions within the chapters. For instance, if a work is discussed in the section titled "Music for Instruments," it will usually not be repeated in the discussion of composers.

I. SOCIOCULTURAL INFLUENCES ON MUSIC

This section includes a discussion of important trends and movements in such areas as religion, economics, government, and social and cultural life that seem to have a bearing on the patronage, types, and styles of music. Because such influences on music are perceived subjectively, only generalizations as to their relationships can be suggested.

II. FUNCTION OF MUSIC

Because composers usually write with a purpose in mind, and because various cultural conditions call for different types of music, the functions of music in a historical period are significant. Moreover, the economic conditions under which a composer lives are partially determined by the demand for, and support of, music with a specific function. Function has a great deal to do with the style and expressiveness of music.

III. STYLE AND PERFORMANCE PRACTICE

Seven fundamental features of music have been identified, each of which is examined for its general stylistic qualities, as are any special devices or techniques that are prominent in the music itself. The features treated in this book are:

1. Formal Organization
2. Melody
3. Rhythm
4. Harmony
5. Texture
6. Instrumentation and Tonc Color
7. Performance Practice

IV. MUSIC FOR VOICES

Each important vocal form is defined, and the general characteristics of its musical substance are commented upon. In addition, specific examples that are representative of the form are suggested. In the case of more important forms, more than one example is given. The instructor or student may substitute or use additional examples as further illustrations. It is realized that no one form can be fully represented by one or two examples.

V. MUSIC FOR INSTRUMENTS

The same approach applies to instrumental forms as in IV. Music for Voices.

VI. COMPOSERS

Composers of major importance are discussed briefly under this heading. They have been chosen for the quality of their works, as well as for their innovations and influence. Biographies of these composers are presented in chronological order according to their dates of birth. An effort has been made to include musicians of quality who may have heretofore been excluded from the mainstream because of gender or race. Selected important works, scores, and recordings are mentioned. From the Classic period on, specific scores and recordings are omitted due to the numerous editions and recordings from which to choose.

These composers are presented in a chronological list by national origin, but without discussion. The authors are aware that this classification is arbitrary, and that it is often only an opinion that places them in one or the other list.

VII. HISTORIANS, THEORISTS, AND MANUSCRIPT SOURCES

Throughout history, writers have provided illuminating accounts of the musical environments of their times. These accounts are important sources for understanding musical styles. With few exceptions, only those writers whose works serve these purposes have been included. Title, place, and date of publication information is given. In addition, a brief statement regarding the contents of the writings is made where pertinent.

Especially in the earlier periods, the only sources for music itself are collections of manuscripts, usually preserved in monasteries or universities. These are of great value to scholars. For this reason, manuscripts are identified in chapters up to and including the Renaissance. Music treatises and printed books dealing with music theory and music history are cited thereafter.

An Outline History of Western Music

Ninth Edition

Chinese Musicians: a wall painting from the caves of Tung-chuan in the province of Kan-su from the time of the Tang dynasty (618–907). Pictured above are a variety of Chinese instruments. No notation or instruments of this period remain today, but the picture reveals a high degree of instrumental development.

1

❧

Ancient Precursors
of Western Music

I. SOCIOCULTURAL INFLUENCES ON MUSIC

Knowledge of ancient music is at best sketchy. In ancient times the preservation
of music depended on oral tradition as the predominant means of transmitting
music among generations. Modern scholars are able to reconstruct accurately but
a few melodic fragments of music composed prior to the Romanesque period.
Music among all peoples existed principally as a form of free improvisation.
Written notation of a consistent form was only developed in the Middle Ages.

Several modern sources provide insight into the nature of ancient music.
First, the study of musical practices of twentieth-century traditional groups,
such as the various African, North and South American Indian, and Oceanic
tribes, allows scholars to reconstruct in part the music of early civilizations.
Second, insight may be gained by studying the musical practices of ancient
civilizations whose cultural institutions are in some measure still in existence

today, such as those of China, India, Indonesia, and Japan. Other sources of study for understanding ancient music include visual representations of instruments, fragments of notation, writings about music, and the few examples of ancient instruments still intact. Such materials have been used to study music of the Mediterranean peoples—Egyptians, Hebrews, and Greeks.

During the twentieth century there has been a surge of interest in the musical expressions of folk and non-Western cultures. The influence of this music on popular and classical music of Europe and America was apparent already in the nineteenth century, but it has become more pronounced since 1950. However, much indigenous music that is heard today has been influenced by the European tradition, especially through the pervasive presence of radio, recordings, cinema, and television. Some cultures have preserved the purity of their folk music despite the widespread influence of the European musical tradition. Performances of such music have acquainted people of the twentieth century with rhythms, melodic systems, and timbres generally unfamiliar to Western art music.

It seems clear that few cultures prior to that of modern western Europe used music as a purely independent art form. Music as an expressive medium is, however, as old as humanity. Music, like the pictorial and plastic expressions of cave paintings, rock carvings, sculptures, ceramics, and painting, was closely associated with the rites of the community as well as with the emotional expressions of individuals. Most references to music, whether written or pictorial, lead to the conclusion that its practice, including the kind of music that was permissible, its manner of presentation, and the instruments employed, was determined by the dominant religion. This did not exclude, however, widespread use of music for secular purposes.

Instrumental music was a part of the temple services of the ancient Hebrews, with professional musicians in charge. Scriptural passages from the Old Testament were chanted. There are indications that antiphonal singing, as well as sung responses by congregations, were common. These practices, as well as hymn singing, were unquestionably of great influence on the early Christians and the role of music in their religious services, where chant played the dominant musical role for more than a thousand years.

Geography often influenced musical practice. Geographic location vitally affected occupational choices and habits, and occupations in turn have influenced folk music as well as classical music of all peoples. Factors of economics, natural resources, and technology have influenced the creation of musical instruments and consequently other musical developments as well. Such influences are found in the music of all early cultures.

The Greek doctrine of *ethos* ascribed ethical values to their music, depending on the tonal relationships within the scales of the modes on which the melodies were built. Melodies in one mode were considered effeminate, others damaging to the morals of youth, and yet others a stimulus to warlike action. Plato, in his *Republic,* assigned a vital role to the type of music that could be used in education.

Picture on a Greek urn of a man playing the lyra, a simple form of a harplike string instrument
of the very early Greeks. The amphora, or Greek wine jar, served as a medium for painting
among the ancient Greeks, and remains of these artifacts record many aspects of Greek life,
among them musical instruments and performance. The lyra had a sound box usually made of a
tortoise shell, and the strings were struck with a plectrum, which is depicted here in the right
hand of the performer. (The Metropolitan Museum of Art, Rogers Fund, 1922)

II. FUNCTION OF MUSIC

In traditional societies, music and ritual were closely connected. Repetitious
incantations and instrumental rhythms commonly accompanied religious rites
and festivals, often achieving a hypnotic or magical character. In ancient civi-
lized societies too, music was mainly associated with religious rituals.

An outgrowth of the combination of music and religious ritual was the musical drama and incidental music in spoken drama. The musical dramas of the Chinese represent a highly developed relationship between music and dramatic presentation. In Greece, music played an important role in the performance of the dramatic works of the classic theater. Unfortunately, there is little or no knowledge of the nature of the music or its precise use.

From paintings, reliefs, and the writings of ancient peoples it also is apparent that secular music existed. Several kinds of secular music, including folk song and dance, were used for festive occasions. Not surprisingly, songs about human experiences such as love and work flourished.

III. STYLE AND PERFORMANCE PRACTICE

In ancient cultures, music was the servant of religious, ritualistic, and festive events that dictated its melodic and rhythmic character. These events also influenced musical structure and the choice of instrumental and vocal timbres. A major difference among music of early Eastern cultures, native peoples, and early western-European musical tradition was the tendency for Eastern musicians to express themselves in a seemingly unending, repetitive, and rhapsodical manner. In contrast, Western composers shaped their music in more clear and formal structures. The repetitive quality of Eastern music was a result of the desire to lend hypnotic expression to their magical and religious rites.

Formal Organization

Generally speaking, ancient music was based on melodic or rhythmic patterns that constituted a point of departure for the performer, who improvised rather freely. The formal organization was the outcome of repetition and rhapsodic variation.

Melody

Melody and rhythm were the two dominant elements of ancient music. Melody had a seemingly unending character, distinguishing it from the melodic expression of Western music. It consisted of spun-out variations in decorative arabesques, trills, turns, and florid scale passages, and was often based on traditional fragments or patterns. As far as can be determined, most non-Western societies have constructed these melodic patterns on a selection of five tones within the octave, a system of melodic construction known as pentatonic. Much of the music of present-day Oriental cultures is built on such a five-tone division of the octave, closely resembling the relationships commonly represented by the first, second, third, fifth, and sixth tones of the modern major scale. Many Oriental systems divided pentatonic scales into very small intervals representing one-fourth, one-eighth, and even one-sixteenth of a modern whole step. In some Indian cultures the octave is divided into as many as twenty-two intervals.

Greek writings demonstrate a vast knowledge of music theory, including the twelve tones of the octave that constitute the modern chromatic scale. The system was derived from arithmetic computations that determined proportional divisions of the string to produce related pitches on the monochord, a rudimentary single-stringed instrument introduced in the fifth century B.C. Pythagoras is credited not only with the instrument's invention, but with the harmonic theory that bears his name.

Their melodies were based on a system of tetrachords that, when performed in sequence, resulted in an octave scale of seven tones similar to those in the modern major scale. Since each of the seven tones might be used as the fundamental tone, a series of seven different modal scales was possible for the construction of a melody. These were the scales or modes to which the Greeks ascribed ethical values.

Rhythm

The second important element of non-Western music was rhythm. In many respects, rhythmic patterns among early, as well as developed groups, achieved a complexity that Western civilization did not cultivate until the present century. Rhythm in music includes quantitative—long and short—beats, as well as qualitative—strong and weak—beats. Rhythmic patterns of seven, ten, and fourteen, for example, are common, especially in India.

Among some African groups the development and cultivation of rhythmic expression resulted in extremely complicated patterns, some of which conveyed specific meanings. In addition to the music of Africa, polyrhythmic expression is frequent in the music of the Javanese and Balinese.

Harmony

In the modern sense of the term, harmony did not exist in ancient music. However, drones and ostinato patterns were probably more widely used than heretofore realized. This is particularly true of the music of southeastern Asiatic societies, such as Java and Bali.

Texture

A variety of musical textures resulted from the combinations of voices and instruments performing the same melody. Accounts of simultaneous performances by hundreds of instrumentalists and singers point to an interest in heterophonic texture, in which a melody is duplicated or ornamented at the unison or octave, or even at other intervals.

Instrumentation and Tone Color

Music and words were closely connected in early musical performance, and the voice was an important medium of expression. Wind, string, and percussion instruments accompanied the voice, generally at the unison or octave. Based on the evidence of present-day performance of African, Indian, and western Oriental music, it is probable that a strikingly high perfection of performance skill was achieved in the use of percussion instruments in ancient cultures. Percussion instruments were made of wood, metal, stone, and even of vegetable fiber, such as gourds. They were divided into groups—those that were accurately pitched according to chosen scales, and those that had no such pitch differentiation. Many of the tuned instruments of these cultures made use of pitches based on intervals smaller than the half steps common to Western music.

Bowed string instruments were of relatively simple construction, normally made with only one string. Plucked string instruments reached a high state of perfection, second only to percussion instruments. Much skill was required in both their construction and performance.

The least developed of the non-Western instruments were the winds that correspond to our present brass and woodwind types. The brasses never advanced beyond a simple natural form (i.e., without valves or slides). They were made of metal, bone, and wood, the primitive mouthpieces being part of the horns themselves. There was a great variety of woodwind instruments, including flutes and reeds. Some were simply-made folk instruments; others were elaborately constructed.

Performance Practice

All performance practices in ancient music relied on the oral tradition because there was no fixed system of written musical notation. The selection of instruments, voices, dynamics, and tempi was determined by contemporaneous taste and tradition. In ancient writings, references to musical performance indicate that particular instruments were used only for certain occasions due to the association of their timbre with moral and ethical values.

The voice also was used differently than in the European tradition. Judging from current practices in cultures other than those of western Europe, various timbres were cultivated by such practices as tightening of the throat passage, falsetto, and guttural grunts. Among some non-Western peoples, especially the east Asians, the use of the voice suggests that it is desirable to make singing as different from speech as possible. The Eastern singer's vocal technique results in sounds that persons in the Western world associate with nasality and restricted resonance. In contrast, vocal technique in Western singing attempts to produce a sustained, and fully resonant sound.

IV. MUSIC FOR VOICES

The improvisational character of ancient vocal music precluded most set formal structures. Furthermore, the absence of notated examples gives us no basis for reconstructing formal designs, if any existed. It is therefore impossible to speak about vocal forms beyond the fact that vocal music, both sacred and secular, was used. It is likely that the narrative nature of the vocal texts influenced the musical form. The written and pictorial records of the time give evidence of accompanied vocal music as well as helpful information about instrumental music.

V. MUSIC FOR INSTRUMENTS

In ancient times, instrumental music, like vocal music, was improvisational, with no known set forms. Purely instrumental music, unrelated to song or dance, was found in some instances. The orchestral groups of percussion instruments used in Java and Bali are notable examples. Instrumental music was usually descriptive and illustrative of poetic or pictorial ideas, as illustrated by the flute and zither music of China and Japan.

VI. COMPOSERS

There is no written record of any composers or extant musical works from this period. Court and archeological records and accounts of performers such as David in the Old Testament are among the records that give an indication of composers as such, since every performer was in fact a composer. Although there are no specific composers to whom compositions can be attributed, examples of ancient music do exist. Recordings of non-Western music are widely available and include such collections as those sponsored by the United Nations Educational, Scientific and Cultural Organization (UNESCO). (See appendix 2 for Ex. 1.1.)

VII. HISTORIANS, THEORISTS, AND MANUSCRIPT SOURCES

Early writers dealt with music either as a mathematical-theoretical system or as a philosophical-ethical matter. Among the former, the most important are those who based their theories on the work of Pythagoras, the early Greek mathematician and theoretician who was concerned with the harmony of the spheres. Among the latter, the most extensive writings are those of the Greek philosophers, although references to music can be found in the works of many ancient writers—Chinese, Indian, Hebrew, and others. What few examples of notated Greek music there are have been deciphered from inscriptions on stone.

Pythagoras (c. 582 B.C.–c. 483 B.C.) was a Greek philosopher and mathematician to whom is ascribed the discovery of pitch ratios. For centuries, only the octave and fifth were considered pure consonances. There is no record of any of Pythagoras's writings, and his theories are known only as they were developed by his followers.

Plato (427 B.C.–347 B.C.) was the great Greek philosopher whose concern with music was almost entirely related to its ethical values. Music played an important role in his educational theories, particularly as it related to the development of character. Passages in *Timaeus* and the *Republic* state his concepts of music and its place in society.

Aristotle (384 B.C.–322 B.C.), a pupil of Plato, also concerned himself with the ethical values of music in several of his writings, notably in the *Politics.*

Aristoxenus (354 B.C.–?) was the most important of the Greek writers on music. Two works, *Harmonic Elements* and *Elements of Rhythmics,* have come down to us, the first complete, the second in fragmentary form. An English edition of these works translated by H. S. Macran was published in 1902.

Cleonides (first half of the second century A.D.) was a Greek writer whose *Harmonic Introduction* was a source of information for Renaissance musicians on classic Greek music. An edition of it was published in Venice in 1497.

Aristedes Quintillianus flourished around A.D. 200. His treatise *De Musica Libri VII* provides a basic source for knowledge of the music of ancient Greece. A German translation by Schafke was published in 1937.

Athenaeus (A.D. 200) was a Greek writer who lived in Rome. Although he was not a musician, his descriptions of musical performance in *Sophists at Dinner* are a valuable source of insight into the place of music in Roman life.

Excerpts from most of the foregoing writings may be found in Strunk, *Source Readings in Music History,* Rev. ed. New York: W. W. Norton, 1996.

King David playing the rotta: an eighth-century miniature from the Canterbury Psalterium. The rotta was a medieval instrument referred to in very early sources. It was probably a psaltery on which the strings, like those of the harp, were plucked by the fingers. Other medieval instruments are pictured: four zinks, or cornetti, and two small, straight flutes, or recorders. The clapping dancers at the bottom of the picture suggest that the music being played is secular in nature. (from *Cott Vespasian* AI f. 30; by permission of the British Library)

2

✦

Early Middle Ages
(300–1100)

I. SOCIOCULTURAL INFLUENCES ON MUSIC

Our knowledge of early medieval music in general is based upon rather meager evidence. While there are examples of early sacred music that were notated and preserved by the Roman Catholic Church, its interpretation is open to question. This is due to a somewhat primitive system of notation, particularly in relation to rhythm. We have even fewer authentic examples of secular music because virtually all writings from the period were by monks, whose function it was to transcribe sacred texts and music. That body of music is commonly referred to by several words: plainchant, plainsong, Gregorian chant, and monody.

Under the patronage of the Roman Catholic Church, music was organized according to the needs of the liturgical services. The many monastic orders that flourished during this period influenced that development and organization of sacred music. In keeping with liturgical practice, the music was set to an ecclesiastical Latin text.

In general, the music of the Byzantine church (the Eastern rite) took its forms and liturgical order from the early Apostolic church and the Jewish service, but modern scholarship is in doubt as to the exact details of such connections. There is also doubt about the degree to which instrumental music was employed in church services. This derives from the fact that only music with texts was sanctioned by the church fathers and notated in the manuscripts of the period. The apparent absence of instrumental music in the church has been interpreted by some as evidence of the medieval ascetic denial of the physical.

The monophonic chant continued its development beyond 1100, but it began to lose its preeminence as a compositional style after the development of polyphony and the consequent introduction of harmony in medieval music. The performance of sacred monophony continues today, especially in monastic settings.

The most important influence on music outside the church during the Middle Ages was feudalism, which paid tribute to patrons and gave rise to a society with a well-developed social consciousness. A large body of secular music and poetry in the vernacular was derived from society's entertainments and the desire for self-expression outside the confines of the church.

II. FUNCTION OF MUSIC

In keeping with the "other-worldly" spirit of early Christianity, plainsong expressed a simple faith in God. This function was achieved by the musical setting of portions of all rituals of the church, the most important of which was the Mass. Other rituals that also used music were the Divine Offices or canonical hours, such as matins, lauds, and vespers. The music of vespers, which includes the Magnificat, was to become especially important.

The liturgy of the Roman Catholic Mass called for the musical setting of eleven texts; the remaining texts were spoken. The musical settings were divided into two parts. The Ordinary, consisting of the Kyrie, Gloria, Credo, Sanctus, Agnus Dei (Benedictus), and the Ite missa est, used an invariable text. The Proper set variable texts in accordance with the church calendar. It consisted of the Introit, Gradual, Alleluia, Offertory, and Communion.

In addition to the Mass and the Divine Offices, plainsong, also called chant, was used extensively in musical settings of hymns, psalms, and tropes. These tropes, nonliturgical texts and music, were inserted between words of liturgical texts.

Much less is known about secular music during this period. It did exist and was used for dancing, to chronicle events, and as a vehicle for the expression of folk tradition.

III. STYLE AND PERFORMANCE PRACTICE

Formal Organization

The organization and forms of sacred plainsong were determined by the Latin text of the liturgy, with pitch and duration generally following the emphasis and duration of the words. In a few instances, mainly in tropes and sequences, the organization was based on freely composed melodic configurations, with little regard for the natural accents of the language. The forms of secular monophony were also determined by the text, but these texts were most often poetic, and consequently the music reveals such patterns as verse with refrain or repeated melodic phrases.

Melody

Plainsong consists of a monophonic melody set to a sacred text. It has a restricted range, seldom extending beyond an octave.

Plainsong melodies were constructed on the intervallic relationships of the church modes (fig. 2.1). These modes differ from one another by the order of steps and half steps within the octave. All the modes are organized around a dominant or reciting tone, and a final or ending pitch. Four modes (I, III, V, and VII) are called authentic modes. The order of steps and half steps in these modes corresponds to the diatonic octave scales based on D (mode I), E (mode III), F (mode V), and G (mode VII) as illustrated in figure 2.1. These modes, however, can be transposed to begin on any pitch. Each authentic mode has a corresponding plagal mode. Each pair of modes (I and II, III and IV, V and VI, and VII and VIII) has the same final. The overriding differences between an authentic mode and its corresponding plagal mode are the range or ambitus and their dominants. The authentic mode has a range within the octave of its final. The plagal mode has a range within the octave of the fourth below its final to a fifth above. The secondary principal tone in each mode is called the dominant.

Figure 2.1 Chart of modes

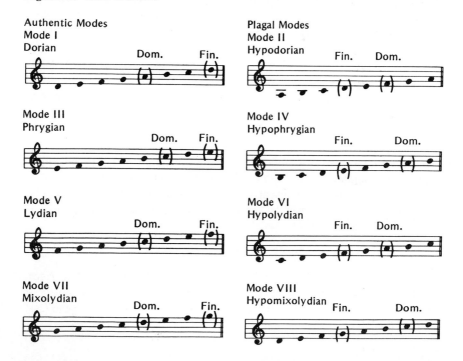

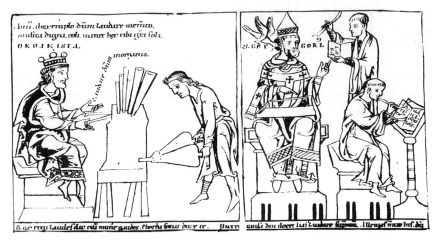

King David playing the organ and Pope Gregory dictating music. The organ was one of the few acceptable instruments for religious services in the Middle Ages. King David is often represented as a performer on the organ. Pope Gregory is shown receiving the inspiration of the Holy Spirit, portrayed as a dove, as he dictates the music of the chant. In actuality, he did not write chants but was responsible for their codification and preservation. (The Bettmann Archive)

Some plainsong, especially those for psalm settings, made use of a reciting tone. This is a tone upon which most of the syllables of the chant are executed and is usually the dominant of the mode. Syllabic chant is one of three plainsong types. In it, each note is set to a syllable of the text. A second type, called neumatic, is one in which a small group of notes is sung to one syllable. Florid, or melismatic chant, is a third type in which extended groups of notes are set to one syllable.

Secular monophony often used a wider range of notes than plainsong. This melodic type was not restricted by the church modes and often approaches tonality. It was usually cast in regular phrases, whereas plainsong was more irregular.

Rhythm

Plainsong rhythm was determined by the rhythmic flow of the prose, which includes the long and short syllabic values of ecclesiastical Latin. As a consequence, metric patterns are absent in sacred monophony. In contrast, secular monophony used the vernacular, in which there are more accents, and its rhythm is most often metric.

Harmony

There was no systematic harmonic practice during the early Middle Ages. However, in both sacred and secular monophony, notes were doubled or embellished on occasion by instruments, and some performance practices, such as drone bass and ostinato figures, were probably present.

As early as the ninth century a practice of singing in parallel fourths and fifths began and was called *organum.* Several types developed that were variously named. They all had the common characteristic of using a preexisting chant, *(vox principalis)*, to which was added one or more melodic lines. Parallel organum added a second voice, *(vox organalis)*, fixed at the interval of a fifth or fourth below the vox principalis (fig. 2.2).

Figure 2.2 *Sit gloria* (parallel organum)

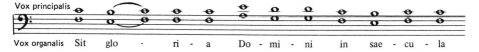

Free organum employed contrary and oblique motion in the vox organalis (fig. 2.3), whereas a later type, melismatic organum, used elaborate decorative note groups in the vox organalis against the very slow-moving values of the vox principalis (fig. 2.4). All styles of organum emphasized the use of the perfect intervals of the unison, fourth, fifth, and octave at cadential points.

Figure 2.3 *Cunctipotens genitor* (free organum)

Figure 2.4 *Cunctipotens genitor* (melismatic organum)

Texture

Because plainsong was monophonic, there was no texture in the sense of a combination of lines or tonal coloring as in later music. However, the austere line of plainsong sung by a priest, or the chant sung in unison or organum by a choir, created a mystic simplicity of linear sound that complemented the stark simplicity of the Romanesque cathedral. A fuller texture was created in secular monophony with its frequent use of instruments. Combined with a wider range, more definite rhythmic patterns, and vernacular texts, it expresses a widening range of human feelings and emotions.

Instrumentation and Tone Color

Plainsong was always vocal. As a rule, instruments were prohibited in the medieval church, although there is some evidence that instruments were occasionally used as accompaniment. The preponderance of secular monophony was vocal, but it was often accompanied by instruments, especially when used as dance music. The instruments used in secular music were plucked and bowed strings, and a variety of woodwind, brass, and percussion instruments.

IV. MUSIC FOR VOICES

Chant

There were five important types of plainsong, or chant, in this era. Collections of these chants document the musical practice in the areas of their origin (Ex. 2.1–2.7). (1) Byzantine chant, begun shortly after 330, was the earliest form of chant developed after the establishment of the Eastern church by Constantine, and it is still sung in the Greek Orthodox church. (2) Ambrosian chant, named for Bishop Ambrose of Milan, comes from northern Italy, and was written largely after his time. (3) Gallican chant was used in France until about 800; no notated manuscripts of it survive. (4) Mozarabic chant was the chant of Spain, with origins prior to the eighth century. (5) Gregorian chant has been the most widely used, and is so named because it was collected and organized under the leadership of Pope Gregory (pope from 590–604). As the secular power of the Roman Catholic Church was consolidated in Rome, Gregorian chant became the prescribed form of chant for liturgical services throughout the Roman Catholic world.

Psalm settings constitute one of the most important bodies of plainsong literature for the Mass and the Divine Office hours. There are three types of psalm settings, defined according to performance practice: (1) responsorial chant, in which a soloist sings the verse and is answered by a choir; (2) antiphonal singing, in which the choir is divided into two groups singing alternately; and (3) direct psalmody, in which the psalm is sung with no refrain by a soloist or a choir.

It is probable that plainsong was sung with little or no vibrato. Only male voices participated in the liturgy, except for the sung services in convents. Chants of the Mass and hours of the Divine Office were sung by the clergy, but the congregation joined in the singing of hymns and some processional chants.

A technique to aid sightsinging, called the hexachord system, was perfected by Guido d'Arezzo in the eleventh century. The six tones of the hexachord were designated by six syllables in order, from the lowest to the highest—ut, re, mi, fa, sol, la—corresponding to the first syllables of successive lines of a hymn to St. John the Baptist (fig. 2.5; see Ex. 2.7). A system of overlapping hexachords was devised that enabled the singer to sing melodies that lay outside the range of a single hexachord.

Figure 2.5 The hymn *Ut queant laxis,* the source of Guido's solmization system

UT que-ant la - xis RE-so -na -re fi -bris MI - ra ge- sto-rum FA-mu-li tu -o - rum,

SOL - ve po -lu -ti LA - bi- i re - a-tum San - cte Jo - an - nes

Organum

The practice of singing in parallel fifths and fourths was probably improvised. It is generally associated with sacred music, but there is evidence that it was also practiced in secular music. Later developments brought the practice of contrary motion and the use of nonperfect intervals (see figs. 2.3 and 2.4). By the end of the eleventh century, organum was so well established that it was referred to in theoretical treatises. Rules were established for avoiding the tritone (the augmented fourth), for arriving at unison cadences, and for identifying those parts of the liturgical chant that were permitted to be used in this manner. The practice of organum led directly to the development of polyphonic forms in the Middle Ages.

Single-Movement Forms and Structural Procedures

With few exceptions, the musical form and organization of specific chants were based solely on the form of the text. Any suggestion of A B A or similar formulae was the result of textual considerations. There were some traditions that placed specific texts in certain of the church modes, and naturally those chants set to the same texts show a degree of similarity. However, there are few distinguishable forms as such. The monophonic Mass is not a true musical form, but rather a composite, a collection of appropriate chant settings of the Ordinary and Proper of the Mass. (Ex. 2.8–2.9)

Among these single-movement forms or procedures are the following:

Antiphon. A short sentence of scripture or other sacred verse sung both before and after the psalm, and after each pair of verses within the psalm. The formal effect was that of a refrain to the psalm. It was mostly in syllabic style. (Ex. 2.10–2.11) A special category of antiphons whose texts celebrate the Virgin Mary are referred to as Marian Antiphons. (Ex. 2.12–2.14)

Alleluia. The alleluia is added at the ends of sections of many chants. It consists of a refrain on the word *alleluia* and is followed by a verse or section with the refrain repeated. The *jubilus* is a vocal elaboration on the final vowel of the *alleluia* that provides a strong impetus for musical form. (Ex. 2.15–2.16)

Trope. Music with a nonliturgical text, that is, texts other than those approved for worship services, inserted between phrases of liturgical text is called a trope. The words provide a commentary on the liturgy. The trope is a musical type that allowed for creative musical expression within the rather rigidly defined liturgy of the church. The practice of interpolating tropes gradually fell into disuse, and they were finally abolished by the Council of Trent in the middle of the sixteenth century. (Ex. 2.17–2.20)

Sequence. The sequence evolved from the practice of troping and consisted of added poetic words to the final jubilus of the alleluia, replacing the verse that followed the alleluia. The texts that provided the musical incentive were usually long and in a free style with repeated sections. Such formulas as A BB CC DD E were common and represented independent compositions. Like the trope, the sequence evolved toward secularism. Four of these sequences were retained in the body of church music. (Ex. 2.21–2.24)

Conductus. The monophonic conductus was probably first sung while a participant in the Mass or liturgical drama was "conducted" or moved from one place to another in the altar area of the church. The text was metric, and not liturgical. The melody was not taken from a chant collection, and was freely composed. This form was first associated with the church but soon became a secular form, and the title was applied to almost any Latin song of a serious nature. (Ex. 2.25)

All of the foregoing types had their origins in sacred music. Secular monophony of the period up to 1100 has not been preserved as well as that of sacred music. No doubt this was largely because there was no institution whose duty it was to maintain and preserve this music.

Secular monophony flourished during the early Middle Ages through the songs of the goliards, jongleurs, and minstrels. Some of the most important of these songs were those of the goliards, who were wandering scholars. The most noted collection of goliard poems is *Carmina Burana,* made famous in modern times by Carl Orff. Among the goliard songs that survive today (most exist only as poems without music) is *O Admirabile Veneris,* which dates from the tenth century. Its melody also appears as *O Roma Nobilis.* It is metric and in strophic form with a refrain. (Ex. 2.26)

The jongleurs and minstrels were itinerant performers who entertained with song, dance, tricks, and juggling. Although they cannot be considered either poets or composers, they sang verses in the vernacular. One of the early types of jongleur song was the *Chanson de Geste,* a narrative song telling of heroic deeds. The most famous of these is the *Song of Roland,* which became a national epic of France. Unfortunately, no authentic music has survived. It is probable that the jongleurs and minstrels helped spread the folk-song tradition that ultimately made its way into art music.

V. MUSIC FOR INSTRUMENTS

Although instrumental music was generally banned in the church, it is known that organs existed in churches as early as 800. We do not know, however, how they were used, or what music was played. It is evident from manuscripts and pictorial representations that instruments were used in secular music both as accompaniment to song and independently as dance music. As is the case with all early medieval secular music, we have little information about specific forms because none of the music has survived in decipherable notation.

VI. COMPOSERS

Because of the improvisatory nature of early music, almost every performer was a composer. This was especially true in secular music, and no doubt the same procedure was responsible for the origin of most of the chants that later became traditional. It is known, however, that the following were composers of some stature and influence during the early Middle Ages.

Notker Balbulus (c. 840–912) was one of the earliest composers identified by name. (The word "balbulus" is the Latin word for stammerer.) He was especially known as a writer of sequences. (Ex. 2.27)

Wipo of Burgundy (d. 1048). The sequence for Easter, *Victimae paschali laudes,* still in use today, is by Wipo.

Hermannus Contractus (1013–1054), also known as Herman the Cripple, was a theorist as well as a composer. His *Alma Redemptoris Mater* achieved great popularity and became the basis for numerous monophonic and polyphonic works.

Abelard (1079–1142) is known to have made a collection of hymns for monks and nuns. One of these nuns, for whom his love is legendary, was the famous Heloise. Their love story has held the interest of the public for many centuries.

VII. HISTORIANS, THEORISTS, AND MANUSCRIPT SOURCES

Most early theoretical writings on music were either interpretations of the music theory of the ancients and subsequent concepts of music as a science, or attempts to link music and religion by means of allegorical writings. They were not derived from contemporaneous musical practices.

Boethius (c. 480–524), one of the earliest theorists, was also a philosopher and mathematician. His chief work was *De Institutione Musica,* in which he related the music of his time to the theories of the Greek philosophers.

Cassiodorus (c. 485–c. 580) was a historian, philosopher, statesman, and the founder of a monastery. His important contribution to the history of music was *Institutiones musicae,* written between 550 and 562.

Isidore of Seville (c. 560–636) was a Spanish scholar. His *Etymologiarum sive originum libri XX* is an encyclopedia of the arts with an account of liturgical music.

Odo of Cluny (879–942), an abbot in France, was a music theorist whose *Dialogus de Musica* contains an account of modes and medieval notation. He was the first to use letters to indicate pitches.

Guido d'Arezzo (c. 997–c. 1050), a Benedictine monk, was the most important writer of his time concerned with the actual practices of music. He dealt with the problems of notation and especially with the technique of singing. His numerous writings have been an important source for modern scholars in interpreting medieval music. He is popularly known today for the system of solmization based on the hymn *Ut queant laxis* (see fig. 2.5). Related to it was the teaching aid known as the "Guidonian Hand."

Musica enchiriadis (c. 900) is a treatise noteworthy for its description of early organum. Its authorship has never been established. For a long time it was thought to have been written by Hucbald (c. 840–930), but recent scholarship has determined that he is not the author. *Musica enchiriadis* covers the whole range of musical knowledge. Most of its material was borrowed from the ancients, including the concept of music as mathematics, the acceptance of Pythagorean theory of numbers, and the division of the scale according to intervallic ratios.

(These writings are not readily available in English. However, important excerpts from each can be found in Strunk, *Source Readings in Music History.*)

Winchester Troper: There are very few extant collections of original manuscripts prior to 1100. The *Winchester Troper* is the most important. It consists of two liturgical manuscripts containing tropes and organum. These are part of the great literature of plainsong melody that has been in the process of being collected, edited, and published by the Benedictines of Solesmes since 1889. Sixteen volumes have been published in the *Paléographie Musicale.*

Further readings on these subjects are identified in the books included in appendix 3.

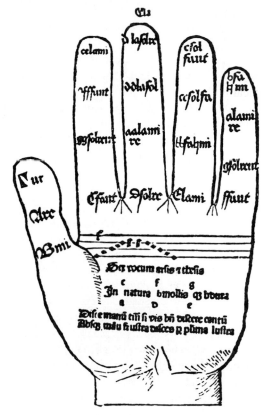

The "Guidonian Hand" was a mnemonic device that assigned scale degrees (ut, re, mi, fa, sol, la) to various parts of the hand. It was used to help singers and other musicians with various aspects of music theory. Attributed to Guido d'Arezzo, it remained in use for several centuries. (Art and History Archive, Berlin)

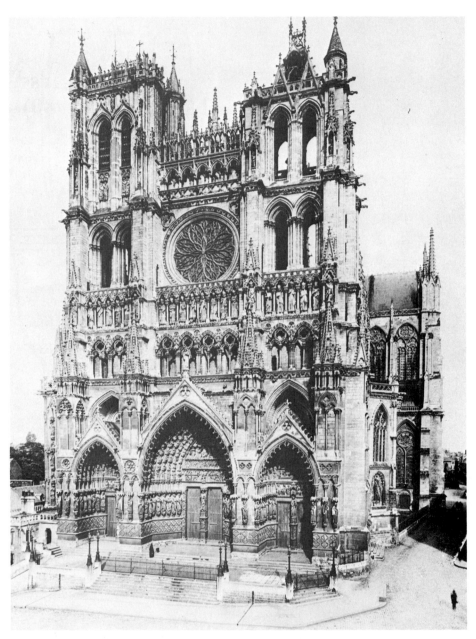

Cathedral at Amiens, France (c. 1225). An excellent example of the great thrust of Gothic architecture. The pointed arches that frame the massive entrance doors and cover the niches of the sculptured figures above the doorways, the greatly elongated openings of the belfry towers, the pointed decorated spires adorning the facade, and the topmost roof all give a breathless feeling of heavenly lift to this massive building.

3

Late Middle Ages: Ars Antiqua–Ars Nova (1100–1400)

CHRONOLOGY

1098	*Abbess Hildegard von Bingen* (1098–1179)
c. 1100	Crusades (1100–1300)
c. 1150	*Troubadours* *School of Notre Dame*
c. 1155	*Perotin* (fl. 1180–1200)
c. 1160	*Leonin* (fl. 1160)
c. 1163	Notre Dame Cathedral (Paris)
1182	St. Francis of Assisi (1182–1226)
	Organum (fl. 9th–12th century)
c. 1200	*Trouvères, Troubadours, and Minnesingers* *Ars Antiqua* (c. 1200–c. 1300)
1215	Magna Carta
1227	St. Thomas Aquinas (1227–1274)
c. 1237	*Adam de la Halle* (c. 1237–1287)
c. 1250	*Franco of Cologne* (fl. 1250–1280)
c. 1260	*Jacques de Liège* (c. 1260–c. 1330)
1265	Dante Alighieri (1265–1321)
1266	Giotto (1266–1337)
c. 1290	*Jean de Muris* (c. 1290–c. 1351)
1291	Philippe de Vitry (1291–1361)
c. 1300	*Ars Nova* (c. 1300–c.1400) *Guillaume de Machaut* (c. 1300–1377) *Marchetto da Padua* (fl. 14th century)
1304	Francesco Petrarch (1304–1374)
1309	Papacy in Avignon (until 1376)
1313	Giovanni Boccacio (1313–1375)
1325	*Francesco Landini* (1325–1397)
c. 1340	Geoffrey Chaucer (c. 1340–1400)
c. 1348	The Black Death (continuing throughout the Middle Ages)

I. SOCIOCULTURAL INFLUENCES ON MUSIC

In art history, the late Middle Ages (the period from c. 1100 to c. 1430) are at times called the Gothic era. The term refers to the architecture characterized by pointed arches, ribbed vaulting, and flying buttresses, and was introduced by seventeenth-century writers who looked upon this style as unclassical and vulgar. They associated it with the medieval Goths of northern Europe. At present, the term merely identifies the artistic style of the period without derogatory implications.

The music of the late Middle Ages is most often divided into the Ars Antiqua and the Ars Nova. The Ars Antiqua is centered in the thirteenth century, and as the term implies, refers to an old tradition. Two major musical contributions of the late Middle Ages, or Ars Nova, are the rise and development of polyphonic forms and the merging of secular and sacred musical styles. In fact, many medieval forms and practices relating to sacred music survived into the twentieth century. Because systems of notation were devised during this period, much music from the late Middle Ages has been preserved. Consequently, modern scholars are able to recreate much of the music with authority and accuracy. These medieval systems of notation made it possible to represent accurately both rhythm and pitch.

In this period the development of music was accelerated by a number of varied sociocultural movements. Among these was scholasticism, a medieval philosophy that systematized all intellectual and religious experience according to rigid rules of medieval logic. This reflected the domination by the Roman Catholic Church over secular and sacred life. The effect of scholasticism on religious music was twofold. First, it regulated the theory and practice of music according to canons of acceptable practice in the church. For example, triple meter was held to be more perfect than duple meter, and perfect intervals were ruled necessary on all strong beats, while dissonant intervals were generally avoided whenever possible. Second, scholasticism also controlled and codified the emotional content of sacred music. Church officials frowned upon ornate melodies because they felt such melodies obscured the meaning of the texts. Any move to make music more emotionally expressive was avoided because it appealed to the senses and not to the soul. Only after a long period of development were expressive qualities allowed in sacred music. Although scholasticism had little direct effect on secular music, there was an indirect influence inasmuch as church composers who rebelled against strict control found freedom in the secular style.

Western society was becoming more and more independent economically, intellectually, and artistically. Toward the end of this era, people were becoming skeptical of the authority of the church to order and control all of life's activities. Communication with the East, the result of the twelfth and thirteenth century Crusades opened new channels of trade, brought new wealth, new ideas, and new incentives for living. New social customs and cultural practices were eventually integrated into Western civilization. As a consequence, a favorable climate for artistic development existed in contrast to the rather severe asceticism of earlier times. Entertainment outside the church became widely cultivated. Even religious music was infused with the new humanism.

The rise of towns stimulated centers of learning in newly established universities, especially in England, the Netherlands, and France. Music became an integral part of education, first as a science and eventually as an art. As well as being associated with the church, the leaders and innovators of medieval music were either at the universities or associated with the courts, where music was given great importance. Beginning with this period, musical leadership came from northern Europe instead of Italy, where musical activity previously had been centered.

The late Middle Ages witnessed the beginning of the struggle between church and state which, in effect, was a struggle between asceticism and humanism, between the power of the church and the individual. In music it took the form of a conflict between the sacred and the secular, a conflict in which each style reached new heights of musical expressiveness.

II. FUNCTION OF MUSIC

Sacred music in the late Middle Ages served the same religious functions as it had earlier. The same liturgical texts were set to music, but in polyphony instead of monophony. An important addition to sacred music was the motet, a form that was later to become one of the most important vocal polyphonic forms. The Gothic spirit precipitated a great program of church building, an activity that in turn led to an increased demand for church musicians. This demand led to the establishment of schools such as St. Martial (Limoges) and Notre Dame (Paris), where sacred music was especially cultivated.

Music took on increased importance in the fabric of medieval society. The rise in the social status of secular music, demonstrated by the nobility of the troubadours and trouvères, shows the wide interest in vernacular secular song. The establishment of courts and the growing power of other secular institutions encouraged strong centers of secular culture in many medieval cities. This was the age of chivalry and the time when courtly love became the subject of lyric love songs. For the first time in music history, individual composers achieved recognition for their creative efforts. Moreover, the most significant developments in music have been traced to these secular composers.

III. STYLE AND PERFORMANCE PRACTICE

Although plainsong and secular monophony continued, the development of polyphonic style was the major concern of late medieval composers. This concern for a defined polyphony marked the beginning of the emancipation of music from its dependence on preexisting materials such as plainsong, a process that was to continue through the Renaissance.

In the twelfth century the Ars Antiqua composers of the School of Notre Dame, mainly Leonin and Perotin, were among the first to develop the basic rules of polyphony. A new movement called Ars Nova emerged in France and Italy during the fourteenth century. In this new movement, rhythm was expanded by the acceptance of duple patterns. In harmony, the use of thirds and sixths were introduced and treated as dissonances.

Formal Organization

All vocal music was organized according to the poetic and syllabic considerations of the text. However, these were frequently made secondary to rhythmic and harmonic considerations. Less is known about instrumental music of this period, but it bears many of the characteristics of vocal forms.

Composers of sacred polyphony organized sections of text into complete units by means of short, repeated rhythmic patterns called rhythmic modes. In the fourteenth century, longer sections were combined on the basis of the isorhythmic principle, a repetition of longer and more complicated rhythmic patterns throughout a composition. Organum continued to be an important organizational principle, even after the introduction of contrary motion and elaborate melismatic settings.

Monophonic and polyphonic secular forms such as the rondeau, virelai, and ballad were known as "formes fixes." They were organized on the basis of two musical phrases combined in repeated patterns: AB AB AB. Some other secular forms also contained a two-line refrain both at the beginning and at the end of each stanza. Those forms that used more than one stanza (strophe) of text to the same musical setting are referred to as strophic.

Secular polyphony made extensive use of canonic imitation as a means of formal organization. The most obvious example is the rondellus.

Melody

Melody was vocal in style; that is, it tended to move stepwise within a limited range. Secular melodies and fourteenth-century sacred forms expanded the range somewhat. Sacred melody in forms other than plainsong usually consisted of short phrases in repeated metric patterns, while secular melody, both monophonic and polyphonic, was often cast in longer phrases and was more lyric. There was no attempt to express the meaning of the text in sacred melody, but secular melody often captured the mood of the text.

All medieval melodies, monophonic and polyphonic, were modal. In the Ars Nova, however, secular songs had a tendency toward intervals that suggested tonality. A common melodic practice of many Ars Nova composers was to move from the leading tone to the sixth tone before proceeding to the tonic. This has been given the name Landini cadence, even though the composer Landini did not initiate the practice (fig. 3.1).

Figure 3.1 A Landini cadence

Rhythm

Rhythmic development held the attention of all composers who were concerned with extending the expressiveness of music. To emancipate musical form from the rhythm of text and to gain some agreement of accent among the voices of polyphonic forms, it was necessary to invent some sort of rhythmic system that was independent of poetic rhythm. To that end, composers devised a system by which rhythmic cohesion could be brought to a melody through repeated notational patterns called rhythmic modes. These rigidly repeated rhythmic patterns were usually separated by a rest before their repetition. There were six rhythmic modes, each identified by a number (fig. 3.2). Some of these rhythmic modes are related to the rhythmic feet used in the analysis of poetry (for example, iamb, dactyl, trochee). In some instances each polyphonic line was set to its own rhythmic mode. In the Ars Nova these modes were extended to longer patterns, which formed the basis of isorhythmic compositions. While the principle of rhythmic modes involved a series of exact repetitions, the practice was to introduce a degree of flexibility by varying the patterns.

Figure 3.2 Rhythmic modes

Rhythmic patterns in triple meter were used extensively in sacred music, whereas secular forms had the freedom of employing either triple or duple meter. Many kinds of beat subdivisions appeared in the fourteenth century (Ars Nova), giving the rhythmic flow more freedom and subtlety. An especially remarkable device of the period was the "hocket," an alternating interruption of the rhythmic and melodic flow among the voices (fig. 3.3).

Crucifixion of St. Andrew. This page of a Flemish-Rhenish Antiphonary (c. 1230–1240) illustrates the art of illumination practiced in the manuscripts of the Gothic period. The elaborate "U" depicting the martyrdom of St. Andrew serves as the first letter of the word *Unus* (one), which begins the text of this antiphon. The notation and the four-line staff of the late Gothic era became the official notational style of the Gregorian chant for the Roman Catholic Church. The translation of the Latin text is: "One of the two who followed the Lord was Andrew, the brother of Simon Peter, alleluja, e u o u a e. Walking by the sea of Galilee, Jesus saw Peter and his brother Andrew and said to them, 'Follow me and I will make you fishers of men.' " In the fourth line of the manuscript, the six vowels following the word "alleluja" are the vowels in the Latin words "seculorum, Amen." This abbreviation is frequently used in chant manuscripts. (The Saint Louis Art Museum)

Figure 3.3 Hockets in the instrumental motet *In seculum* (From *The Historical Anthology of Music,* edited by Archibald T. Davison and Willi Apel. © 1950 by the President and Fellows of Harvard College; renewed 1978 by Alice D. Humez and Willi Apel. Reprinted by permission of Harvard University Press, Cambridge, MA.)

One of the most significant innovations in medieval music was the development of a system of notation. After the emergence of a system of lines and spaces in the eleventh century, pitch designation was fairly accurate, although there was no practical means of notating duration and stress. By the thirteenth century, mensural (measured) notation had been developed, principally by Franco of Cologne, introducing for the first time a codified system for recording notes of varying duration and emphasis. This system, with many variations, was to remain in use until c. 1600. Black notes used in the thirteenth and fourteenth centuries were changed to white notes in the fifteenth century. The relative durational values of these notes within the mensural system and their modern equivalents are illustrated in figure 3.4. Unlike modern notation, which assumes a

Figure 3.4 Mensural notes—their names and modern equivalents

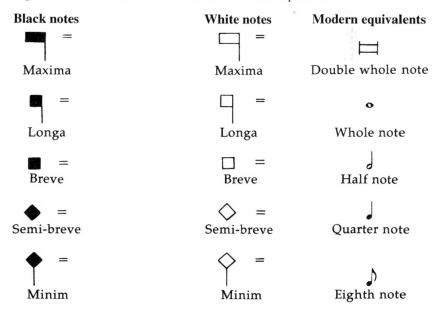

Black notes	White notes	Modern equivalents
Maxima	Maxima	Double whole note
Longa	Longa	Whole note
Breve	Breve	Half note
Semi-breve	Semi-breve	Quarter note
Minim	Minim	Eighth note

division of any note into two notes of the next smaller degree, mensuration divided the notes into either two or three notes of the next smaller degree. The divisions of the longa, breve, and semi-breve were named as follows:

MENSURAL DIVISIONS INTO 3	MENSURAL DIVISIONS INTO 2
Modus perfectum	Modus imperfectum
1 longa = 3 breves	1 longa = 2 breves
Tempus perfectum	Tempus imperfectum
1 breve = 3 semi-breves	1 breve = 2 semi-breves
Prolatio major	Prolatio minor
1 semi-breve = 3 minims	1 semi-breve = 2 minims

The division of the longa, breve, and semi-breve into two or three smaller units was indicated by the use of symbols of mensuration as follows:

1. A circle indicated tempus perfectum, the division of the breve into three semi-breves. In prolatio minor the semi-breve was divided into two minims (fig. 3.5A).
2. A broken circle indicated tempus imperfectum, the division of the breve into two semi-breves. Here again in prolatio minor the semi-breve was divided into two minims (fig. 3.5B).
3. As stated in number 1, the circle indicated tempus perfectum. However, the addition of the dot within the circle indicates the further division of the semi-breve into three minims, prolatio major (fig. 3.5C).
4. As stated in number 2, the broken circle indicated tempus imperfectum. When the dot was added within the broken circle, prolatio major was indicated (fig. 3.5D).

Figure 3.5A Tempus perfectum: Prolatio minor,

which corresponds to the modern notation of 3/4

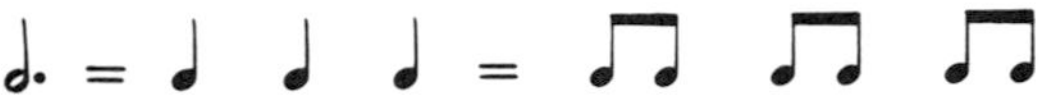

Figure 3.5B Tempus imperfectum: Prolatio minor,

which corresponds to the modern notation of 2/4

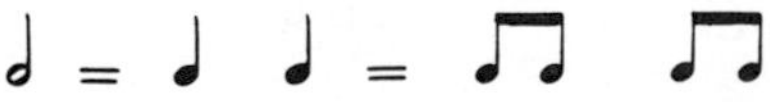

Figure 3.5C Tempus perfectum: Prolatio major,

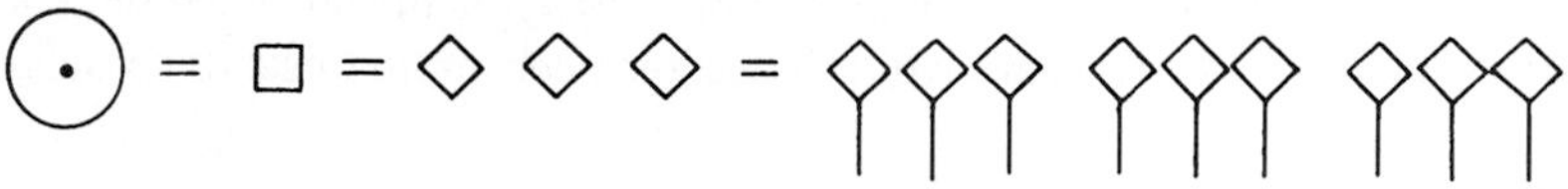

which corresponds to the modern notation of 9/8

Figure 3.5D Tempus imperfectum: Prolatio major,

which corresponds to the modern notation of 6/8

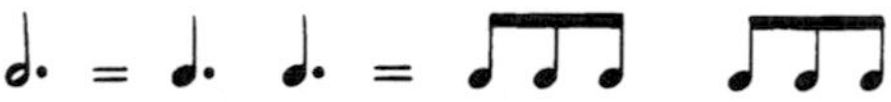

Harmony

Medieval harmony was the result of polyphonic texture. Because there was no systematic chordal structure, there were often sharp and unresolved dissonances among the voices. This was partly due to the fact that in the early Ars Nova, each of the upper voices related to the lowest voice and not to one another.

Because melodies were composed in modes, harmony was also modal, although secular polyphony on occasion tended toward major and minor tonality. The harmonic vocabulary was largely limited to the use of perfect fourths, fifths, and octaves. All other intervals were considered dissonant. In the Ars Nova, thirds and sixths were considered imperfect consonances and were utilized first in secular forms and then in sacred music.

Chromaticism was not generally used as an expressive device. Chromatic alterations were often introduced in cadences (fig. 3.6), and were used to avoid the intervals of the augmented fourth or diminished fifth (called tritones) above

Figure 3.6 Avoiding a tritone using *musica ficta*

the lowest tone. One aspect of chromaticism, the practice of *musica ficta* or false music, enabled performers to introduce flats or sharps into the modes in order to avoid certain intervals, or to make intervallic adjustments for the sake of "beauty."

Texture

Polyphonic texture prevailed in almost all medieval music after 1300. Prior to this time, secular music was monophonic and religious music was either set to traditional plainsong or organum, an early form of polyphony. Three-voice polyphony was the most common, but four voices were in frequent use by the end of the fourteenth century. Virtually all of this polyphony was based on preexistent chant melodies that were "held" (It. *tenere*) in the tenor, usually in slow or augmented note values.

In three-voice polyphony, the cantus firmus was normally the lowest voice. The other voices usually moved more rapidly and were often orna-mented. In four-voice polyphony, the cantus firmus was assigned to the tenor, and the lowest part was the contratenor, later named the bassus. It had approx-imately the same range as the tenor and frequently crossed the tenor line. The voice immediately above the tenor was called altus, and the voice above the altus was designated sovrano or superius.

There was no distinction between the textures of sacred and secular poly-phonic music of the period. The different voices retained their melodic inde-pendence and frequently crossed. At the same time, there was an openness about the sound of early polyphony due to extensive use of the intervals of the fourth, fifth, and octave, which lack the harmonic direction of other intervals.

Instrumentation and Tone Color

Music for voices dominated both sacred and secular music. Melodic instruments of all kinds could be substituted for the cantus firmus in polyphonic forms. No doubt instruments also doubled vocal parts, especially in secular polyphony. Secular monophony was usually accompanied by instruments, most commonly the lute, viol, and harp. Combinations of instruments were also used for dances and out-of-doors music, but because this kind of music was either improvised or played from memory, few actual written examples have survived.

The instruments of medieval times in many instances bear little similarity to the instruments of today. (A description of these and other instruments may be found in appendix 1.)

IV. MUSIC FOR VOICES

Single-Movement Forms and Structural Devices

Secular monophony was music of the troubadours, trouvères, and min-nesingers. It included many forms such as the formes fixes: the virelai (Ex. 3.1–3.4), rondeau (Ex. 3.5–3.7), and ballade (Ex. 3.8–3.10). The troubadours were poet-musicians of southern France who wrote in Provençal French. They were often men and women of high birth and wealth who could afford to hire performers to sing their songs. Trouvères, who lived in northern France, were a counterpart of the troubadours. The songs of the troubadours and trouvères were mainly amorous, including love songs to the Virgin Mary. The minnesingers were German poet-musicians who were inspired by the troubadours and trouvères. Their songs were often didactic or devotional. Individual songs were poetic types designated according to subject matter. Minnesingers limited themselves to four formal types, each derived from a well-known strophic form already in existence: the hymn type, the litany type, the rondel type, and the sequence type.

The Italian *canzo* (Ex. 3.11–3.13) is an example of the hymn type. Each stanza has six or seven lines, with the melody of the first two lines repeated for the second two. The last two or three lines use a different melody. For example, AB AB CD. The German version, found in the literature of the minnesingers, is called *bar form.* (Ex. 3.14–3.15)

The French *rotrouenge,* an example of the litany type, is a form in which the same melody is used for all the lines of the poem except for the last two. The pattern is AA AA BB. (Ex. 3.16)

The *virelai* is a French form of the rondel type, incorporating the refrain and stanza principle. The general musical pattern is: AB CC AB AB. The verse pattern is: AB CD EF AB. The Italian *cantiga* and *lauda* also used this pattern. (Ex. 3.17–3.18)

The *lai* is derived from the sequence with one melody to every two lines of poetry. The lai text is usually addressed to the Virgin Mary and is cast in irregular stanzas of six to sixteen or more lines. The musical form consists of AA BB CC DD. In Germany, the French *lai* was called *Leich.* This form was commonly used by the trouvères and minnesingers. (Ex. 3.19–3.20)

In the thirteenth century, a type of polyphony called *Notre Dame Organum* was developed. The principle of organum was restricted to those portions of the chant which were normally sung by a solo voice. Other sections were sung in plainsong. In the organum, the tenor sang the plainsong melody in long pedal tones, while the upper voice or voices sang free, usually metric, melodies above it. (Ex. 3.21–3.29)

The *clausula* was a polyphonic form that used a melismatic section of a chant as a cantus firmus. It was often only a section of an organum. The upper voices move in a quick but measured rhythm against the tenor, which moves in notes of even lengths. Because the melisma used only a few syllables, or at the most two or three words, there was no meaningful text to the clausula. All parts were vocalized on the vowel sounds of the tenor line. (Ex. 3.30–3.32)

The *conductus* is a two-, three-, or four-voice form in which the lowest voice is a freely invented melody on a Latin text. One of its important features is the syllabic and rhythmic unity among the voices, giving the effect of chords. (Ex. 3.33–3.35)

The *motet* was the most important vocal form in the thirteenth and fourteenth centuries in both secular and sacred practice. In the earlier motet the lowest voice, the tenor or cantus firmus, was a melody selected from plainsong or secular sources in a slow-moving rhythmic mode. The two upper voices, the duplum (or motetus) and the triplum, moved more quickly, each with its own text. At times, even the language of each text was different. Because the tenor notes were an elongation of the original cantus firmus, its text was unimportant, and it was common practice to play the tenor line on an instrument. The titles of motets are made up of the *incipits* of the several voices. (Ex. 3.36–3.42)

The *isorhythmic motet* was developed in the fourteenth century and had many of the same characteristics as the earlier motet. In the isorhythmic motet the rhythmic modes were extended. The isorhythm consisted of a rhythmic pattern called *talea,* which was repeated a number of times to form the rhythm of a melody, called *color.* The melody was usually repeated, but its repetition did not always coincide with the beginning of a talea (fig. 3.7A, B). This led to a much more complex and interesting rhythmic structure. While the isorhythmic principle was first applied to the tenor, in later works it was often present in all voices. (Ex. 3.43–3.46)

The *rota* is a medieval round, or canon, in which each singer returns from the end of the melody to the beginning. The phrases of the melody are so composed that their interaction makes functional harmony. All voices end on a cadence at the completion of any phrase. The rota is usually a secular form. In the famous example *Sumer is icumen in,* the rota is accompanied by an ostinato bass line in canonic style. (Ex. 3.47)

The *ballata* is an Italian secular form for two or three voices derived from the virelai. The ballata consists of a chain of stanzas, each with six lines. A two-line refrain precedes and follows each stanza. The ballata has two melodies, one for the refrain and one for each of the two first pairs of lines from each stanza. The third pair of lines uses the refrain melody. The resulting pattern is A b b a A. (Ex. 3.48–3.52)

The *caccia* is a hunting song that appeared in the fourteenth century. It often has three voices, and when it does, the two upper voices move in strict canonic imitation. The lower voice was independent and was probably performed on an instrument. The French version of the form is called *chace.* (Ex. 3.53–3.55)

The fourteenth-century *madrigal* is a lyric poem in which each stanza consists of three lines followed by a two-line couplet called a ritornello. The entire text is set for two or three voices. The same music is used for each stanza, while the ritornello is set to different music. The upper voice is usually ornamental. Instruments frequently doubled or substituted for the lower voice parts. (Ex. 3.56–3.57)

Figure 3.7 Tenor from three-part isorhythmic motet: *S'il estoit nulz*

Composite Forms

Polyphonic Mass

The polyphonic setting of the sung portions of the Mass is the only music of the late Middle Ages that is a composite, multisectional form. Although the Mass is not a musical form in itself, composers at this time began the practice of setting the liturgical texts of the Ordinary of the Mass with some semblance of unity among the various sections. This unity is achieved by means of motives common to each section, by similarity of moods, and by similarity of imitative devices. (Ex. 3.58–3.61)

Liturgical Drama

Dramatic presentations of biblical scenes were a further outgrowth of troping. The earliest liturgical drama was based on the story of the three Marys and the angel at the tomb of Christ at Easter, and is known from its opening words, "Quem quaeritis." (Ex. 3.62)

V. MUSIC FOR INSTRUMENTS

Single-Movement Forms and Structural Devices

Notated instrumental forms were slow to develop. Most dances during this period were still improvised. Many medieval dances were cast in two sections—dance and after dance. There was usually a slow-moving section in duple time followed by a faster section in triple time. Sometimes the section in triple time was based on the same melody as the first or duple section. Because of the improvisatory nature of these dances, very few have come to us in notation.

Conducti, motets, and even polyphonic sections of the Mass were sometimes played instead of sung. It was common practice to perform vocal music on instruments. Many vocal forms derived from dance melodies. (Ex. 3.63–3.64)

The dance form most commonly notated in the thirteenth and fourteenth centuries was the *estampie*. It is similar to the vocal sequence and consists of a number of sections called *puncti*, which were repeated. Its form is AA BB CC. (Ex. 3.65–3.68)

VI. COMPOSERS

Hildegard von Bingen (1098–1179), an abbess, mystic, poet, and composer, who wrote prodigiously, is known for the liturgical drama, "Ordo virtutum," in which the sixteen virtues do battle with the devil over the human soul. (Ex. 3.45) Her influence over the highest clerical and political figures of her time was remarkable.

Leonin (fl. 1160) was the first of the great masters of the Notre Dame School. Noted for his style of organum, he made extensive use of the syllabic technique, and foreshadowed the motet principle by lengthening the notes of the plainsong as a cantus firmus with a freely moving voice above it. He wrote a cycle of two-part liturgical settings for the church calendar known as the *Magnus Liber Organi* (The Great Book of Organum). (Ex. 3.23, 3.25, 3.28)

Perotin (twelfth century) succeeded Leonin at Notre Dame. He developed organum from the Leonin style by instilling a greater rhythmic accuracy, and by making additions and modifications to the *Magnus Liber Organi.* His tenor voices were written in a series of rhythmic motives that were the precursors of the rhythmic modes. He expanded organum to three and four voices. In addition, his music shows evidence of canonic imitation. His most famous work is *Sederunt principes,* a quadruple organum. (Ex. 3.24, 3.26, 3.29, 3.69)

Adam de la Halle (c. 1237–1287), one of the best-known trouvères, was both a poet and a composer. Many examples of his monodic as well as his polyphonic compositions survive. Besides many rondeaux and virelais, his musical play *Le jeu de Robin et de Marion,* written for the entertainment of the Aragonese court at Naples, is still performed. (Ex. 3.51, 3.70)

Guillaume de Machaut (c. 1300–1377), leader of the French Ars Nova, was the most important composer of the fourteenth century. In addition to being a musician, Machaut was also a poet and theologian, holding many important ecclesiastical posts, including that of Canon of Rheims. He was also secretary to King John of Bohemia. Among Machaut's musical innovations was the development of more lyric melodies and a more suave harmonic texture using thirds and sixths to soften the dissonance of earlier organum. He was the first to compose a complete polyphonic setting of the Ordinary of the Mass with some degree of unity among sections. He wrote in all the musical forms of his time, sacred and secular. Among the secular forms, he excelled in the ballad, bringing to it an ingenuity of imitation, a sonorous harmony, and an expressive melody that foreshadowed Renaissance style. (Ex. 3.5, 3.7–3.10, 3.45, 3.46)

Francesco Landini (1325–1397) had the distinction of being the most famous Italian Ars Nova composer of the fourteenth century. Blinded in his youth, he became a virtuoso performer on a number of instruments but was best known as an organist. His skill as a performer and as a composer won him legendary fame in the annals of Italian music. Landini's compositions number more than 150 and include every form of secular music, although the greater portion are two-part and three-part ballatas. His melodies are very expressive, and the resulting harmonies are exceedingly smooth and fluid. (Ex. 3.48–3.50, 3.55, 3.56, 3.71, 3.72)

ADDITIONAL COMPOSERS

A. France
   Franco of Cologne (fl. 1250–1280)
   Philippe de Vitry (1291–1361)
B. England
   Leonel Power (c. 1370–1445)

C. Italy
   Giovanni da Cascia (Giovanni da
   Firenze), (fl. 1330–1350)

VII. HISTORIANS, THEORISTS, AND MANUSCRIPT SOURCES

Medieval writers still considered music the servant of the church, and their philosophy is mainly a repetition of the earlier authors. However, major portions of their writings are concerned with practical problems of music, mainly those of rhythm and notation. An especially important subject was the interpretation of rhythmic notation.

The conflict between the more conservative style of early medieval music with that of the fourteenth-century Ars Nova was made articulate by medieval writers. This controversy is made especially clear in the writings of Jacques de Liège and Jean de Muris. The former was an ardent foe of the new style and a champion of the more traditional manner of composition.

Franco of Cologne (fl. 1250–1280) was a medieval theorist and a practical musician. A number of medieval writings were attributed to Franco, but only *Ars cantus mensurabilis* has been authenticated as genuine. Franco's primary contribution to notation, which took his name, "Franconian," was in developing a system of precise durations for notes, indicated by their shapes. In other areas of musical knowledge his writing is based on the earlier theorists.

Marchetto da Padua (fl. fourteenth century), an Italian who wrote an account of the musical practices in Italy, was also the author of a theoretical treatise, *Pomerium,* that was a justification of duple time in music.

Jacques de Liège (c. 1260–c. 1330), a Belgian, was the author of *Speculum musicae,* written about 1325. It was an attack on modern musical practices and more particularly an attack on the writings of Jean de Muris. In addition to its controversial nature, the *Speculum* is a compendium of all medieval knowledge about music.

Jean de Muris (c. 1290–c. 1351) was a writer on music, astronomy, and mathematics. He was the author of *Musica speculativa secundum Boetium* and the important treatise, *Ars novae musicae.* He championed the cause of the "new style" and also dealt with the interpretation of rhythmic notation.

Philippe de Vitry (1291–1361) was the first writer to theorize on the "new art." His treatise, *Ars nova,* in which he describes the new way of measuring time, gave the name to this period first in France and then in Italy. De Vitry was also known as a composer.

(The writings of the foregoing theorists and historians are not readily available in English. However, important excerpts from these can be found in Strunk, *Source Readings in Music History.*)

There are a large number of manuscript collections from the twelfth to the fourteenth centuries. The following are generally recognized as the most important:

(a) St. Martial MSS of the twelfth century is a collection of early organum.

(b) Two important collections of motets from the thirteenth century are the Codex Montpellier and the Codex Bamberg.

(c) Fourteenth century Italian secular music is adequately represented by the Codex Squarcialupi. It contains works by Francesco Landini and other Italian composers. Forms included are madrigals, ballatas, and caccias.

Further source readings are identified in appendix 3.

Sixteenth-century woodcut from *Der Weisskunig,* depicting a large number of Renaissance instruments. The number of instruments and the conditions of performance indicate the great rise in instrumental performance and the secular nature of court music in this period. (The Metropolitan Museum of Art, Gift of William Loring Andrews, 1888)

4

⚓

Renaissance
(1400–1600)

CHRONOLOGY

c. 1400 *Guillaume Dufay*
         (c. 1400–1474)

c. 1420 *Johannes Ockeghem*
         (c. 1420–1496)

1430   Rule of the Medici family
         (1430–1495)

1440   Sandro Botticelli
         (1440–1510)

         Meistersingers in Germany
         (c. 1440)

         Josquin des Prez
         (c. 1440–1521)

1449   Lorenzo de Medici
         (1449–1492)

c. 1450 *Heinrich Isaac*
         (c. 1450–1517)

1452   Leonardo da Vinci
         (1452–1519)

         Jacob Obrecht (c. 1452–1505)

1454   Johannes Gutenberg
         (c. 1390–1468) invented
         printing from moveable type
         Bible printed

1469   Niccolò Machiavelli
         (1469–1527)

1471   Albrecht Dürer (1471–1528)

1473   Nicolaus Copernicus
         (1473–1543)

1475   Michelangelo Buonarroti
         (1475–1564)

1477   Tiziano Vicelli (Titian)
         (1477–1576)

1480   Matthias Grünewald
         (1480–1528)

1483   Raphael Sanzio (1483–1520)
         Martin Luther (1483–1546)

c. 1490 *Adrian Willaert*
         (c. 1490–1562)

1496   *Johann Walter* (1496–1570)

1501   *Ottaviano Petrucci*
         (1466–1539) printed the
         Harmonice musices
         odhecaton

1517   Luther's 95 theses
         Beginning of the
         Reformation

c. 1520 *Andrea Gabrieli*
         (c. 1520–1586)

c. 1525 *Giovanni Pierluigi Palestrina*
         (c. 1525–1594)

1532   *Orlando di Lasso*
         (1532–1594)

1534   Church of England separates
         from the Papacy

1540   Founding of the Jesuit
         Society

c. 1540 *Maddalena Casulana*
         (fl. 1566–1583)

1543   *William Byrd* (1543–1623)

1545   *Council of Trent*

1553   *Luca Marenzio* (1553–1599)

c. 1557 *Giovanni Gabrieli*
         (c. 1557–1612)

c. 1560 *Don Carlo Gesualdo*
         (c. 1560–1613)

1564   William Shakespeare
         (1564–1616)

I. SOCIOCULTURAL INFLUENCES ON MUSIC

In its narrowest sense, the term *renaissance* means a rebirth of interest in the ideas and forms of classic antiquity as applied to the artistic and cultural life of Italy during the fifteenth and sixteenth centuries. In its broader sense, however, renaissance implies a general renewal or rebirth of interest in the dignity and inherent value of humankind, a trend already indicated in the late Middle Ages. This trend is reflected in all the political, religious, and social institutions of the period as well as in the arts. It is most adequately expressed in the philosophy of humanism. Music reflected the movement only in the broader sense, and found its greatest expression in the works of the Burgundian and Netherland composers until the final half of the sixteenth century. At that time the Italians, educated in the style of the period by the long influx of northern composers, blossomed into a dominating school. With the contributions of these later schools of composition, the Renaissance witnessed a rebirth of music.

The Protestant Reformation exercised a greater influence upon religious music specifically, and European music generally, than any other movement initiated in the Renaissance. Both the Huguenot and English Reformations gave rise to musical expressions appropriate to these movements, resulting in psalm settings in the vernacular in France and England, and to the creation of an entirely new musical liturgy in the Anglican church. It was, however, the positive inclusion of music by Luther as a vital and important part of the religious liturgy, especially in the form of congregational chorale singing, that contributed substantially to the musical renaissance in German-speaking lands. It was this movement that ultimately led to the great influence of German and Austrian music from the middle of the seventeenth to the end of the nineteenth century.

The Roman Catholic Church remained the leading patron of musical production even though there was a growing tendency toward secularization. Evidence of the concern of the Catholic Church in counteracting the increasing secularization of religious music, as well as the influence of Protestantism, can be seen in the abolition of tropes and all but four sequences, and secular *canti firmi* for the composition of motets and masses by the Council of Trent (1545-1563). The Council's determination to stem the great wave of secularization almost resulted in the banning of all polyphonic settings of liturgical music and a return to the exclusive use of traditional plainsong. The Council and its repercussions were part of the Counter Reformation.

The rise of wealthy and powerful aristocratic patrons in the ruling courts of Burgundy in the fifteenth century, the Holy Roman Empire of Charles V and Philip II, and the princely courts such as those of Florence, Mantua, and Venice, were powerful influences on music. Usually these aristocratic rulers were as influential in religious as in secular affairs, because they maintained important chapels within the courts and became patrons of composers for their religious as well as secular compositions.

Prior to the sixteenth century, with a few notable exceptions, women played insignificant roles in musical life. This changed from midcentury, with the influence of the composer-teacher Casulana (fl. 1566–1583) and the *Concerto di Donne,* a group of talented women performers at the court of Ferrara.

The invention of the printing press in the fifteenth century led to the first successful music printing from moveable type at the beginning of the sixteenth century. Ottaviano Petrucci (1466–1539), an Italian, was the first to employ this method to print an edition of part music, the *Harmonice musices odhecaton,* in 1501. Pierre Attaignant, a Frenchman, published the first collection of French chansons, using moveable type, in Paris in 1528. Thomas Tallis (c. 1505–1585) and William Byrd (1543–1623) published the first English collection of motets in 1575. By the end of the sixteenth century, large numbers of printed musical works were available, particularly editions of secular music such as madrigals, airs, and chansons. Although the aristocracy and wealthy upper middle class were the principal purchasers of such works, the multiplicity of printed copies tended to spread the musical works of important composers over a wider area than was heretofore possible through limited manuscripts.

II. FUNCTION OF MUSIC

The primary purpose of sacred music in the Renaissance was liturgical and devotional. It served both the traditional Roman Catholic and the newly founded Protestant service. The Roman Catholic Church had the more highly organized liturgy, and, therefore, the greater body of religious music was composed in the service of Catholicism.

Secular music provided a highly cultivated group of amateur performers among the aristocracy and upper middle class with appropriate music for singing and playing. Cultivated ladies and gentlemen of the Renaissance were often capable singers or players, and frequently both.

During the last half of the sixteenth century, instrumental music was employed to provide a select society with entertainment performed by professional and skilled amateur players. These performances took place in the salons of the nobility and the homes of wealthy burghers. Music was written in response to the demand for dancing at formal court functions. Popular songs and dances of folklike character supplied the great mass of people with music that was appropriate to festivals and other social occasions, both religious and secular.

III. STYLE AND PERFORMANCE PRACTICE

Much of the music of the Renaissance was based on polyphonic practices. There was a unity of style in both secular and religious music that applied equally to vocal and instrumental compositions as well. The Renaissance represents the last period of music history in which there is such unity of style in all forms.

Formal Organization

Renaissance music shows a unity of formal organization except in the case of small secular poetic and dance forms. One general unifying technique employs a cantus firmus derived primarily from plainsong literature or from folk-song sources, giving rise to works that were basically polyphonic elaborations of a preexisting melodic idea. The cantus firmus was generally placed in the tenor voice, which in the early Renaissance was the lowest voice.

The imitative use of melodic material became an increasingly important organizational device. In order to give variety to such practice, several forms of imitation were used:

(1) In canonic imitation, all voices sound the same melodic material, but each voice begins at a different time. Canonic imitations vary from strict to free imitation of the original melodic materials, and can be constructed so that the pitches of each voice are at the same or at different pitch levels (fig. 4.1).

Figure 4.1 Canon in three voices at the unison: *Illumina oculos meos*

Palestrina

(2) In imitation by inversion, the direction of the original melodic intervals was changed so that the ascending interval in the original melody becomes a descending one in the inverted version, and vice versa. In the excerpt that follows (fig. 4.2), the middle and upper voices present the ascending five-note melody, while the other three voices invert the pattern.

(3) In imitation by retrogression, the original melody is repeated note for note in reverse order. This device is also called crab canon or *cancrizans*. It can also be used in combination with imitation by inversion.

In Machaut's *Ma fin est mon commencement* (My end is my beginning), voice 1 (beginning to end) is identical to voice 2 (end to beginning). Continuing with the intent of the title, voice 3 is a true retrograde, reading identically from beginning to end and from the end to the beginning (fig. 4.3). (This work is from the medieval period, but it is included here because of its clarity in illustrating imitation by retrograde motion.)

Figure 4.2 Canon in inversion: *Jeremiae Prophetae Lamentationes* (1585)
Orlando di Lasso

Figure 4.3 Imitation by retrograde motion: *Ma fin est mon commencement* (rondeau)

Guillaume de Machaut

Continued.

Figure 4.3—*Continued*

(4) In imitation by augmentation, a melody is presented in two voices, one of which is in longer note values than the other (fig. 4.4).

(5) In imitation by diminution, the original melody is answered in a second voice with the same melody, but in shorter note values (fig. 4.5).

Figure 4.4 Imitation by augmentation

A different kind of imitation employed preexisting material in new compositions such as the Parody Mass, which went so far as to employ complete, short polyphonic works in larger works.

In strictly polyphonic works formal organization was episodic. Compositions consisted of a number of sections, each treating its thematic material individually and exhaustively. In highly developed polyphonic forms, such as the motet and Mass, there was rarely any repetition of a previously used musical section or text. Each section constituted the complete treatment of a line of text.

Secular poetic song forms were often characterized by a formal organization that used a principal refrain in contrast to its other musical phrases. Dance forms were based on folk idioms and generally consisted of an application of the principle of repetition and contrast. As opposed to the Mass, all these works are in single rather than multiple movements.

Figure 4.5 Imitation by diminution

Melody

Expression in Renaissance music often was the result of varied melodic treatment. Melodic form was determined by textual rather than musical considerations. Harmony and rhythm cannot be analyzed apart from melodic structure. Melodies were modal, largely vocal in conception, and limited to a range that rarely exceeded the octave. Wide skips were avoided, and most melodic movement was diatonic or restricted to the tones of a particular modal scale. Chromaticism was rare in the early works of the Renaissance, but is frequently found in the secular music of the late Renaissance. (See musica ficta, page 34.)

Rhythm

The restrictive isorhythmic devices of the Middle Ages disappeared in the fifteenth century, although there are some examples of this method of rhythmic organization among early Renaissance compositions. Renaissance rhythms were free from strict metrical phrasing, although many rhythmic formulas were used, including syncopation. Rhythmic phrases were generally long, and free from metrical accent. The rhythms of the polyphonic voices often overlapped (fig. 4.6).

The rhythms of Renaissance music are often complex as a result of the polyphonic writing and the metric intricacies of the texts. One aspect of this complexity is exemplified in the musical puzzles that delighted Renaissance composers. These musical puzzles were based upon a variety of clefs and mensural signatures, leaving the performer to find the key to their solution. They varied from the rather simple to the very intricate, often with instructions for

Figure 4.6 *Zwischen Berg und tiefem Tal:* overlapping rhythmic phrases (bar lines added)

Heinrich Isaac

their solution (fig. 4.7). In its original notation, the puzzle appears simple. However, when transcribed into modern notation, its rhythmic complexity becomes more apparent (fig. 4.8).

Figure 4.7 *Agnus Dei "Ex una voce tres":* a mensuration canon from *Missa L'Homme armé*

Josquin des Prez

Figure 4.8 A transcription of figure 4.7

Josquin des Prez

Harmony

In Renaissance music, harmony results from the simultaneous sounding of more or less independent lines of melody, not from planned harmonic progressions. Composers did not build their music on chordal assumptions within a tonal system. Such a predetermined function of harmony gradually made its appearance at final cadences, however, and began to point the way to the dominance of harmonic considerations over melodic voice leading. One of the most common is the authentic cadence (fig. 4.9). Other cadences that were commonly used are the plagal, Landini (fig. 3.1), Lydian, and Phrygian.

Figure 4.9 A perfect authentic cadence

Harmony was essentially intervallic rather than chordal. The relation between the tones of the melodic lines, particularly in reference to the cantus firmus, was of prime importance in determining the melodic progression and the treatment of dissonance. Since rules and conventions governing voice leading were determined by the treatment of intervals among the voices, that which strikes the ear as harmonic progression today is a result of voice relationships rather than harmonic construction.

Texture

Polyphony was the predominant texture of Renaissance music. Even in the late Renaissance, when a tendency toward homophonic treatment was found in secular songs, the accompanying voices were treated more or less as independent melodies rather than as chordal accompaniments. In the sixteenth century there were works in which harmonic texture was used as a contrast to the predominating polyphonic texture. These homophonic passages were called the *familiar style* (fig. 4.10), suggesting that this might have been a practice generally used in folk or popular music.

Figure 4.10 Familiar style, from the motet: *Magnus es tu, Domine*

Josquin des Prez

Tu   pau - pe - rum re - fu - gi - um,

An engraving of equestrian musicians. This ensemble is performing festive outdoor music on what appear to be sackbuts, cornamuses, and shawms. (The Bettmann Archive)

Instrumentation and Tone Color

The human voice, in solo and ensemble, was the most commonly accepted medium of performance for all Renaissance music. Voice ranges, cantus or superius (soprano), altus, tenor, and bassus became the framework for all vocal compositions. Voices were reinforced by instruments of all kinds in both sacred and secular music. Instruments such as the organ, harpsichord, and clavichord were used independently in the sixteenth century, and string and wind ensembles became increasingly popular.

The English *full consort* was an ensemble in which a consistency of tone color was achieved. These were most commonly groups of viols or recorders in different ranges. Variety in tone color was accomplished by mixing the various types of instruments in performance. This was referred to as a *broken consort.* The lute, which held a place of importance parallel to the piano in the nineteenth century, was the most popular instrument. (A description of these and other instruments may be found in appendix 1.)

Performance Practice

Composers rarely indicated specific voices or instruments for their music. This was left to the judgment of the performers, who selected from whatever performers were available. Notation indicated relative pitch because at the time there was no absolute or fixed pitch such as A = 440 cps. Accommodation to vocal and instrumental ranges determined the actual pitch of any given performance.

Clefs were used before the Renaissance to designate the pitch names and relationships of the notes on the staff. By the sixteenth century, however, regular use was made of the C and F clefs to designate the ranges corresponding to our modern soprano, alto, tenor, and bass voices. The G or treble clef began to displace the soprano C clef in the latter part of the sixteenth century.

No interpretive directions (tempi, dynamics, or phrasing) are to be found in the music of the period until the time of Giovanni Gabrieli. The use of accidentals written above the notes in modern editions indicates the editor's decision that these were included in performance, but not in notation, a practice known as *musica ficta* (described in chapter 3). The performers understood this common practice and added appropriate accidentals to avoid inappropriate voice leading and dissonance. This dependence on the common practice explains the chromatic differences occurring between the notated and performed music of the Renaissance. Another term, concerning which there is little agreement, is *musica reservata.* Several of its interpretations suggest that performance was often regulated by commonly understood practices of improvisation for which no detailed directions were necessary at that time.

The fifteenth-century French practice of using a succession of first inversion triads or sixth-chords was known as *fauxbourdon.* The English *faburden* created similar sounds but was an improvised technique. The composer duplicated a soprano melody at the sixth below, and a singer extemporized a fourth below the soprano. This practice marked the beginning of the use of the third and the full triad as a basic harmonic element (fig. 4.11).

Polychoral singing was cultivated particularly in Venice, due in part to the architecture of St. Mark's Cathedral. The large choral compositions of the Venetian School of the late Renaissance lent themselves to a division of choral forces into two or more groups that were placed in different parts of the cathedral. The success of this practice gave rise to many compositions for divided choral groups, and their placement in various parts of the church was widely adopted by choir directors throughout Europe, extending well into the Baroque era. Two choral groups alternating in performance results in antiphonal singing.

Figure 4.11 Fauxbourdon from *Supremum est mortalabus bonum*

Dufay

IV. MUSIC FOR VOICES

Single-Movement Forms and Structural Devices

Motet

The motet continued to be an important vocal form during the fifteenth and sixteenth centuries. The isorhythmic motet (see chapter 3) continued in use until the middle of the fifteenth century. (Ex. 4.1)

Many new methods of composition were applied to motet writing, but the cantus firmus in long-note values continued in use through the last half of the fifteenth century. The principal motet form of the Renaissance was developed by Josquin des Prez and consisted generally of a work in four to six voices with imitative treatment. The motet was usually made up of a number of sections, nonrepetitive, each of which treated a portion of the text. The texts were always in Latin and taken either from the liturgy of the Mass or from the Bible. In polyphonic writing of this period, the voices seldom concluded textual lines simultaneously. Consequently, well-defined harmonic cadences were few, except at such marked divisions in the music as occur with changes in meter or at the conclusion. (Ex. 4.2–4.14)

Hymn

Hymns were polyphonic strophic settings of Latin poetic religious texts in which each verse of text was repeated to the same musical setting. The upper voice was usually melodic. (Ex. 4.15–4.16)

Chorale

The hymn tunes and their four-part chordal settings adopted for use in the German Protestant church by Luther and his musical collaborators are known as chorales, German Protestant Chorales, or Lutheran Chorales. The texts were in the vernacular—principally German. The tunes were often taken from older Latin hymns or specifically composed to appropriate texts, but a rich source was the secular folk melody. These chorales in their simple form are usually binary, with a repeated first section. The melodies, predominantly in the upper voice, are slow moving, and the cadences are very marked and strong. (Ex. 4.17–4.19)

Psalms

The psalm compositions of the French Protestants (the Huguenots) were simple settings, generally in chordal style, with some free polyphonic treatment. The dominant melody, as in the German Chorale, was in the upper voice. Rhythmically, these psalm settings were somewhat more lively than the German Chorales, and the texts were French metrical translations. In the Anglican church, psalms were sung antiphonally, with the choir divided into two groups, placed on either side of the area in which the service was performed. (Ex. 4.20–4.21)

Anthem

Similar to the motet, anthems were introduced by the Anglican church. They followed the general structure of the Renaissance motet, but were sung in English. Two types evolved. The *full anthem* was sung in motet style; that is, with the entire choir participating throughout. In contrast, the *verse anthem* presented soloists and chorus with instrumental forces in varying combinations. (Ex. 4.22–4.25)

Frottola

This derivation of a dance form represents the most important of the strophic forms developed in the late fifteenth and early sixteenth centuries in northern Italy. It is a sophisticated folk song, generally chordal in structure, and characterized by variously arranged patterns of two contrasting musical ideas. One pattern commonly used is ABAABAB. The frottola was written for three or four voices. The lower parts were probably played on instruments, as well as sung. (Ex. 4.26–4.28)

Madrigal

The madrigal is the most highly developed of all Renaissance secular vocal forms. It originated in Italy and flourished in the latter half of the sixteenth century. Composers of all schools, even outside Italy, set the lyrics of Italian poets in madrigal form. Three stages of development are discernible: the chordal style represented by Arcadelt and Verdelot; the more highly developed imitative polyphonic style, often in five voices, represented by Palestrina, Lasso, and Rore; and the highly dramatic and expressive madrigals of the late Renaissance, represented by Marenzio, Gesualdo, and Monteverdi. The madrigal became very popular in England, where for a short time an independent school of composers rivaled the Italians in quantity and quality. The largest body of madrigals by English composers was set to English lyric poetry, though some were written in Italian.

The Renaissance madrigal was a through-composed (nonrepetitive) polyphonic composition contrasting with the verse-refrain madrigal of the fourteenth century. It varied from the chordal, much as in the frottola, to the imitatively polyphonic. In some respects the madrigal was a secular counterpart to the sacred motet, as were all these highly developed secular forms.

There were madrigals that were humorous, and others of a more serious nature, often treating the subject of unrequited love. Instances of the deliberate use of musically expressive devices to fit the text were frequent. These so-called "madrigalisms" consisted of textual interruptions by rests, chromaticism, or naive attempts to make the music illustrate the text by means of rhythmic and melodic tone painting. Frequent changes of rhythm were often used. Madrigals were commonly written in three to five voices. Toward the end of the sixteenth century there was a distinct tendency to write madrigals in homophonic style with a predominating or solo voice. The *ballet madrigal,* most common in England, was a strophic form with a "fa-la" refrain. (Ex. 4.29–4.40)

Chanson

Fifteenth-century chansons were generally in the repetitive, fixed forms of the rondeau or virelai. In the sixteenth century, the fixed forms were abandoned, and there was a truly polyphonic treatment in imitative style. The term *chanson* embraced the whole of the polyphonic secular writing to French texts of the fifteenth and sixteenth centuries. Like the motet, chansons were usually sectional and through-composed. The sections, however, were short and marked with simultaneous cadences in all voices, and tended to be homophonic. Their rhythms were faster and lighter than in the motet. Most sixteenth-century chansons were for four voices, and the top voice usually carried the principal melody. (Ex. 4.41–4.47)

Polyphonic Lied

The German counterpart of the Italian and English madrigal, as well as the French chanson, was the polyphonic *Lied.* Almost without exception, they were polyphonic settings of folk-song melodies. In some instances these settings were predominantly chordal. However, an imitative polyphonic treatment developed in the last half of the fifteenth and first half of the sixteenth centuries. (Ex. 4.48–4.49)

Quodlibet

The quodlibet was a polyphonic composition in which two or more popular, folk, or sacred songs were combined to make an imaginative polytextual unit. (Ex. 4.50–4.51)

Ayre

In England the ayre was a late development of the Renaissance. These largely homophonic songs were strophic. The accompanying voices were normally played on the lute, though in some instances (such as Dowland) they were sung as vocal ensemble music much as the madrigal was. Its most distinguishing characteristic was its strophic form. (Ex. 4.52–4.53)

Miscellaneous Secular Forms

A large body of traditional strophic forms such as the *villancico, virelai, ballata, and rondeau* employed both monophonic and polyphonic styles in the fifteenth and sixteenth centuries. They retained their fixed forms, although they were often more simple in form and rhythmic structure than earlier. The principal melody was placed in the uppermost part, and settings were generally chordal with little imitation. The formal musical structure of these songs was determined by their strict poetic forms. (Ex. 4.54–4.58)

Composite Forms

Mass

The Mass is the only important composite form used in the Renaissance. It is built up of a series of movements, each of which is similar in structure and form to the motet. Each of these movements provides a musical setting for one of the five principal parts of the Ordinary of the Roman Catholic Mass: Kyrie, Gloria, Credo, Sanctus, and Agnus Dei. As in the motet, the composer employed secular, sacred, and freely invented *canti firmi,* as well as imitative techniques for organizational purposes. Renaissance Masses, for the most part, were based on preexisting material: plainsong, folk song, motets, or polyphonic secular works.

One type, often called the *Plainsong Mass,* was constructed on appropriate and different canti firmi for each of the parts of the Mass (e.g., the Kyrie on a plainsong Kyrie, the Gloria on a plainsong Gloria). This procedure was in use since the late Middle Ages.

The *Cantus Firmus Mass* was the most frequently composed type in the Renaissance. It used a single cantus firmus that appeared in each of the several parts of the composition. The cantus firmus might consist of an entire preexisting melody or only a portion of it. It might be quoted literally or paraphrased in all movements, though always initiated in the tenor voice. In contrast, it may be paraphrased throughout each movement and appear in all voices imitatively. (Ex. 4.60–4.61)

A special type of Mass, the *Parody Mass,* was developed in the sixteenth century. This form is an even more complex extension of the technique of basing the parts, as well as the whole, on a preexisting form. In the Parody Mass, a polyphonic motet was used as a basis for imitative development. The motet could be used in its entirety or in fragments throughout the several movements of the Mass. A motet was often selected from among the composer's own works as the basis for Parody Masses. (Ex. 4.64)

Names given to the preceding mass types were taken from the motets or canti firmi from which they were derived (that is, *Missa Pange Lingua*). Relatively few masses were composed entirely on original, freely invented material. (Ex. 4.63, 4.65)

V. MUSIC FOR INSTRUMENTS

Single-Movement Forms and Structural Devices

Although instruments were popularly used in musical performance in the Renaissance, there was little independent instrumental writing until very late in the sixteenth century. Consequently, there are very few purely instrumental forms that are unrelated to polyphonic vocal music. Except for dance music, instrumental performances duplicated or substituted for voice parts in polyphonic vocal music. Some works written specifically for instruments in the sixteenth century displayed a consideration for the special technical capabilities of those instruments then in use.

Ricercar

The instrumental equivalent of the vocal motet, the ricercar, was constructed in several sections, each of which had a musical theme that was treated imitatively and contrapuntally. The ricercar written for instrumental ensemble was closely patterned after the vocal motet, with numerous sections and melodic themes. The fact that many such works were published with instructions "to be sung and played" indicated their affinity to vocal forms.

There were nonimitative ricercars for the lute, organ, and instrumental ensemble. They seem to have been written more for study purposes, since they tend to exploit the technical possibilities of the instruments. (Ex. 4.66–4.68)

The organ ricercar, although basically the same construction, tended to have fewer themes and sections, and therefore the treatment of the themes was longer and more elaborate. Contrapuntal imitation was its principal formal ingredient.

Canzona

The instrumental canzona, which appeared in the sixteenth century, was at first a mere instrumental arrangement, or transcription, of the vocal chanson. It was written for either lute or keyboard. Subsequently, composers wrote original instrumental works in the style of the vocal chanson that also borrow the name *canzona*. Keyboard canzonas, as well as those for instrumental ensembles, varied from the conventional imitative and sectional character of the vocal chansons to the spectacular polychoral type of the Venetian school. These Venetian compositions presented alternating sections in varying rhythms and textures, and were performed by alternating choirs of instruments. (Ex. 4.69–4.71)

In Nomine

In nomines were instrumental works based on the antiphon *Gloria tibi Trinitas,* which was derived from a cantus firmus mass of the same name by John Taverner. They were written exclusively in England. (Ex. 4.72)

Toccata

A form of keyboard composition deriving its name from the Italian *toccare* (to touch), the toccata exploited a rather improvisatory style in which florid homophonic scale and choral passages were combined with imitative sections. Most characteristic of the toccata is its adherence to the keyboard idiom and its unchanging tempo. (Ex. 4.73–4.74)

Fantasia

This rather ambiguous title was given to instrumental compositions in the sixteenth century. The name probably referred to the improvisatory nature of such works as the ricercar, which combined a free form with strict contrapuntal style. The title "Fantasia" was used to cover a wide variety of compositions published at the very end of the sixteenth century, many of which were free ricercars and chansons printed in tablature. (Ex. 4.75–4.76)

Prelude

This term was applied very loosely to a variety of compositions which originally served to introduce a liturgical ceremony. In the fifteenth and sixteenth centuries it was used to designate free, idiomatic keyboard music. The prelude was often very short and in homophonic style, and usually exploited the technique of the keyboard. Unlike the canzona or ricercar, the prelude does not derive from any vocal form, but represents the first truly instrumental music. English virginal composers often used the term to describe virtuoso keyboard compositions. (Ex. 4.77)

Variation

This form is basically repetitive, using a newly invented or a preexisting melody presented in a succession of alterations. Composers of variations faced the problem of maintaining the relationship among the successive versions and at the same time providing interest through the alterations. In the sixteenth century, early versions of this form varied the contrapuntal texture by the use of imitative figures, or by embellishing the melody by ornamentation and rapid scale passages.

Variations for vihuela (lute) or keyboard in the early sixteenth-century Spanish school illustrate the contrapuntal type, whereas the keyboard variation of the English school is representative of the figured type. (Ex. 4.78–4.80)

Dance Forms

There are only a few instrumental dances in polyphonic style to be found in the fifteenth century. Those that are known come from the *Münchener Liederbuch* and the *Glogauer Liederbuch,* the two large collections of dances and songs dating from c. 1460. The sixteenth century, however, is dominated by dance forms and is often called the century of the dance. These dances are

characteristically paired—*pavane-galliard* and *passamezzo-saltarello.* In
these pairs, the first dance is in slow duple meter, followed by the second in
fast triple meter. In many instances the second dance is a rhythmically
changed version of the first dance. This was particularly true of the German
Tanz and *Nachtanz,* or *Tanz* and *Proportz.* In this case the second dance
assumes the characteristics of a variation on the first. The form of the dance
is binary. (Ex. 4.81–4.86)

Composite Forms

At the end of the sixteenth century, the pairing of dances and the grouping of
several dances indicated a desire to write instrumental works of larger scope.
These combinations are among the first examples of the instrumental suite,
which became a standard form in the Baroque period. (Ex. 4.87)

VI. COMPOSERS

In the Middle Ages, artworks in all media were for the most part anonymous
efforts. Renaissance composers commonly began to be identified by name
with their works. Moreover, many of those whose names we now know were
innovators in style, or leaders of particular schools of composition. During the
Renaissance there were two distinctive schools, the Burgundian and the Flemish, or Netherlands schools. The Burgundian school flourished during the first
half of the fifteenth century and included Dufay and Binchois. The Flemish
school, from about 1450 to 1600, included such composers as Ockeghem,
Obrecht, Josquin des Prez, and many others who were to spread the Flemish
innovations to various sections of Europe. Although their works represent
Renaissance music of high quality, mention of them here does not mean that
their works were always superior to composers whose names have been omitted. In addition there were vital musical centers or schools in England, Spain,
Germany, and Italy, particularly in Rome and Venice.

    John Dunstable (c. 1380–1453) was an English composer and early mas-
ter of counterpoint. He is especially noted for his interesting contrapuntal lines
composed around plainsong melodies. He was an important influence on the
composers of the Burgundian school. (Ex. 4.1, 4.2, 4.88–4.89)

    Guillaume Dufay (c. 1400–1474) is considered the master of the Burgun-
dian school. His works show a strong preference for the upper voices, both
melodically and rhythmically. The use of instruments is often implied. He
wrote in all the religious and secular forms of his time. (Ex. 4.15, 4.42–4.43,
4.61, 4.90–4.91)

    Gilles Binchois (c. 1400–1460), also one of the Burgundian group, is best
known for the excellence of his secular works, especially the chanson. Like
others of his time, his stylistic features were essentially the same in both
sacred and secular polyphony. (Ex. 4.41, 4.92–4.93)

A fifteenth-century illuminated manuscript depicting Guillaume Dufay (1400–1474) and Gilles Binchois (1400–1460), two outstanding composers of fifteenth-century Burgundy. On the left is a portative organ, on the right an early harp. (The Bettmann Archive)

Johannes Ockeghem (c. 1420–1496), a pupil of Dufay and the leader of the Flemish school, developed devices of imitation that served as models for those who later perfected the *a cappella style*. He was also one of the first to write four-part polyphony that created a seamless fabric. His writing was generally for low voices. (Ex. 4.57, 4.59, 4.94–4.97)

Josquin des Prez (c. 1440–1521) of the Flemish School, was one of the greatest composers of all time. The rhythmic freedom, lyricism, and clarity of texture of his music sets him apart from his contemporaries. He was fortunate to have the majority of his compositions published during his lifetime. Because of this fact, coupled with his genius, he was well known and had great influence on other composers. In general his sacred works are contrapuntal, but many of the secular works tend toward homophony, perhaps due to the influence of the Italian frottola. (Ex. 4.4–4.6, 4.44, 4.62–4.63, 4.98–4.101)

Heinrich Isaac (c. 1450–1517), although a Flemish composer, was at one time court composer to Maximilian in Vienna, bringing the Flemish style to Austria. He wrote many masses and motets, but it was his polyphonic settings of chorale melodies that make his music memorable. (Ex. 4.49, 4.102)

Jacob Obrecht (c. 1452–1505) was born in the Netherlands. He carried on the innovations of Ockeghem, adding an expressive quality that followed the meaning of the texts. In his four-voice writing, the lowest part became a true bass line, leading to frequent authentic cadences. He was also one of the first composers to have a large number of his works published during his lifetime. (Ex. 4.3, 4.103–4.104)

Clément Janequin (c. 1485–1558), a prolific composer from the south of France, is most remembered for his programmatic chansons. These compositions imitated many sounds from nature or experience. Among the better-known chansons are *Le chant des oiseaux* and *La guerre.* Additionally, he composed many settings of the psalms in the French language. (Ex. 4.46–4.47, 4.105)

Adrian Willaert (c. 1490–1562) was a Flemish composer who became the founder of the Venetian school, numbering among his pupils such masters as Andrea Gabrieli and Zarlino. He held the post of Master of the Chapel at St. Mark's, where he introduced a style of writing for antiphonal choirs. His sacred music is of high quality, but he is perhaps best known for his madrigals, a form that he raised far above the level of the popular frottola. (Ex. 4.66, 4.106)

Ludwig Senfl (c. 1486–1543), whose name means "little mustard," was Swiss, but held musical positions in Germany. He was known as a singer and a composer of church music. As a pupil of Isaac, he cultivated the Flemish style. He was also known for the charm of his polyphonic settings of the German Lied. Luther praised Senfl as the "Prince of all German music." (Ex. 4.48, 4.107)

Thomas Tallis (c. 1505–1585), an English organist and composer, was the first to use the English language in settings of the liturgy of the Anglican church. He also wrote a large number of motets and masses in Latin. (Ex. 4.23, 4.108–4.109)

Jacobus Clemens (c. 1510–c. 1556), a Flemish composer known as "Clemens non Papa" to distinguish him from a pope of similar name, was one of the more progressive composers of the early sixteenth century in his use of chromatic harmonization. His best works are masses and motets, but he is also important as the first composer of polyphonic settings of psalms in the vernacular (*Souterliedekens*). (Ex. 4.110)

Antonio de Cabezon (1510–1566), an important Spanish composer and organist, strongly influenced many European composers for the organ and other keyboard instruments. He also made keyboard arrangements of the vocal music of Josquin des Prez and other Flemish composers. (Ex. 4.111)

Andrea Gabrieli (c. 1520–1586), an Italian composer of the Venetian school, studied with Adrian Willaert, and was the uncle and teacher of Giovanni Gabrieli. After extensive travel in Germany and Bohemia, Andrea became organist at St. Mark's in Venice, where he achieved a great reputation as organist. He was a prolific composer of both choral and instrumental music, ranging from massive sacred works to madrigals. Many of his larger compositions exhibit the polychoral tradition of the Venetian school established by Willaert. (Ex. 4.67, 4.69, 4.112–4.113)

Philippe de Monte (1521–1603), a Belgian, and a friend of Roland de Lassus (Orlando di Lasso) was influenced by the Flemish style. He is best known for his expressive madrigals. (Ex. 4.114–4.115)

Giovanni Pierluigi Palestrina (c. 1525–1594), an Italian composer, is generally considered the greatest master of Renaissance Catholic music. His most important post was that of director of the Cappella Giulia at the Vatican. Palestrina is noted for the perfection of a purely vocal style, commonly known as the *a cappella* style. His music is characterized by a high degree of technical perfection, with diatonic melodies and smooth textures that culminated in a rare beauty of sound that is almost transcendental. His *Missa Papae Marcelli* became a model of pure Catholic music. (Ex. 4.11–4.12, 4.64–4.65, 4.116–4.118)

Roland de Lassus, or, *Orlando di Lasso* (1532–1594), was also a product of the Flemish school but was international in his music. He wrote more than two thousand compositions. His fame rests mainly on his religious music. However, his writing was equally effective in Italian madrigals, German polyphonic Lieder, and French chansons. Historians rank him as the greatest of the Flemish composers, and along with Palestrina, one of the most important of the Renaissance composers. (Ex. 4.8–4.9, 4.119–4.120)

Maddalena Casulana (b. ca. 1540) was a renowned Italian singer and the composer of sixty–six extant madrigals. Philippe de Monte's first book of madrigals was dedicated to her, and Monteverdi conducted a wedding piece by Casulana at the wedding of Wilhelm IV of Bavaria to Renée of Lorraine. She was also an influential teacher.

William Byrd (1543–1623) was one of the greatest composers in English history. He is best known for his superb polyphonic settings of sacred texts, including masses for three, four, and five voices. He was equally skilled in keyboard music for the organ and virginal. His *Carmen's Whistle,* a set of variations for virginal, was very popular during his lifetime. (Ex. 4.13, 4.24, 4.121–4.122)

Tomás Luis de Victoria (c. 1549–1611), a leading representative of the Roman school in Spain, studied in Rome, probably with Palestrina. However, his music has a dramatic intensity and spiritual fervor that is thoroughly Spanish. He is best known for his motets, of which there are many in four, five, and six parts. He also wrote a large number of other works, including a *Requiem Mass,* considered his masterpiece, and a book of hymns for four voices. (Ex. 4.123–4.124)

Luca Marenzio (1553–1599) was an important Italian madrigalist. His writing demonstrates the work of a progressive composer who made many innovations in chordal relationships and expressive chromaticism. (Ex. 4.31–4.32, 4.125–4.127)

Giovanni Gabrieli (c. 1557–1612) was a nephew and pupil of Andrea Gabrieli. The greatest composer of the Venetian school, he extended the grand musical tradition at St. Mark's Cathedral. He was one of the first to write expressly for combined voices and instruments. Among his best-known works in this medium are the collections called *Sacrae Symphoniae.* He achieved massive sonorities with his polychoral technique. He is often regarded as the first to develop orchestration, and to indicate varied dynamics as in his *Sonata Pian'e Forte.* (Ex. 4.70, 4.128–4.129)

Thomas Morley (1557–1602) was an English composer of madrigals and ballets. He published the *Triumphs of Oriana,* a set of twenty-five madrigals by twenty-three composers—each madrigal in honor of Queen Elizabeth I. He was also the author of the first treatise on music printed in England, *A Plaine and Easie Introduction to Practicall Musicke.* (Ex. 4.130–4.133)

Don Carlo Gesualdo (c. 1560–1613) was an Italian madrigalist whose works represent the extreme of chromaticism reached in the last years of the Renaissance. The harmonic results achieved by Gesualdo, while often described as mannerism, are indicative of a growing consciousness of the strength of musical expression and of the ideals of the dawning Baroque era. (Ex. 4.35, 4.134–4.135)

John Dowland (1563–1626) was one of the greatest lutenists of all time, and England's finest composer of lute songs. He lived a most exciting life, having been involved, at least peripherally, in a plot to assassinate Queen Elizabeth I. Of his instrumental music, the *Lachrimae* is perhaps the best known, and its opening melodic gesture was widely imitated by other composers of the period. His compositional style also allows him to be considered a Baroque composer. (Ex. 4.136)

Hans Leo Hassler (1564–1612) flourished in the period that bridged the Renaissance and the Baroque. He was a German who studied in Italy with Andrea Gabrieli, adapted the Venetian style to the German Lied, and created a strong German musical style. He wrote in all the current vocal and keyboard forms, both Renaissance and early Baroque, but was best known for his settings of German polyphonic songs and chorales. (Ex. 4.137–4.138)

Claudio Monteverdi (1567–1643), like Hassler, spans the final years of the Renaissance and the beginning of the Baroque. He was one of the first composers to employ consciously two different practices: a *prima prattica (stile antico),* and a *seconda prattica (stile moderno).* Although he wrote sacred choral music and madrigals in the first practice, typical of the Renaissance, it was his use of the second practice that marked his contribution to the emerging Baroque and made him historically important. (Ex. 4.40, 4.139)

Thomas Weelkes (c. 1575–1623), one of the greatest of the English madrigalists, was well in advance of his time in his characterization of text. He wrote numerous anthems and services for the Anglican liturgy. (Ex. 4.140)

ADDITIONAL COMPOSERS

A. Austria
Paul Hofhaimer (1459–1537)
Jacobus Gallus (Handl)
(1550–1591)
B. England
John Taverner (c. 1490–1545)
John Bull (c. 1562–1628)
Giles Farnaby (c. 1565–1640)
John Bennet (c. 1570–c. 1614)
John Wilbye (1574–1638)
Orlando Gibbons (1583–1625)
John Farmer (fl. 1591–1601)
C. Germany
Conrad Paumann (c. 1410–1473)
Heinrich Finck (1445–1527)
Johann Walter (1496–1570)
Johannes Eccard (1553–1611)
Melchior Franck (c. 1579–1639)
D. Italy
Marchetto Cara (c. 1470–c. 1525)
Constanzo Festa (c. 1480–1545)
Cipriano de Rore (1516–1565)

Annibale (Il Padovano)
(c. 1527–1575)
Claudio Merulo (1533–1604)
Marco Antonio Ingegneri
(c. 1545–1592)
Orazio Vecchi (1550–1605)
Giovanni Gastoldi (d. 1622)
Raffaella Aleotti (c. 1570–c. 1646)
Caterina Assandra (fl. 1609)
E. Mexico
Hernando Franco (1532–1585)
F. Netherlands-Burgundy (French)
Pierre de La Rue (c. 1455–1518)
Nicholas Gombert (c. 1490–1556)
Claudin de Sermisy (c. 1490–1562)
Jacob Arcadelt (c. 1505–1568)
Cipriano de Rore (1516–1565)
Claude le Jeune (c. 1528–1600)
Philippe Verdelot (d. 1552)
Thomas Crécquillon (d. 1557)
G. Spain
Juan del Encina (1468–c. 1529)
Luis Milan (c. 1500–1561)
Cristóbal de Morales (c. 1500–1553)

VII. HISTORIANS, THEORISTS, AND MANUSCRIPT SOURCES

The theoretical treatises on music written during the Renaissance were generally in Latin, the language of scholars, and in a learned style that, today, often obscures rather than illuminates. These treatises are the sources of most of our knowledge of Renaissance music not revealed by the music itself. Without these sources, little would be precisely known about Renaissance notation, rhythm, tempo, tuning, performance, instrumental construction, or rules of theory. Many of these works contain examples from the music of the times that would otherwise be unavailable. In cases in which more than one treatise was written by a theoretician, the most important has been listed below with its original title and date of writing or publication, as well as any modern edition or translation.

Johannes Tinctoris (1435–1511) was a Belgian theorist and composer. His *Terminorum musicae diffinitorium* (Naples 1473) is the oldest known dictionary of musical terms. An English translation appeared in London in 1849. Several of his writings were published in Coussemaker's complete edition of the writings of Tinctoris in 1875.

Bartolome Ramos de Pareja (c. 1440–1491) was a Spanish theorist. His *Musica practica* (Bologna 1482) is a landmark in the science of harmony, particularly concerning intonation. Ramos, through his division of the monochord, established the ratios of 4:5 and 5:6 for the major and minor thirds.

Franchino Gaforio (1451–1522), an Italian theorist, dealt with rules of counterpoint and compositional practice, as well as the current performance styles in his magnum opus, *Practica musicae Franchino Gaforio Laudenis . . . in IV libris* (Milan 1496).

Martin Agricola (1486–1556) was a German theorist whose *Musica instrumentalis deudsch* (Wittenberg 1529) remains an authoritative work on the instruments of the time. It is a valuable source for the history of notation.

Henricus Glareanus (1488–1563) was a Swiss philosopher, theologian, historian, poet, and musical scholar. His *Dodechachordon* (Basle 1547) advocated the completion of the modal series to twelve and greatly influenced the concept of modality and tonality. A German translation of this work was published in 1888.

Pietro Aaron (1489–1545) is one of the most important Italian theorists of the early sixteenth century. *Thoscanello della Musica* (Venice 1523) contains descriptions of contrapuntal rules, the chord formations employed in his day.

Gioseffo Zarlino (1517–1590) discussed various topics concerning music of his day in the four books that make up his major work *Instituzioni harmoniche* (Venice 1558). This treatise includes rules of counterpoint, intonation, treatment of text, and the general excellence of music.

Thomas Morley (1557–1602) wrote and published the earliest treatise on music published in England. *A Plaine and Easie Introduction to Practicall Musicke* (London 1597) is a discourse on all phases of music making. Reprinted in 1937, this is the most important English book on musical theory from the Renaissance. Another modern edition was published in 1952.

(Important excerpts in English from several of the foregoing works can be found in Strunk, *Source Readings in Music History.*)

Until music printing became a practicality in the sixteenth century, the manuscript collections constituted the most valuable source of notated music of the Renaissance. These manuscripts were usually made by anonymous copyists and were treasured by the libraries of monasteries, churches, and royal courts. Of the countless manuscripts written before the end of the fifteenth century, when the printing of music had not yet displaced the collecting of musical works in handwritten form, certain monumental collections stand out as important. In many cases these are the sole sources of folk and composed music.

Old Hall MS, written about 1450 at the Catholic College of St. Edmunds in Old Hall, England, contains a large number of Mass compositions and hymns. A modern edition of this work was published from 1935 to 1938 by Ramsbotham and Collins.

The *Trent Codices* contain sacred and secular polyphonic music of the fifteenth century in six volumes. They include perhaps the richest collection of music by most of the masters of fifteenth-century polyphony. A large part of this collection has been printed in modern notation in the *Denkmäler der Tonkunst in Oesterreich* (vols. 7, 11, 19, 27, 31, and 40).

Among the collections of purely secular songs, the *chansonniers* and *Liederbücher* of France and Germany, respectively, are especially noteworthy. The *Copenhagen Chansonnier* of the fifteenth century contains thirty-three polyphonic chansons, and is representative of a number of such collections. It is available in modern edition also. Of the German collections, the *Glogauer Liederbuch,* the *Lochaimer Liederbuch,* and the *Münchner Liederbuch* contain vocal and instrumental polyphonic and monophonic settings of German folk songs and composed works. All three of these are published in modern editions.

Further source readings are identified in appendix 3.

Exuberantly decorated organ cases were the hallmark of Baroque organ builders. This example includes typical angel musicians high on the organ case. (Historical Pictures/Stock Montage, Inc.)

5

Baroque
(1600–1750)

c. 1666   *Elisabeth-Claude Jacquet de la Guerre* (c. 1666–1729)

1668   *François Couperin (1668–1733)*

1678   *Antonio Vivaldi (1678–1741)*

First public German opera house opens in Hamburg

1681   *Georg Philipp Telemann (1681–1767)*

1683   *Jean-Philippe Rameau (1683–1764)*

1685   *Johann Sebastian Bach (1685–1750)*

Domenico Scarlatti (1685–1757)

George Frideric Handel (1685–1759)

1689   Peter the Great, Tsar of Russia (1689–1725)

1700   *Sauveur measures sound vibrations*

1709   *Cristofori builds the first pianoforte*

1710   *Giovanni Battista Pergolesi (1710–1736)*

I. SOCIOCULTURAL INFLUENCES ON MUSIC

The term *baroque* probably derived from the Portuguese word *barroco,* meaning an irregularly shaped pearl. It was first used as a term of scorn for works of art, particularly architecture, produced from the end of the sixteenth century to the middle of the eighteenth century. The word no longer carries a derogatory meaning and is widely used to designate the arts and music of this era. The term applies to a long period of history and to such diverse countries as Italy, France, England, and the vast territories that came under Germanic influence. So generous was the artistic output of the Baroque that it is normally divided into three phases: early, middle, and late. In general, Baroque art is considered elaborately decorative, dramatic, flamboyant, and emotional. There is a tendency to fuse the arts wherever possible. Architecture, painting, and sculpture, for example, are combined in the domed ceilings of seventeenth- and eighteenth-century churches. Music, literature, painting, architecture, and sculpture are all combined in the opera, or *dramma per musica.* The intense desire to express an idea, a feeling, or the artists' deep convictions and emotions often led to excesses in all forms of art. The tendency to ascribe these violent expressive qualities to lack of taste or to the desire to cover poor workmanship placed the arts of the Baroque in disfavor in the late eighteenth and nineteenth centuries. A reappraisal of the Baroque in the twentieth century as representative of a period of violent and revolutionary upheavals, however, gives new insight into the deep-lying motives that found expression in what seems at first to be the arts of excess.

The Baroque movement had its inception in Italy as a part of the Counter-Reformation. Its influence and spirit spread rapidly into all parts of Europe, particularly into southern Germany and Austria, where the Roman Catholic Counter-Reformation was most successful in its struggle with the Protestant north. Despite its first association with the Counter-Reformation, the Baroque spirit became an equally vital part of the Protestant Reformation, and in fact pervaded spiritual and secular forms of artistic expression. Several important movements in religion, government, economics, and science influenced the artistic activity of the Baroque.

The struggle between Roman Catholics and Protestants over religious issues, political power, and the ownership of land brought about the Thirty Years' War. It dominated the first half of the seventeenth century, especially in northern and central Europe, widening the cultural and musical differences between Roman Catholics and Protestants. Roman Catholics in the south were influenced primarily by the Italian style, whereas Protestants in the north worked to expand and elaborate on the chorale tradition. This devastating war delayed the development of Baroque musical life in the German lands for more than a generation. However, both the Roman Catholic Church, which in this series of wars partially regained its political influence, and the Protestant churches, which developed a clearcut form of its own, adapted the prevailing magnificence of Baroque style for their own purposes.

The rise of absolute monarchies and the unification of national states played an important part in the creation of national styles, because the monarchs and princes were among the most important patrons of a lavish musical life. The courts of Louis XIV and Louis XV of France, and the Hapsburgs of Spain and Austria, were centers that stimulated the production of large, spectacular forms of musical expression like the opera. Smaller courts, such as those of the German princes and dukes, were influential in cultivating intimate music for salon and chapel. The courts of the Dukes of Weimar and the Princes of Anhalt-Cöthen are examples of these smaller but highly cultural courts.

Worldwide intensive colonization during the seventeenth and eighteenth centuries gave rise to a wealthy merchant class. This wealth supplied the basis for rich, independent cities that were to provide a suitable climate for the establishment of a commercial theater and its musical production, the opera. Venice and Hamburg are good examples of such concentrations of merchant wealth, and their musical theaters became internationally famous during the period.

Scholarly inquiry became much more important in the Baroque era. Discoveries through the application of inductive reasoning were most spectacular in the sciences of physiology, astronomy, mathematics, and physics. The success of scientific examination in these fields influenced musicians to apply methods of science to problems of music, and led to a systematic development of the techniques and materials of musical art. Such works, discoveries, and devices as Bach's *Art of the Fugue,* Rameau's *Treatise on Harmony,* the practice of well-tempered tuning, and the perfection of the violin family are all examples of the urge to systematize, and to investigate through scientific inquiry.

Literature and music abounded in affectations and expressive feeling. Architecture achieved these by means of such devices as the arch without a keystone and the twisted stone columns as decorative elements whose function no longer was architectural but expressive. Music achieved these same qualities in the tension created by dissonance within the tonal system of Baroque harmony. Related to this was the *doctrine of affections,* a philosophical position that assumed that the arousal and sustaining of feelings and affections was the primary purpose of music. This doctrine expected that a consistent emotion be evoked and sustained throughout a movement or composition. As the doctrine was practiced, numerous musical formulas were devised for the evocation of particular emotions. It was a calculated and planned emotional music.

II. FUNCTION OF MUSIC

While much of the religious music was written for purely liturgical purposes, especially for the Lutheran church, an increasing amount of religious music for instruments was used for nonliturgical purposes. Some of this nonliturgical music was used for preludes, postludes, and musical background for quasi-religious purposes such as marriage ceremonies, dedications of new buildings, and the installation of civil or religious officials.

Much music in the latter part of the Baroque was written for amateur musicians who performed in the households of the aristocracy and the wealthy class. Music for private entertainment was cultivated in these households, where small bands of musicians provided both the compositions for and performances of dinner music, dances, and even ensemble concerts that ranged in style from the purely utilitarian to that of significant aesthetic quality. A substantial portion of this music was instrumental; however, vocal music was also very important. This was truly chamber music, meant more for the pleasure of the performer than for an audience.

In the large wealthy courts, ballets and operas were first performed as special entertainments for princes and courtiers. Opera soon developed into a popular form of public entertainment, occurring first in Italy and in private theaters, and thereafter in public theaters throughout Europe. Performances of purely instrumental music were rarely given for the general public.

The oratorio was the religious counterpart of the opera. Because of its subject matter and presentation without staging, gesture, costumes, or lighting, it was not as popular as opera, but it found success as a public choral concert.

Special festive occasions called for vocal as well as instrumental music. Secular cantatas were often presented for such events with texts that referred directly or allegorically to the occasion.

The musical arts were taught in cathedral and orphanage schools. In addition, young boys who showed interest and talent either were taught by their own musical fathers or relatives or were attached to the households of composer-performers. Without doubt, many compositions were written for the teaching of such prospective musicians. Such works as the *Orgelbüchlein* (Little Organ Book), by J. S. Bach, were in part to provide exercise material for his four musical sons. *The Art of Playing on the Violin,* by Geminiani, was a systematic approach to instrumental pedagogy. Instruction in performance and composition was restricted to the aspiring musician and to the households of the aristocracy and wealthy burghers.

III. STYLE AND PERFORMANCE PRACTICE

For the first time in the history of western European music, two styles flourished side by side: (1) the Renaissance style, the *stile antico* or *prima prattica,* which carried over into the Baroque period; and (2) the new Baroque style itself, often called *stile moderno.* The following characterizations apply to the *stile moderno,* which is typically Baroque. It must be realized, however, that the music of many composers, including some of the most important, continued to possess characteristics of Renaissance style.

Stile moderno was characterized by several stylistic compositional devices peculiar to the Baroque itself. One of these devices was given the Greek name of *monody.* This was a manner of writing in which melodic line was supported by a very simple chordal accompaniment. Strictly speaking, therefore, it is in homophonic style. Originally, the melodic line was something midway between speech and song and was called *stile rappresentativo.* It was characterized by freedom of rhythm, dramatic pauses, and asymmetric phrases. The alleviation of the monotony of the musical declamation by means of passages that were more melodic eventually gave rise to the distinction in monodic style between recitative and aria.

Another characteristic of Baroque music was the *stile concertato.* In concertato style, the composer used instrumental and vocal forces in compositions that were harmonic or contrapuntal in style. The style includes planned contrasts of instruments or voices against one another either as soloists or as groups. Many of the vocal and instrumental forms of the later Baroque are derived from this style of writing.

Stile concitato, or excited style, was a practice in which music illustrated the words or moods of the dramatic action. The use of tremolo in the strings of the orchestra or rapidly sung syllables to a repeated note by the voice are typical of this style.

Formal Organization

Thematic material continued to be developed in works that were wholly or partially contrapuntal—the fugue, toccata, and the chorale prelude. New homophonic forms, particularly in instrumental music, generally depended upon simple statement and contrast of melodic material. The variation principle was a logical expansion of these forms, and evolved homophonically and contrapuntally into the theme and variation, passacaglia, or chorale variation.

A great number of solo instrumental works for keyboard instruments, especially organ and harpsichord, were written in a style which suggested improvisation. Rapid scale passages, decorations, or chordal figurations in a free style were characteristic of such compositions, often called *fantasias.* Sometimes such improvisatory passages were used to display a brilliant technique, and were dictated by this consideration rather than purely musical ones.

As in the Renaissance, text continued to dominate vocal musical forms, but in different ways. In the new recitative the text was declared in an almost theatrical style attempting to replicate vocal delivery in the Greek theater.

The establishment of major and minor tonalities led to distinct phrase and period construction in formal design. This was common to instrumental and vocal music, as was the frequently used device of sequential patterning in formal organization.

Melody

Melodic writing varies from the declamatory style of the recitative to the extremely florid style of late Baroque arias and instrumental melodies. An example of the latter is referred to as *fortspinnung,* a process of melodic writing in which short figures are developed into melodic lines of substantial length and complexity. In recitative, the declamatory style, which to modern ears may appear to be a negation of melody, dominated the formal structure.

The recitative, a creation of early Baroque composers, represented a melodic idea, the structure of which was determined solely by verbal considerations. Two forms of recitative were employed. One was known as *recitativo secco* (dry recitative), in which only a thorough bass accompanied the voice (fig. 5.1). The second, *recitativo accompagnato* (accompanied recitative), was more dramatic and was accompanied by an ensemble of instruments (fig. 5.2). Accompanied recitative style was usually used to introduce an aria in cantatas and the dramatic forms of opera and oratorio.

In a real sense the opera was the progenitor of the *bel canto* (beautiful singing) style, which emphasized beauty of vocal sound and brilliant florid technique. Composers provided for this demand by writing melodies that were musically scintillating and often dramatically expressive. In conformity with this demand, melodies often deteriorated into spectacular vocalises with ornamentation either written in or left to the discretion of the singer.

In the Baroque, melody gradually assumed vocally and instrumentally idiomatic styles, but these were often interchangeable. However, in the early decades of the seventeenth century, publications appeared that designated specifically whether the music was to be sung or played. It was not uncommon to find purely vocal design applied to instrumental writing and vice versa. Both instrumental and vocal music employed melodic lines of extended range. The desire for vocal display and the use of homophonic style account for this

Figure 5.1 Recitativo secco from the *Historia der Geburt Jesu Christe*

Heinrich Schütz

phenomenon, while the continued perfecting of keyboard and stringed instruments made an extended instrumental range possible.

In homophonic music, melody was essentially one of balanced phrase and period, usually in four or eight measures. Although the upper melodic line was dominant, there existed a kind of polarity between the melody and the bass line, which was in itself a melodically conceived part (fig. 5.3).

Figure 5.2 Recitativo accompagnato from *Unser Mund sei voll Lachens*, Cantata #110

J. S. Bach

Figure 5.3 Tenor aria from *Ich hatte viel Bekümmernis*, Cantata #21, showing polarity of bass and melody

J. S. Bach

Rhythm

Except for recitative, repeated metrical units became the standard in Baroque music. Tempos were more constant, in part because of the importance of the moving basso continuo, which gave a certain driving, almost motoric, feeling to both instrumental and choral works written in contrapuntal style. The rapid change of harmony induced by the basso continuo also made for a driving harmonic rhythm, the movement given to music by changes in harmony, which added its force to the total rhythmic motion.

Harmony

A fundamental change in harmony occurred during the Baroque. The reliance on modal systems of the past gradually yielded to the major-minor system of tonal relationships. This system dominated Western music until the twentieth century. Even in works that were essentially contrapuntal, Baroque counterpoint was based on major-minor tonalities rather than the modality of the Renaissance.

The chordal nature of harmony was reflected in a system of numbers placed under the notes of the bass line, called "figured bass." The harmonic figurations of the bass line, suggesting rapid changes of harmony, especially in the works of the late Baroque, were then realized by the keyboard performer. The bass line and its performance were called by various names: thorough bass, figured bass, basso continuo, or continuo. (Figure 5.4A illustrates a figured bass, and figure 5.4B presents a possible realization of the same bass.)

Chromaticism and dissonance were freely employed in Baroque music for expressive purposes. Tempered tuning of keyboard instruments was introduced, and made possible the chromatic changes that were necessary for extended modulations. Bach's *Das Wohltemperierte Klavier* (The Well-Tempered Clavier) illustrates, in a series of forty-eight preludes and fugues, how tempered tuning made it possible to play in all keys, major and minor, without retuning the instrument.

Texture

Homophonic textures appeared with increasing frequency in vocal and instrumental forms. There are abundant examples in opera and in arias of all kinds, as well as in instrumental forms, such as the sonata da camera, keyboard sonatas, and suites. The tendency in purely homophonic forms to include contrapuntal techniques and the harmonic richness of contrapuntal forms tended to make the texture of most Baroque music rather thick and opaque.

The interest in homophonic texture did not exclude polyphonic textures, which were achieved by tonal counterpoint. Such counterpoint was used in religious choral works as well as in many types of instrumental compositions, such as the fugue, chorale prelude, or variations on a ground. The trio sonata, with its polarized polyphony, was greatly favored by Baroque composers. In it, two melodic lines and an active continuo part (figured bass) comprised the style, in which polyphonic writing, often in imitation, predominated.

Figure 5.4A Soprano aria from *Ich hatte viel Bekümmernis,* Cantata #21, showing unrealized figured bass

There was great emphasis on contrasting textures, especially in concertato style. The common contrast of large and small groups was enhanced by the general use of contrapuntal treatment for the large group and homophonic treatment for the smaller group.

Instrumentation and Tone Color

Many of the instruments of the Baroque era were forerunners of modern instruments. The violin family, for example, was perfected and gradually displaced

Figure 5.4B Soprano aria as in figure 5.4A, showing realized figured bass

J. S. Bach

Seuf -zer, Trä - nen,Kum - mer,

the viols by the end of the period. Composition became increasingly idiomatic as composers wrote for the possibilities and limitations of specific instruments.

Trio sonatas were written for one of the most popular chamber music ensembles of the Baroque. Despite its title, it most frequently consisted of four instruments: two treble melodic instruments (often interchangeable), a bass instrument to play the continuo part (wind or string instrument), and a keyboard instrument to realize the figured bass (usually a harpsichord or organ). Such instrumentation is not always employed. For example, Bach wrote six trio sonatas for organ, alone, as well as solo sonatas for violin that are essentially trio sonatas as well.

In the Baroque, the *solo sonata,* whose name again belies the instrumentation, consisted of three instruments: a melody instrument, and bass and keyboard instruments which comprised the continuo.

The instrumentation of the orchestra was not fixed. Orchestras accompanied vocal dramatic works and performed as independent musical organizations. The

The high altar, Augustin Church of Freibourg, Switzerland (1592–1601), by Peter Spring. Four of the angelic host from this central group are playing instruments that are clearly identifiable; left upper, a harp; left lower, a zink (cornetto); right upper, a lute; right lower, a sackbut (trombone). The sculptured group represents the acceptance of instrumental music in the church art and music of the Baroque era. (Bärenreiter-Bildarchiv)

Baroque orchestra was smaller than the modern orchestra and consisted mainly of strings and woodwinds, with brass and percussion added for special effects. At the beginning of the period the brass instruments were natural; that is, without valves. Much solo music was written for the high or *clarino* register of the natural trumpet, often called the *clarin trumpet.*

The Baroque organ was an instrument of great clarity and mellowness of tone, but it could only execute crescendos by adding stops. Contrasts in dynamics generally followed the Baroque practice of contrasting sonorities, achieved on the organ by changes in registration. Its limited volume and pureness of tone made the Baroque organ an ideal instrument for realizing the transparent contrapuntal texture of the organ music of the period. Many great composers of the Baroque wrote for the organ and were organ performers.

The term *clavier* referred to all types of keyboard instruments, especially the harpsichord and the clavichord. The former, known variously as *clavecin, cembalo, gravicembalo, spinet,* and *virginal,* was the more widely used instrument. The harpsichord was eventually displaced by the *pianoforte,* invented in 1709 by Cristofori, but not universally adopted until after the Baroque era. The name pianoforte derives from the instrument's mechanical capacity for graded dynamic contrasts. Much solo and ensemble music was written for the harpsichord, especially in the last half of the Baroque. (Appendix 1 includes further information on instruments.)

In addition to the traditional vocal classifications of soprano, alto, tenor, and bass, which have persisted throughout history, the Baroque added male, or artificial, sopranos known as *castrati.* The power, range, and technical facility of the castrati voices made them a great favorite with Baroque opera audiences and account for many arias in Baroque operas that are extremely difficult for modern singers. The *countertenor,* or male alto, which used a falsetto voice in singing, continued from the Renaissance, but now in a solo role as well as in sacred ensemble music.

Performance Practice

With few exceptions, the Baroque was the last period in which improvisation was a definite requisite of every performer. Such improvisatory techniques as the realization and actual addition of ornaments in both vocal and instrumental performance were not only tolerated but expected. In fact, composers often only outlined the melodic line with the full expectation of having the performer add not only ornamentation but passing tones, scale passages, and even melodic fragments to the notated melody. Vocal music was particularly given to such improvisatory additions at highly expressive points, often dictated by the texts, and known as *gorgia.* In the later Baroque, brilliant rapid ornamentation of a virtuoso type was known as *coloratura,* and it sometimes designated a particular soprano voice type.

In all music, performers were expected to extend cadences, especially climactic cadences near the end of a movement or work, with elaborate improvisation. Such improvisations came to take the name of *cadenzas*. In solo arias of operas and in solo instrumental concertos, cadenzas became integral parts of the works, and performers used them not only to exhibit their ability at improvisation but also their command of technical skill. Organists practice improvisation to the present day.

Closely allied to pure improvisation was the realization or completion of the harmonies indicated in the figured bass by keyboard performers. Where figuration was present, the realization consisted of improvising suitable chordal and rhythmic patterns or even contrapuntal lines (see fig. 5.4B). Much music, however, was not even figured, so the keyboard realization demanded the choosing of both the proper harmony and its patterns.

Various systems of tempered tuning were adopted during the Baroque. Mean-tone temperament was the most consistently employed, but by the end of the Baroque period the tendency toward a system of equal temperament was indicated by the ever-increasing modulatory practice of composers. Tuning of some instruments varied, such as the altered tuning of the violin, known as *scordatura*, a tuning used to achieve unusual chordal effects and note combinations that would otherwise be impossible.

Writing for instruments became more and more idiomatic, but there was still freedom of choice of instruments in certain compositions. Recorders and the new transverse, or German flutes—as well as oboes and violins, were often interchangeable in ensemble music. Tremolo and pizzicato were performance techniques for strings introduced in this period. Dynamic markings such as *p., f., cresc., dim.,* were introduced but used very sparingly. Most dynamic variations were achieved by contrasting instrumental groups of varied size or quality.

Signs and symbols were increasingly used to designate particular ornaments in the Baroque. Performers were expected to improvise ornamentation even though it was not marked by the composer. Although some of the signs were in common usage, many of them took on the personal meanings of composers or schools to which they belonged. This has given rise to many differences of interpretation in the works of the Baroque. Tempo designations such as *allegro, andante,* and *grave* were also introduced but bore imprecise meanings.

Almost all composers were recognized as virtuoso performers as well. This was especially true of keyboard performers. Both Bach and Handel were celebrated as skillful performers of the organ. Corelli, Tartini, and Biber made notable advances in the techniques of violin playing, with double stops, triple stops, arpeggios, and so forth. In the performance of opera, the castrato Farinelli and others became internationally known as virtuoso singers in opera.

IV. MUSIC FOR VOICES

Single-Movement Forms and Structural Devices

Recitative

Vocal passages written in a style of highly inflected declamation are known as recitatives. This is the declamatory form of the *stile rappresentativo* that came to be separated from the lyrical parts of the monody. By the end of the seventeenth century the clear distinction between recitative and aria had been accomplished. The recitative served to carry the narrative and acted as a prelude to and the connecting material between the highly emotional points represented by the arias. Recitatives took no formal structure, such as the aria. They were rhythmically free and served as a vocal vehicle for the prose dialogue. In some situations recitative might be accompanied by full orchestra. In quick-moving operatic narrative, it was often accompanied only by the continuo that performed from the figured bass. In the former case it was known as *recitativo accompagnato* and in the latter, was called *recitativo secco*. (Ex. 5.1, 5.2)

Aria

The more melodic passages of the *stile rappresentativo* took on a formal character and finally separated from the declamatory parts as arias. The most typical form these arias assumed was the three-part, or *da capo aria,* in which a musical statement was followed by a contrasting section, which was in turn followed by a repetition of the original section with ornamentation. This form was almost universally adopted by the writers for all musical dramatic works, secular and religious. The aria form was often applied to ensembles such as the *chamber duet.* (Ex. 5.3, 5.4)

Arioso

The *arioso* was a free vocal form for solo voice that emerged from the declamatory style of the recitative and moved toward the lyrical style of the aria. Like the aria, the arioso was accompanied by full orchestra, often with repeated figures. The arioso was often used to express rapid changes of mood by means of the vocal line and the orchestral accompaniment. More brief than the aria, the arioso was cast in free designs. (Ex. 5.5, 5.6)

Chorus

Choral and ensemble works or passages took on no new formal characteristics. Contrapuntal texture generally prevailed in the oratorio and mass, whereas homophonic texture frequently invaded operatic writing. Because of the emphasis on solo singing, choral passages were infrequent in Baroque opera, and occurred only when dramatic incidents required it as part of the action. (Ex. 5.7)

Motet

Baroque composers continued the Renaissance tradition of the unaccompanied choral motet. Typically, however, the motet was moving toward tonal counterpoint as opposed to the modal counterpoint of the past. The motet was generally liturgical and was used in both the Roman Catholic and Lutheran services. (Ex. 5.8–5.10)

Geistliche Konzerte

Works variously known as *concerti ecclesiastici* and as *Geistliche Konzerte* were frequently composed in concertato style. They were restricted to a few voices with continuo or sometimes a few concerted instruments. Many were for a single voice. German composers of the seventeenth century used spiritual concertos most frequently because they could be used in much the same manner as a cantata in the Lutheran service. (Ex. 5.11–5.14)

Anthem

Baroque composers continued to write anthems (see Renaissance vocal compositions) for the Anglican church. The *verse anthem* with an introduction of dramatic style was most typical of the Baroque era in England. (Ex. 5.15)

Solo Song

Solo songs, though not constituting a major form, were being written in many parts of Europe. The English *lute song* is sometimes associated with the Renaissance, but it is arguably an expression of the Baroque as well. Like the German *Lied,* lute songs were often strophic. They are also treasured for the rich quality of their poetry. Baroque Lieder were usually of folk character, in binary or ternary form, resembling small arias, and with instrumental accompaniment. The accompanied solo madrigal, from Italy, is distinguished from its sixteenth-century predecessors, which were unaccompanied part songs. (Ex. 5.15–5.21)

Composite Forms

Opera

The most significant composite vocal form originating in the Baroque period was the dramatic opera, first called *dramma per musica.* The first impulse toward this form was by certain intellectuals, noblemen, poets, and musicians who met in Florence. They formed a group known as the Florentine Camerata, who wished to create theatrical pieces in which words would dominate the music and dictate the rhythm. This was a seventeenth-century attempt to recreate what was thought to be the role of music in the classical tragedies of ancient Greece. The expression of this desire came to be called accompanied monody (fig. 5.5).

Opera libretti were generally concerned with secular themes shaped into dramatic form. Early operas were based on Greek myths, but later works dealt with historical, legendary, and fictional heroes and heroines, and were referred to as *opera seria.* The comic *entr'actes* of the *opera seria* were brought together at the end of the seventeenth century, constituting an independent

Figure 5.5 Excerpt from *Orfeo* showing the accompanied monodic style (Monteverdi L'ORFEO, *COLLECTED WORKS OF CLAUDIO MONTEVERDI,* edited by G. Franceso Malipiero. Used by kind permission of European American Music Distributors Corporation, sole U.S. and Canadian agent for Universal Edition A.G., Vienna.)

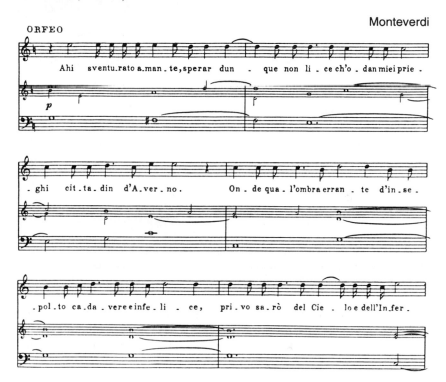

comic opera form called *opera buffa* (comic opera). The *opera buffa* (Italy), and the similar forms of *opéra comique* (France), *Singspiel* (Germany), and even the *ballad opera* (England) became commercially successful to a large degree due to their use of the vernacular, their focus on comedy, and on characters of greater realism than those of *opera seria*.

Opera was written for soloists, chorus, and orchestra, and was staged with appropriate scenic settings and dramatic presentation. Elaborate stage machinery was often important in staging of opera. While the first operas were performed for private groups in such surroundings as palace halls and theaters, opera houses were soon built for public presentations.

Musically, the opera used a variety of formal sections such as arias, choruses, dances, duets, and other ensemble numbers. The music was largely homophonic in texture. Choral passages, generously used in the early operas, were finally reduced to insignificance, whereas solo arias received increasing attention.

An eighteenth century stage set for Handel's *Giulio Cesare* showing the famous castrato
Bernardi Senesino (left) as Giulio Cesare and Francesca Cuzzoni, the celebrated Italian soprano,
as Cleopatra. (Corbis-Bettmann)

Because of the great public appeal of opera by the end of the seventeenth
century, certain characteristics were attached to it by virtue of its national origin. Four general schools of opera can be discerned, namely Italian, French,
English, and German.

The Italian school was the first and most widely disseminated. Its main centers were Florence, Venice, Rome, and Naples, from which it spread to
all the great political and economic centers of Europe. By the end of the
seventeenth century, most Italian opera had become little more than an elaborate
display of solo singing. Arias in *bel canto* style, often with obbligato instruments
displaying elaborately embellished and virtuoso passages, were held together
loosely by dramatic narrative sung in recitativo secco. The orchestra provided an
overture and an unobtrusive accompaniment for the vocal passages, which added
little to the dramatic intensity of the work. (Ex. 5.22–5.26)

The centers of French opera were the royal courts of France, especially
during the reigns of Louis XIV and Louis XV. French opera differed from
Italian opera in language and general emphasis. French composers, influenced by the great popularity and prestige of classic French drama, tended to
emphasize dramatic sincerity and action, and wrote arias of simpler melodic
line with less demands on virtuoso technique. A clear difference was the
inclusion of ballet episodes, an attempt to give national character to French
opera by continuing the tradition of the *ballet de cour.* In French opera the

orchestra provided an overture in the French style. It also provided the music for the dances as well as accompaniment for the singing. (Ex. 5.27–5.30)

English opera is represented by very few works. Their general character-istics were adopted from French and Italian models. The tradition of the Eng-lish dramatic form of the masque, to which music was often added, was influ-ential in the few operas written. (Ex. 5.31–5.32)

In Germany, opera found wide acceptance, and although the Italian style was well entrenched, a considerable number of important German composers were active. Most of their works were in the Italian style, even when written to German texts. The *Singspiel,* a native German form in which popular songs were combined into a new musical entertainment that included spoken dia-logue, was the only original form comparable to opera. (Ex. 5.33–5.34)

Oratorio

The oratorio employed the same forces as the opera, but was distinguished from it in that it usually did not use dramatic action, costumes, or stage set-tings for presentation. Originally performed in the oratory of churches in Italy, by the end of the Baroque it had become a dramatic musical form based on a religious but nonliturgical theme, most often on Old Testament topics, and pre-sented in concert form. The oratorio employed soloists but tended to empha-size the chorus and usually contained a number of large choral movements.

The forms of the solo and small ensemble movements were identical with those of opera, though often of more reserved character. The choral move-ments, however, were almost exclusively contrapuntal, ranging from strict to free fugal forms. The oratorio frequently used a dramatic character known as the narrator (*storicus* or *testo*), who introduced and often narrated the story by means of recitatives. (Ex. 5.35–5.37)

Passion Music

The settings of the Passion of Christ as narrated in the four gospels of the New Testament were frequently set for both Roman Catholic and Lutheran use. These settings were actually oratorios whose texts were restricted to Biblical quotations concerning Christ's trial and crucifixion, and such other commen-tary as the composer might select in keeping with this subject. A narrator took the part of the evangelist and sang all the narration that was not in direct quo-tation in recitative style. Other soloists took the parts of Biblical characters or sang solos that were commentary on the story. The chorus, *turba,* represented crowds, soldiers, and priests, and its members also sang choruses based on the commentary. In many passion settings for the Lutheran church, German Protestant chorales were used. Otherwise these works were mostly constructed in the same manner as the oratorios of the period. (Ex. 5.38)

Cantata

In the publications of the early Baroque, title pages used the word *cantade* and variants thereof to instruct that the contents were to be sung. From that beginning the cantata developed in several forms and for several purposes.

Solo and choral cantatas were written for liturgical and nonliturgical religious purposes, as well as secular occasions.

The structure of these cantatas was essentially the same in all instances. Small instrumental groups were employed for accompaniment, with solo instruments often used in obbligato fashion with the voice. Soloists and chorus provided the vocal forces. The forms of the aria, ensembles, and choruses were the same as those used in opera and oratorio; cantatas might be regarded as miniature oratorios. The primary difference between solo cantatas and choral cantatas was the forces employed. Whereas solo cantatas were obviously written for a single solo voice, choral cantatas, in addition to the chorus, employed soloists as well.

Roman Catholic and Protestant composers wrote cantatas, but those written by Lutheran composers in the sixteenth and seventeenth centuries comprise the greatest wealth of church music of this period. These were liturgical cantatas and might be said to represent a kind of musical sermon, since most cantatas were written for specific holy days in the church calendar. (Ex. 5.39–5.45)

Mass

The Roman Catholic Mass continued to be set, now in typical Baroque style. It took on a dramatic character with the addition of orchestral accompaniment and frequent division of its various sections into solo and ensemble as well as choral settings. Even the da capo aria form was employed in some instances. Most masses continued to be written for use in liturgical services. However, some masses were nonliturgical because of their treatment of the text or the forces demanded in performance. Bach's *Mass in B minor* is one notable example. (Ex. 5.46–5.47)

V. MUSIC FOR INSTRUMENTS

There were no specific instruments designated for much of Baroque instrumental music. Keyboard compositions could be performed on the harpsichord, clavichord, or even the organ. Violins, flutes, and oboes were often interchangeable in ensembles, as were the bassoon, cello, and string bass. In some works, instruments such as the natural trumpet or oboe d'amore were specified but could be substituted by other instruments of the same range.

Single-Movement Forms and Structural Devices

Toccata

The toccata, frequently called *prelude,* grew out of the improvisatory style and was a continuation of the Renaissance toccata. In mature Baroque style, the improvisatory toccata was followed by a section in imitative contrapuntal style. A final crystallization of form was revealed in the toccata, which framed a fugue between two rhapsodic improvisatory parts. The toccata was frequently treated as a single movement independent of the fugue, with which it was often paired. In this case it was likely to be purely improvisatory. (Ex. 5.48–5.49)

Prelude

This name is freely used to describe an introductory movement, usually improvisatory. It is often applied to the toccata form itself. In the late Baroque, preludes coupled with fugues were usually free and in indefinite form. (Ex. 5.50–5.53)

Ricercar

The ricercar is an imitative contrapuntal form for harpsichord or organ. The Baroque ricercar, in contrast to that of the Renaissance, is a work in which one theme is developed imitatively throughout. The distinction between ricercar and fugue is more one of rhythmic drive than of formal organization. The ricercar is frequently modal, exploiting its thematic material with less climactic contrast, making less use of sequential treatment, and using thematic material that is slower and potentially less significant rhythmically. (Ex. 5.54)

Fugue

The fugue employs imitative counterpoint and is built on a single theme or subject repeated in two or more individual voices. The presentation of the subject alternately on tonic and dominant pitch levels (the latter form of the subject is known as the answer), emphasizes the tonic-dominant relationship as a means of achieving formal development. Fugues, in contrast to ricercars from which they were developed, used subjects of more melodic and rhythmic character. Fugues commonly employ the imitative devices of stretto, inversion, augmentation, and diminution. They often employ a countersubject. These are developed through various key changes, rhythmic treatments, or sequential appearances. Episodes, or sections in which the subject does not appear in its entirety, alternate with repeated appearances of the subject in some or all of the voices. Although the fugue is generally a single movement of comparatively brief duration, it is possible to present the fugal material in a great variety of key relationships so that the single movement can be extended. A fugue with two subjects is called a double fugue.

Essentially an instrumental form, the fugue is especially well adapted to organ and other keyboard performance; however, fugal writing is found in many other instrumental forms and in large choral works of the Baroque. It represents the highest development of harmonic contrapuntal technique of the period. (Ex. 5.55–5.57)

Fantasia

An instrumental composition, the fantasia was originally closely related to the ricercar. In the Baroque it became a loosely structured, improvisatory-sounding composition for various solo instruments or small ensembles. Some composers, such as Telemann, wrote solo fantasias that were more on the order of Italian sonatas than the early ricercar. The term *fancy* was used in England to designate works similar to the fantasia written for an ensemble or consort of viols or wind instruments. The name fantasia was also given to improvisatory single movement works that were later paired with fugues, as were preludes and toccatas. (Ex. 5.58–5.59)

Orchestral Overture

Although this term was used variously, two forms growing out of Italian and French opera are typical of the multiple-section works generally called overtures. The French and Italian overtures differ mainly in the order of the three sections. The *French Overture* consists of a slow section with pompous, dotted rhythms and rich harmonies followed by a lively, driving fugal section. It concludes with a return to the opening slow section, or at least a part of it. The *Italian Overture* reverses the order of movements to fast, slow, fast. Both types were used as purely orchestral forms as well as orchestral openings to operas. (Ex. 5.60)

Theme and Variation

This was an extension of the same form used in the Renaissance in which a melody, either original or more often preexisting, is presented in a number of variations. In the Baroque, theme and variation writing became more idiomatic, exploiting the technical possibilities of specific instruments. Two kinds of variations were employed. One was of a contrapuntal character in which the melody remained intact as it wandered from voice to voice while the counterpoint changed in each variation. The other was essentially homophonic, in which the harmony remained the same throughout while the melody above the harmony was ornamented or changed in subsequent variations. (Ex. 5.61–5.66)

Ritornello Form

In music of the late Baroque and early Classic periods, ritornello form (It. *ritorno,* meaning return), was used to indicate the alternation of orchestra and soloists in concerti. It is also sometimes the designation for the full orchestra or *tutti* in printed scores. The *Italian Concerto* of J. S. Bach is an example of this form, as are many of his cantata choruses.

Passacaglia and Chaconne

While these two names designate different forms, both are variations on a repeated musical element of four to eight measures, and the distinction between the two is often unclear. In the passacaglia, the ostinato is most often a repeated bass line, but the melody can be found in voices other than the bass. The chaconne is based upon a repeated harmonic progression. Passacaglias and chaconnes were written for all types of instruments and ensembles, although those for keyboard are more common. (Ex. 5.65–5.66)

Chorale Prelude

Organ music in which a chorale tune is the basis of the composition is called a chorale prelude. In some instances the chorale tune acts as a theme for a set of variations. Such works are known as *chorale partitas* or *chorale variations*. In other instances the chorale tune forms the basis for a fantasia, and the work is then known as a *chorale fantasia*. By far the most popular, however, was a single setting of the chorale tune that might vary from a highly developed fugal treatment to a rather simple homophonic presentation. This last form probably originated as a prelude to the singing of the chorale by the congregation in the Lutheran church. (Ex. 5.53, 5.67–5.69)

Composite Forms

Suite

The idea of extending an instrumental piece by joining a number of dance movements of different rhythms and tempos is an extension of the Renaissance device of pairing dances. The typical early suite (*Partita* in German, *ordre* in French) was written for harpsichord and combined four or more dances to form a complete work. The four most common dances are the *Allemande, Courante, Sarabande,* and *Gigue.* Generally, each dance is in binary form, with the first part ending in the dominant key and the second half returning to the tonic. Each dance retains its original rhythmic character but is cast in an idealized form with no practical use in mind. The dances have no thematic relationship to one another, and the only unifying factor is the constancy of key among all the dances. While the four dances named were considered the basic dances of the suite, other dances, even those in then-current ballroom use, were often added to, or substituted for, the original dances. Such optional dances, frequently following the sarabande, might include the *Minuet, Bourrée, Gavotte,* and *Loure.* This is especially true of the French ordre. (Ex. 5.70–5.72)

Orchestral Suite

As in the chamber sonata, there was no set number or order of dances in the orchestral suite. The orchestral suite was often called an overture because the first movement was frequently in the form of the French overture. (Ex. 5.73)

Sonata da Chiesa (Church Sonata)

These compositions evolved from the sectional canzona of the Renaissance into a rather freely designed multimovement form that became one of the most important in chamber music of the Baroque period. Although there are no definite forms for individual movements, these compositions generally used alternating slow and fast tempos with contrapuntal or fugal style in one or more movements. The sonata da chiesa (fig. 5.6) was written for various instrumental combinations: any solo melodic instrument with continuo, or more frequently, for two violins or other melodic instruments and continuo (trio sonata).

Musical score, dance, and costume illustration from *Neue und Curieuse Theatralische Tanz–schule*; Nürnberg, 1716. (AKG, London)

Figure 5.6 *Sonata da chiesa,* Opus 5, No. 1 (© Stainer & Bell Ltd., London, England. Reprinted by permission.)

Arcangelo Corelli

Continued.

Figure 5.6—*Continued*

Dance forms were regularly found in the sonata da camera, and movements of the sonata da chiesa were sometimes in dance forms though not necessarily so designated. The sonata da chiesa often went by the simple name *sonata,* especially in the late Baroque. (Ex. 5.74–5.76)

Sonata da Camera (Chamber Sonata)

This is the ensemble form of the suite written as a solo sonata or trio sonata, but often using larger groups. The four basic dances were less likely to be found in the chamber sonata. Additional and substitute dances were often used. A prelude frequently preceded the chamber sonata, and movements other than dances, such as the aria, were often present. (Ex. 5.77–5.80)

Keyboard Sonata

The original use of the term sonata to differentiate instrumental from vocal works was often retained in the Baroque period. A number of keyboard compositions therefore bear the title sonata, though they do not resemble either of the two typical sonata types of the Baroque, sonata da chiesa or sonata da camera. Some of these sonatas consisted of several movements, whereas others had only one. Generally, simple binary or ternary forms were used for individual movements, which varied from dancelike character to song types, usually homophonic in texture. The greatest exponent of the keyboard sonata in the Baroque was Domenico Scarlatti. (Ex. 5.81)

Solo Concerto and Concerto Grosso

Two forms of the concerto, the solo concerto and the concerto grosso, were the final instrumental contributions of the Baroque period. These two forms differed only in that the solo concerto used a single instrument as soloist, and the concerto grosso used a group of soloists, generally three, in contrast to the larger mass of orchestral sound.

Three movements are most frequently employed: first, an allegro; then a slow movement in a closely related key; and finally, a shorter fast movement in the original key. Each of the movements is constructed on the concertato principle, alternating soloist or soloists (concertino) and full orchestra (tutti or ripieno). Soloists and orchestra may be given different themes, but usually all of the thematic material is presented by the full group and then developed by the soloist or soloists in turn. The solo concerto and the concerto grosso were at times designed to display the technical virtuosity of the soloists. As well, they offered the Baroque composer the possibility of combining the concertato idea, the polarity of bass and treble melody, the concept of clear major-minor tonalities, and the use of a number of separate movements into a single idealized instrumental form. (Ex. 5.84–5.89)

VI. COMPOSERS

Giulio Caccini (c. 1550–1618) was an Italian singer and composer associated with the Florentine Camerata. His performance of the new type of monodic composition, *musica in stile rappresentativo,* was looked upon as the ideal of this style. His most important work was the collection of madrigals and arias published under the title *Le Nuove musiche.* Its preface contains one of the clearest and most detailed descriptions of the manner of performance of the new monodic style. (Ex. 5.16, 5.90–5.91)

Jacopo Peri (1561–1633), a member of the Florentine Camerata, composed the opera *Dafne.* It was one of the earliest operas in the new monodic style. Peri was known for his masterly handling of pedal-point basses, a device that suited his delight in somber subject matter. (Ex. 5.22, 5.92)

Jan Pieterzoon Sweelinck (1562–1621) was a celebrated Dutch organist and composer. His two outstanding contributions to organ literature are the development of the organ chorale variation, leading to the organ prelude, and his use of monothematic treatment in the ricercar, which resulted in the form known as the fugue. While he also wrote a great number of vocal works in Renaissance style, his organ compositions belong to the early Baroque. As the teacher of many German pupils he was to become the founder of the famous north German organ school. (Ex. 5.58, 5.93–5.94)

Claudio Monteverdi (1567–1643), the greatest of the early Italian Baroque composers, was the creator of *Orfeo,* the first operatic masterpiece in modern style. In it he adapted the Florentine recitative style to closed forms of the aria and dance song. He was equally at home in the Renaissance polyphonic and the Baroque monodic idioms. His madrigals are among the finest of the Italian school, but even here he shows his association with the modern school of the Baroque through his close attention to word and mood expression. Monteverdi expanded the orchestra and, unusual for his time, in some cases scored for specific instruments in his dramatic works. His harmonic writing was for expressive purposes and caused much adverse criticism, particularly by one Giovanni Artusi. Among his works are eight books of madrigals, dramatic scenes, religious music, and a number of operas. The most important operas are *Orfeo* (see fig. 5.5), *Il ritorno d'Ulisse in patria,* and *L'Incoronazione di Poppea.*

Claudio Monteverdi. Portrait by Bernardo Strozzi (1567–1643). (Tiroler Landesmuseum Ferdinandeum, Innsbruck, Austria.)

Michael Praetorius (1571–1621), a German composer and theorist, devoted himself extensively to the writing of Lutheran choral works. His most important contribution to music history was made in his treatise, *Syntagma musicum.* (Ex. 5.95–5.96)

Girolamo Frescobaldi (1583–1643), an Italian organist and composer, was an important link in the history of fugal form. Although he wrote no works that were actually called fugues, his monothematic ricercars were among the most important forerunners of the fugue. As a teacher of Froberger, his influence in the development of composition and performance of the south German organ school was equalled only by Sweelinck's influence in the north. He was recognized as one of the greatest organists of his day, and was appointed organist at St. Peter's in Rome. His compositions include toccatas, capriccios, ricercars, and canzonas, typical organ forms of the early Baroque. A collection of these works for church use appeared in his *Fiori musicali* (Musical Flowers). (Ex. 5.48, 5.97–5.98)

Heinrich Schütz (1585–1672) was the greatest German composer before J. S. Bach. Evidence of his importance is the oft-repeated designation of Schütz as the father of German music. He was the composer of the first German opera, *Daphne.* His contacts with Italian music of the late sixteenth and early seventeenth centuries led him to write many dramatic religious vocal works to German texts that introduced the new Baroque style into Germany. He adapted the recitative, the thorough bass, and the concertato principle to works for the Lutheran service, and laid the foundation for the great art of dramatic church music in his

Symphoniae sacrae (Sacred Symphonies), *Cantiones sacrae* (Sacred Songs), and *Kleine geistliche Konzerten* (Little Sacred Concerti), which later blossomed into the cantatas and passion music of Bach and his contemporaries. Recent performances based on research into Schütz's music have revealed a starkness and simplicity of dramatic presentation. These characteristics are apparent in such works as *Die Sieben Wortte . . .* (The Seven Last Words), *Historia, der freuden-und gnadenreichen Geburt Gottes und Marien Sohnes, Jesu Christi* (The Christmas Oratorio), *Auferstehungs Historie* (The Resurrection of Our Lord), and his passion settings to the Gospels of Matthew, Luke, and John. (Ex. 5.11–5.13, 5.99–5.100)

Johann Hermann Schein (1586–1630), another German, also helped introduce Italian monody and instrumental music into Germany. His choral adaptations for organ were representative of the great interest in this form. A collection of twenty suites for strings called *Banchetto musicale* represents some of the earliest instrumental works written in Germany. Schein also wrote numerous vocal compositions. (Ex. 5.14)

Francesca Caccini (1587–1640), the daughter of Guilio Caccini, was a performer on several instruments, but was best known as a singer and composer. She sang at the wedding of Marie de' Medici and King Henri IV of France. She composed for such courts as the Pitti, and her opera, *La liberazione di Ruggiero dell'isola d'Alcina,* is the first known opera by a woman composer, and was the first Italian opera to be performed outside Italy.

Samuel Scheidt (1587–1654) is often considered the most important German organ composer of the first half of the seventeenth century, particularly in his treatment of the chorale in true organ style. His greatest published work, *Tabulatura nova,* was a collection of figured chorales, toccatas, fantasias, hymns, and other works for the organ. Though his main contribution was in organ composition, he wrote many choral works as well. (Ex. 5.62, 5.101)

Pier Francesco Cavalli (1602–1676) was celebrated as an opera composer in his native Italy, where he held the position of Maestro di Cappella at St. Mark's in Venice. He was also well known in France and Austria. Though he wrote church works, he gained wide recognition from his forty-one operas. His greatest operatic successes were *Giasone, Cerce,* and *Ercole amante* (Hercules, The Lover). Cavalli's wide recognition attests to the rapid rise and acceptance of Italian opera in other countries. (Ex. 5.24, 5.102)

Jacques Champion Chambonnières (c. 1610–1672) is regarded as the founder of the French clavecin school. As the teacher of Couperin the Elder, d'Angelbert, and others, his influence was felt not only in France, but throughout Europe. He was first chamber musician to Louis XIV. His wide recognition influenced German harpsichord composers from Froberger to J. S. Bach. His compositions were exclusively for harpsichord. (Ex. 5.103)

Giacomo Carissimi (1605–1674), an Italian composer, applied the new devices of the monodic style to religious music, particularly the oratorio. His masterpiece, *Jepthe,* is a composition of the highest musical and dramatic quality. He is regarded as the founder of the oratorio. (Ex. 5.35, 5.104)

Johann Jakob Froberger (1616–1667) was a German organist and pupil of Frescobaldi, whose techniques he introduced in Vienna. He wrote many works for the organ and is credited with having created the keyboard suite and establishing the order of its dances: Allemande, Courante, Sarabande, and Gigue. (Ex. 5.70–5.71)

Barbara Strozzi (1619–c. 1664) was the composer of eight published volumes of cantatas and arias for solo and basso continuo. She was a champion of women in society, rebelling against and successfully changing some of the repressive and sexist conventions of her day.

Antonio Cesti (1623–1669) gained wide recognition as an Italian opera composer. *Il pomo d'oro* (The Golden Apple), produced in Vienna in 1667, is regarded as his masterpiece. (Ex. 5.105)

Jean-Henri d'Angelbert (c. 1628–1691) was a French composer and pupil of Chambonnières. His collection, *Pièces de clavecin* (Pieces for the Harpsichord) contains suites, arrangements of airs from Lully's operas and variations, as well as instructions on how to play figured bass. (Ex. 5.106)

Jean-Baptiste Lully (1632–1687) was the most distinguished opera composer of seventeenth-century France, though he was actually an Italian by birth. He succeeded in establishing a true French opera, which was in effect a reform of the traditional Italian opera with its many musical excesses. He gave French opera a greater measure of dramatic sincerity through his handling of dramatic recitative, arias, and instrumental accompaniment. Lully established the French overture as well as the ballet as parts of French opera. His musical production was not exclusively operatic, however. He composed a great number of ballets for Molière's plays, some independent instrumental music, and religious choral works. Among his operatic masterpieces are *Cadmus et Hermione, Alceste, Armide et Renaud, Thésée,* and *Persée.* (Ex. 5.27, 5.60)

Marc-Antoine Charpentier (1634–1704), a French composer and pupil of Carissimi, was mainly concerned with writing masses, motets, and oratorios. He also wrote operas and smaller dramatic works for the stage, but his popularity suffered from Lully's disfavor. (Ex. 5.46, 5.107)

Dietrich Buxtehude (1637–1707) was a famous German organist and composer. Buxtehude influenced J. S. Bach, who made a two-hundred-mile journey on foot in 1705 from Arnstadt to Lübeck to hear Buxtehude play. Buxtehude's works included all the current forms of organ music, much choral music, and a variety of chamber and harpsichord compositions. (Ex. 5.40, 5.67)

Johann Pachelbel (1653–1706), a German organist and composer, wrote mainly organ works, though he also wrote for other keyboard instruments. His fugues are of utmost importance, not only because of their influence on Bach's writing, but for their intrinsic artistic value. (Ex. 5.49)

Arcangelo Corelli (1653–1713) was an Italian composer of great importance, as well as a violin virtuoso. He is looked upon as the founder of modern violin technique, with its intricacies of bowing, performance of double stops, and chordal effects. He was not a prolific composer. His entire output consisted of six opus numbers or collections, of which four are devoted to trio sonatas, one to violin and keyboard, and one to the concerto grosso. The latter represented a new form of composition of which Corelli is recognized as the creator. Handel was acquainted with Corelli and was undoubtedly influenced by his instrumental writing. (Ex. 5.74–5.75, 5.78)

Henry Purcell (c. 1659–1695) was England's most famous Baroque composer. Despite a very short life, his works are numerous and represent all areas of composition. He was equally gifted as an instrumental and vocal composer. Among his most important works are numerous anthems and religious choral compositions, the collection of twelve trio sonatas published during his lifetime, and his one opera, *Dido and Aeneas,* a work still frequently performed. Purcell was singularly gifted in his ability to compose on a ground (a recurring melodic pattern, usually in the bass), one of which is Dido's lament, *When I am laid in earth.* (Ex. 5.31, 5.108)

Johann Kuhnau (1660–1722) was a German composer whose works for the harpsichord are the most important among his other instrumental and vocal compositions. He was J. S. Bach's immediate predecessor as cantor at St. Thomas Church in Leipzig. His most important works are his sonatas for harpsichord, especially the group of six entitled *Biblische Historien* (Biblical Sonatas). These are early examples of music in which stories are illustrated by means of musical allusion. (Ex. 5.109)

Alessandro Scarlatti (1660–1725) was known mainly for his contributions to the style of the Neapolitan opera, of which he wrote over one hundred. He also added a rich literature of chamber and orchestral music as well as religious cantatas and masses to Italian music of the Baroque. Scarlatti established the *da capo aria* in the Neapolitan opera, a form which was generally adopted for all dramatic arias. (Ex. 5.41, 5.110–5.111)

Elisabeth-Claude Jacquet de la Guerre (c. 1666–1729) was patronized by King Louis XIV. She was a performer of exceptional skill and imagination. Her compositions included many cantatas, sonatas, suites, and an opera.

François Couperin (1668–1733), a member of a famous French family of musicians, was known as Couperin le Grand, because of his enormous skill as an organist. His religious compositions, mainly for the organ, constitute a large part of his works. His most numerous and renowned compositions, however, are those instrumental works written for the harpsichord during the last part of his life. The many ordres or suites for clavecin consist of dances that are often programmatic. He also wrote *L'Art de toucher le clavecin* (The Art of Playing the Clavecin), which had wide influence. Among his best-known works are the *Concerts Royaux* (Royal Concerts), the four volumes of *Pièces de clavecin* (Pieces for the Clavecin), and *Les Gouts réunis* (Gathered Tastes), the latter consisting of a number of concerted pieces written for strings and clavecin. Couperin's works are characterized by simple harmonies, generous ornamentation, and short phrases, all typical of the *galant* style of his time. (Ex. 5.79, 5.112–5.114)

Antonio Vivaldi (1678–1741) was the most celebrated of all the Baroque Italian masters and probably the most musically prolific. He wrote a large number of operas, oratorios, secular cantatas, and church music; however, his present fame rests on his concerti grossi and solo concerti. These number over four hundred. Vivaldi was a priest in the Roman Catholic Church and for many years was in charge of the musical program of the Ospidale della Pietá in Venice, a home for orphaned and foundling girls. It was in discharge of this duty that he wrote most of his instrumental and smaller choral works. These were performed by the girls in the institution. Among the most famous of the concerti grossi are the works known as *L'estro harmonico* (Harmonic Whim), *Il cimento dell' armonia e dell' inventione* (The Struggle between Harmony and Invention), including *Le quattro stagione* (The Four Seasons). J. S. Bach was especially influenced by Vivaldi's concertos and transcribed several for clavier. (Ex. 5.88–5.89, 5.115)

Georg Philipp Telemann (1681–1767) was perhaps the most prolific German composer of the late Baroque era. Some concept of his enormous output can be gained from the fact that he wrote more than forty operas, about three thousand cantatas and motets with orchestra or organ, six hundred overtures, forty-four passion settings, and equally numerous works for special occasions such as funer-als, weddings, coronations, and consecrations. His fame was considerably greater during his lifetime than that of J. S. Bach. The last forty-six years of his life were spent in Hamburg, where he was director of music for the city. He took this posi-tion in preference to that of cantor of St. Thomas Church in Leipzig. The latter position was then assumed by Bach, who after Telemann was second choice of the church council. Telemann remained relatively unknown during the nineteenth and early part of the twentieth centuries. However, the revival of interest in Baroque music during the past fifty years has brought his music to the fore again, particularly the orchestral and chamber music. (Ex. 5.59)

Jean-Philippe Rameau (1683–1764) was well known in his day as a musi-cal theorist, organist, and composer. His early career was devoted to organ playing in several of the great cathedrals of France. While serving in this capacity at Clermont-Ferand, he wrote his famous *Traité de l'harmonie* (Trea-tise of Harmony) in 1722. In this work he stated his system of chord building on superimposed thirds; the conception of a chord in all its inversions as one and the same entity; and the idea of a fundamental bass by which chord pro-gressions are determined. His fame as a composer, however, is based mainly on his dramatic compositions, of which the works *Les Indes galantes* (The Gallant Indians) and *Castor et Pollux* are his masterpieces. In addition to many ballets, operas, and much incidental music for drama, Rameau wrote fre-quently for clavecin and chamber groups typical of the Baroque period. Rameau's dramatic works were exceptional for their expressive melodic line, originality of instrumentation, and richness of harmonic idiom. Rameau's ideas aroused violent interest (both antagonistic and favorable), first between those who favored him and those who favored Lully, and later between his adherents and the *Encyclopédistes*. The latter exchange was known as the "War of the Buffoons." The perennial charges against operatic innovators that were leveled against Monteverdi, Gluck, and Wagner were leveled at Rameau. His critics found that his works lacked melody, were filled with illogical harmony, and used orchestral instruments in a noisy fashion. (Ex. 5.5, 5.28–5.29)

Johann Sebastian Bach (1685–1750) certainly was one of the greatest composers of all time. He was a member of what is perhaps the most interesting musical family in history. During a period encompassing several generations, more than one hundred members of the Bach family in Thuringia were occupied in musical activities. Of this number, some twenty were performers and composers of special significance, including both ancestors and offspring of Johann Sebastian.

At fifteen years of age Bach spent a short time studing with his brother Johann Christoph in Lüneburg. A year as violinist in the orchestra of the Duke of Saxe-Weimar was followed by his first real post as organist in Arnstadt in 1704. He left Arnstadt in 1707 to become an organist in Mülhausen. In 1708 he moved again, this time to Weimar, where he was made court organist and chamber musician to the Duke of Weimar. In 1714 he was raised to the rank of chamber musician and remained in this post until 1717. During this time he earned a reputation as one of the great organists of his day, as well as a composer of a wide variety of works in secular and religious forms. In 1717 he accepted the post of chapelmaster and director of chamber music to the Prince of Anhalt at Cöthen. Here Bach composed most of his orchestral and chamber music. His wife Barbara died in 1720, and in 1721 Bach married Anna Magdalena Wülcken, a gifted musician whose handwriting is often found in early manuscripts of Bach's works.

In 1723 Bach succeeded Kuhnau as cantor of the Thomas School in Leipzig, a post he held until his death in 1750. As organist and director of music at the two principal churches in Leipzig, Bach composed most of his great church music during the next twenty-seven years.

Among the many visits he paid to other cities in the capacity of organist, organ installer, and composer, none was more famous than the one to the court of Frederick the Great in Potsdam. Bach's second son, Karl Philipp Emanuel, was chamber musician there. It was during this visit that Bach improvised upon a theme given him by Frederick, a theme which he later used as the basis for the *Musikalisches Opfer* (Musical Offering). An unsuccessful eye operation in 1749 caused Bach to become totally blind, and in 1750 he died from a stroke. Bach represents the culmination of an era, particularly through his great emphasis on contrapuntal style. He was a master of the art of tonal counterpoint, and his *Kunst der Fuge* (Art of the Fugue) is an exhaustive treatise dealing with all manner of contrapuntal devices illustrated in the canons and fugues that comprise the work. His skill in handling fugal treatment is evident

Johann Sebastian Bach (1685–1750). (Corbis-Bettmann)

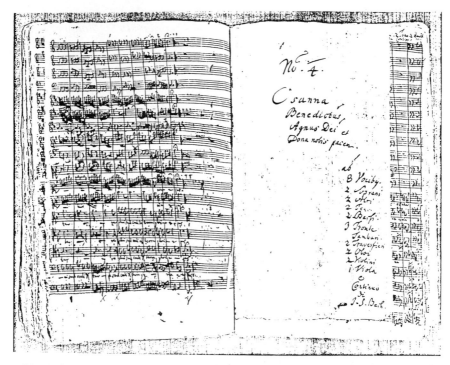

Manuscript page from Bach's *"B minor Mass,"* showing the instrumentation of the *Osanna.*

in all of his compositions: instrumental, vocal, secular, and religious. In his use of instruments he foreshadowed the future. He composed in every conceivable form except opera. Although the preponderance of his works were written for the church, much of his instrumental output is strictly secular. Even the smallest works, however, demonstrate his care and attention to compositional excellence. His mastery of counterpoint within the tonal system is comparable to that of Palestrina within the modal system.

No measurable appreciation of his great contribution to the history of music was realized until more than a half-century after his death. Mendelssohn brought Bach to the attention of the musical world of the nineteenth century with a performance of the *Saint Matthew Passion* in Leipzig in 1829.

Many of Bach's works were lost in manuscript; a comparatively small number was published during his lifetime. Despite this great loss, the complete edition, begun in 1850 by the Bach Gesellschaft, contained forty-seven volumes. A second complete edition was begun in 1954. Bach's works were not given opus numbers. Today they are most commonly referred to by BWV (Bach Werk Verzeichniss) numbers. A more logical thematic catalogue is that by Wolfgang Schmieder, published in 1950 (Rev. edition, 1990). (In this catalogue, the numbers are preceded by *S.*)

Among his great masterpieces remaining today are the following:

Vocal works: *Mass in B minor, The Passion According to St. Matthew, The Passion According to St. John, The Christmas Oratorio,* a *Magnificat,* approximately one hundred and ninety church cantatas, more than twenty-five secular cantatas, and many other shorter works.

Instrumental works: *Kunst der Fuge* (Art of Fugue), *Musikalisches Opfer* (The Musical Offering), the *Italian Concerto, The Goldberg Variations, Das Wohltemperierte Klavier* (The Well-Tempered Clavier), suites, partitas, and inventions for harpsichord, four overtures (suites) for orchestra, six *Brandenburg Concerti,* six unaccompanied *Suites for Violoncello,* three sonatas and three partitas for solo violin, numerous works for organ, including chorale preludes, toccatas, preludes, fantasias, and fugues, and concertos for harpsichord and violin as well as numerous sonatas for instrumental combinations. (Ex. 5.6, 5.10, 5.38, 5.42–5.44, 5.47, 5.51–5.53, 5.55–5.56, 5.65, 5.67–5.68, 5.73, 5.80, 5.84, 5.87)

Domenico Scarlatti (1685–1757), the greatest of the Italian composers for the keyboard, was one of the most original composers in the history of music. Although he wrote works for the church and for the operatic stage, his greatest contribution was his more than five hundred compositions for the harpsichord. He was the son and pupil of Alessandro Scarlatti. After a very productive youth in Italy, he took a post with the Portuguese court in Lisbon, where he became music master to Princess Maria Barbara. It was for her that he composed the works that were to make him famous, the *Esercizi per gravicembalo* (Exercises for the Harpsichord), which are usually referred to as sonatas. When the princess married the heir to the Spanish throne, Scarlatti moved to Madrid, where he spent the remainder of his life (from 1729 to 1757) as master of the salon. His sonatas are the finest example of late Baroque writing for the harpsichord. Scarlatti managed to exploit the instrument to the utmost in these works, and in so doing laid the foundation for future keyboard technique. Many of the works call for such innovations in performance as the crossing of the hands. The sonatas of Scarlatti reflect the whole gamut of moods from gay and dancelike, which often include Spanish rhythms, to lyric and romantic. (Ex. 5.81)

George Frideric Handel (1685–1759) was a compatriot of Johann Sebastian Bach, and one who shares with him the distinction of bringing the Baroque era to a close. In contrast to Bach, Handel was a cosmopolitan composer who added to his German heritage a wide study and firsthand knowledge of Italian musical style. He practiced these accomplishments during most of the last fifty years of his life, which he spent in England. Handel was something of a musical prodigy; after instruction in organ, oboe, and harpsichord, as well as counterpoint and fugue, he assumed a position as assistant organist in Halle, his native city, at the age of twelve. During this year he also composed a number of choral and instrumental works. In 1702 Handel went to Hamburg, where he was associated with the opera until 1706. In the same year

George Frideric Handel (1685–1759) (Free Library of Philadelphia)

he went to Italy and became successful as a composer of Italian opera and dramatic oratorios. Handel returned to Germany in 1710 as *Kapellmeister* to the Elector of Hanover, a relationship that resulted in his going to England when the German prince took over the throne of England.

From this time on, Handel was occupied with a variety of activities, such as teacher, director of the Royal Academy of Music (an institution that produced Italian opera in London), composer, opera impresario, and traveler. His main compositional area was opera until 1741, when he turned to the composition and production of oratorios. It is in the latter field that he achieved his most lasting fame.

His compositions of both secular and religious drama reveal a spirit of grandeur, for there is always something of the pomp of the court about his work. He wrote twenty-seven oratorios and more than forty operas, as well as a great quantity of other vocal works including anthems, cantatas, and vocal solos and ensembles. Handel was also a prolific composer of instrumental compositions that include all the Baroque forms: concerti grossi; harpsichord suites; organ concerti; chamber music for strings, winds, and keyboard; and large orchestral works. Among his numerous works, a few stand out as masterpieces: the oratorios (*Messiah, Samson, Judas Maccabaeus, Solomon, Israel in Egypt, Saul*); the operas (*Alcina, Giulio Cesare, Rinaldo, Xerxes*); the orchestral music (*Water Music, Fireworks Music*); and twelve concerti grossi for strings.

Several incomplete and often inaccurate editions of the works of Handel have been issued from time to time. In 1955, work was begun on a new complete edition issued by the Georg Friedrich Händel Gesellschaft of Halle. (Ex. 5.26, 5.36, 5.86, 5.116)

Manuscript page from the bass aria, *"But who may abide the day of coming?"* from Handel's *Messiah* (The Bettmann Archive)

Giovanni Battista Pergolesi (1710–1736), whose short life fell entirely within the eighteenth century, was, however, still a representative of the Baroque style of composition. He wrote both instrumental and vocal music, but his *opera buffa* compositions brought him fame. Pergolesi wrote three of these works, which were performed between the acts of his serious operas. The most famous of these, *La Serva padrona,* which was the rival opera to Rameau's works that were the focus of the War of the Buffoons (1752), is still found in the modern opera repertoire. Although a large number of trio sonatas, solo sonatas, and concertos in the Baroque style were once ascribed to Pergolesi, it is now certain that many of them are not his works. A number of his religious works were published during his lifetime; the best known today is *Stabat Mater.* (Ex. 5.25, 5.117)

ADDITIONAL COMPOSERS

A. Austria
    Heinrich Ignaz Franz von Biber
    (1644–1704)
    Johann Joseph Fux (1660–1741)
B. England
    Henry Lawes (1596–1662)
    Matthew Locke (c. 1630–1677)
    Pelham Humfrey (1647–1674)
    John Blow (c. 1648–1708)
C. France
    Louis Couperin (c. 1626–1661)
    Robert Cambert (c. 1628–1677)
    Michel-Richard Delalande
    (1657–1726)
    Jean-Marie Leclair (1697–1764)
D. Germany
    Melchior Franck (c. 1579–1639)
    Franz Tunder (1614–1667)
    Johann Kaspar Kerll (1627–1693)
    Johann Christoph Bach
    (1642–1703)
    Johann Krieger (1651–1735)
    Georg Muffat (1653–1704)
    Philipp Heinrich Erlebach
    (1657–1714)
    Georg Böhm (1661–1733)
    Reinhard Keiser (1674–1739)
    Christoph Graupner (1683–1760)
    Johann Gottfried Walther
    (1684–1748)
    Johann Friedrich Fasch
    (1688–1758)
    Johann Adolph Hasse (1699–1783)

E. Italy
    Emilio del Cavalieri (c. 1550–1602)
    Adriano Banchieri (1568–1634)
    Salomone Rossi (1570–c. 1630)
    Sigismondo d'India (c. 1582–c. 1629)
    Stefano Landi (c. 1590–1639)
    Domenico Mazzochi (1592–1665)
    Biagio Marini (1597–1665)
    Francesco Cavalli (1602–1676)
    Giovanni Legrenzi (1626–1690)
    Giovanni Battista Vitali
    (1632–1692)
    Antonio Draghi (1635–1700)
    Alessandro Stradella (1644–1682)
    Agostino Steffani (1654–1728)
    Giuseppe Torelli (1658–1709)
    Antonio Lotti (c. 1667–1740)
    Giovanni Bononcini (1670–1747)
    Tomaso Albinoni (1671–1750)
    Evaristo Felice dall' Abaco
    (1675–1742)
    Francisco Durante (1684–1755)
    Benedetto Marcello (1686–1739)
    Nicola Porpora (1686–1768)
    Francesco Geminiani (1687–1762)
    Francesco Maria Veracini
    (1690–1768)
F. Mexico
    Manuel de Zumaya (c. 1678–1755)
    Ignacio de Jerúsalem (c. 1710–1769)
G. Peru
    Tomás de Torrejón y Velasco
    (1644–1728)
    José de Orejón y Aparicio
    (c. 1705–1765)

VII. HISTORIANS AND THEORISTS

Giovanni de' Bardi (1534–1612) was an Italian aristocrat who, because of his philosophical and literary interests, helped found the Florentine Camerata, the group whose investigations led to the first operatic composition. His writings, all in Italian, are concerned with speculations concerning the new music. Among them is the *Discorso mandato a Caccini sopra la musica antica e 'l cantar bene* (c. 1578), in which he discusses ideas about ancient music and vocal performance.

Giovanni Maria Artusi (c. 1540–1613) was an Italian writer on music. *L'Artusi, overo delle imperfettioni della moderna musica* (Artusi, concerning the imperfections of modern music), printed in Venice in 1600, is a representative critical essay. Artusi was very conservative in his musical philosophy and is remembered mainly for his criticism of the new style as represented by Monteverdi at the opening of the seventeenth century.

Michael Praetorius (1571–1621), a German musician, composer, and theorist, wrote his three-volume *Syntagma Musicum* (Musical encyclopedia) between 1615 and 1618. The first, written in Latin, deals with ancient church music and secular instruments. The second volume, in German, is an exhaustive treatise on the instruments of the Baroque period and is the most important source of information concerning instruments of the early Baroque. Forty-two woodcuts depicting the principal instruments add to its importance. The third volume contains accounts of secular music. His writings are among the most valuable treatises on music written during the Baroque period. Reprints of the second and third volumes were made in 1929 and 1916, respectively.

Marin Mersenne (1588–1648) was a French theorist. His *Traité de l'harmonie universelle* (Treatise Concerning Universal Harmony), Paris 1627, was published in an expanded form in 1936 and 1937 as *Harmonie universelle.* It includes a discourse on harmonic theory and an especially valuable description, both verbal and pictorial, of all the instruments of the seventeenth century. An English version of this work was published under the title *Harmonie Universelle: The Books on Instruments,* published in The Hague in 1957.

Christopher Simpson (c. 1610–1669), an English violist and composer, wrote *The Division Violist or an Introduction to the Playing Upon a Ground* in 1659. It is a book of instruction for improvisation and the playing of the viol. A modern edition was published in London in 1958.

Johann Joseph Fux (1660–1741) was a German composer and theorist whose most important work was *Gradus ad Parnassum* (Steps to Parnassus), published in Vienna in 1725. It became a standard text in contrapuntal instruction and was studied by such masters as Mozart and Haydn, and used by such distinguished teachers as Cherubini and Albrechtsberger. It was of great influence in the teaching of counterpoint for well over a century. An English translation was published in 1943.

François Couperin (1668–1733) was a French composer, organist, and clavecinist. *L'Art de toucher le clavecin* (The art of playing the harpsichord), Paris 1716, described Couperin's manner of performance of his clavecin pieces. It is of greatest importance in its description of the manner and style of playing the keyboard literature of the seventeenth and eighteenth centuries.

Jacques Hotteterre (1674–1763) was a French flutist. His *Principes de la flute traversière ou flûte d'Allemagne, de la flûte à bec ou flûte douce et du hautbois* (Principles of playing the transverse or German flute, the recorder, or sweet flute and oboe), Paris 1707, is the earliest work on the performance of these three woodwind instruments.

Johann Mattheson (1681–1764) was a German composer and writer. He wrote a biographical dictionary, *Grundlage einer Ehren-Pforte, woran die tüchtigsten Capellmeister, Componisten, Musikgelehrten, Tonkünstler, etc., Leben, Werke, Verdienste, etc., erscheinen sollen* (Foundation for a triumphal arch on which the lives, works, and success of the greatest directors, composers, learned musicians, and artists shall be inscribed), Hamburg 1740, which is a source of historical information of the period.

Jean-Philippe Rameau (1683–1764) was a French composer and theorist. His *Traité de l'harmonie reduite a ses principes naturels* (Treatise on Harmony), Paris 1722, presented the revolutionary idea of a harmonic system in which the chords were built on thirds and were classified in all their inversions as the same chord. Rameau's treatise also established the primacy of chords on I, IV, and V in a given key.

Francesco Geminiani (1687–1762) was an Italian violinist, composer, and writer. *The Art of Playing the Violin,* London 1730, was first published anonymously, and was the first method for violin instruction to be written. In 1751 it was published under Geminiani's name as *The Compleat Tutor for the Violin.* However, some scholars today believe that this is an incorrect attribution. A facsimile edition was published in 1952. This work is of utmost importance in the study of principles of violin playing of the Baroque era.

Giuseppe Tartini (1692–1770), Italian violinist, composer, and theorist, wrote a number of theoretical works dealing with his discovery of combination tones and other theories concerning harmonic structure. The performance of *agréments* is discussed in *Traitée des agréments de la musique,* Paris, 1771.

Important excerpts in English from several of the foregoing works can be found in *Source Readings in Music History* by Strunk.

The Mozart family in performance. Leopold Mozart and his children, Wolfgang and Nannerl in an engraving after a watercolor by Louis Carrogis. (Art and History Archive, Berlin)

6

Classic
(1750–1820)

I. SOCIOCULTURAL INFLUENCES ON MUSIC

The term *classic* is used here to designate the music of the eighteenth century. This term has also been used by historians to describe those arts that are concerned mainly with problems of form, logic, balance, and restrained expression, and that were also based on models of Greek and Roman art. Unfortunately, there are no such models for Classic music to emulate. Consequently, the term as applied to music refers to the works of those eighteenth century composers whose music gives the impression of clarity, repose, balance, lyricism, and restraint of emotional expression. In the opinion of many, the Classic period is one of the high points of music history and was nourished by a number of important developments in the patronage and function of music during this time.

An important feature of the late eighteenth century, affecting many areas of society—theology, philosophy, science, morality, politics, and the arts— was the movement called the Enlightenment. Among its chief characteristics was a shift from traditional Christian theology to a morality based on social equality, and a shift from absolutes in governmental authority to greater independence and freedom of thought and behavior. Among the effects of the Enlightenment on music were changes in the nature of patronage, particularly regarding the church and the courts of the aristocracy.

Austria and Germany became centers of vital musical activity. In these countries numerous courts were able to maintain their independence. This was in contrast to France and England, where almost all aristocratic life had come under the influence of a central power. In Austria and Germany, however, these small courts gave up much of their political and economic independence but maintained their artistic and social status. There was even greater rivalry among them in artistic and social matters. Moreover, a long tradition of instrumental music, an abundance of talent, a natural love of music among all classes, great artistic ambition combined with great wealth—together these made the perfect conditions for an enthusiastic patronage.

Composers depended upon the patronage of a court or aristocratic society that was very discriminating in its tastes. This society was not only sophisticated and elegant but disclaimed any affinity for being profound or showing emotion. The Age of Reason and Enlightenment had placed a premium on intellectual pursuits and looked with a good deal of suspicion on any reliance upon feelings.

The concert hall and opera house became established institutions, making it possible for all classes to enjoy the fruits of creative activity, whether aristocratic or not, and women played increasingly important roles in the public performance of operas and church music.

Publishing houses became well established and exerted a strong influence on both composers and the public. Not only did publishers make performances of musical works more widespread; they were in a position to champion certain composers, often to the detriment of others.

There was a general decline in the patronage of the church toward music. There were certain reform movements in both Protestantism and Catholicism during the eighteenth century, but none of them provided a suitable climate for a continuous growth of religious music. Certainly, the rather shallow attitude of aristocratic society did little to maintain religious music at the level of the Baroque.

II. FUNCTION OF MUSIC

Music in the Classic era served a highly sophisticated and aristocratic society. Its most common function was to provide delightful entertainment for guests in exclusive salons. Unlike Baroque music, which often had a descriptive character, Classic music was more abstract and tended to avoid representation. (See *Empfindsamer Stil.*) However, one movement in this period, *Sturm und Drang* (named after a literary movement), belies to a degree this assertion with its emphasis on dynamic power and high emotions.

A larger but still discriminating audience patronized public concerts of orchestral music and the elegant spectacle of opera.

Music also served an important function in the home, for this was an era of amateur musical performances, both vocal and instrumental. Many composers were called upon to write chamber music as well as vocal solos and ensembles for amateur consumption. Naturally, music for dancing was in popular demand for a society that loved gaiety and entertainment. Although the church was not a major patron, it still demanded that composers write sacred music for its services in the spirit of secularism that prevailed.

III. STYLE AND PERFORMANCE PRACTICE

The following characteristics of style applied to some extent to all vocal and instrumental forms in the Classic era.

Formal Organization

Classical compositions were typically constructed around one melody contrasted with a second melody in A B A form. This was partly in protest against the complications of polyphony, and partly an effort to create a form that could be grasped and enjoyed by all, aristocrat and bourgeois alike. Classic music was characterized by a symmetry of form that was precise and clear, with sections clearly marked off by cadences. Musical periods tended to be balanced, often in units of four-measure phrases.

Folk music in all its forms and idioms was gradually introduced into classical music, including chamber and symphonic writing as well as opera and song. This was especially true in the works of Haydn, who used Croatian melodies and rhythms, among others, in his music. No doubt the use of folk music was due to the great diversity of the Classic audience.

Melody

There was an emphasis on lyricism with smooth, melodic contours. Melodies were extended to double phrases and more, in contrast to the generally short, cryptic melodic devices of earlier music. Ornaments (often written out) became a part of the lyric melody, and sequential patterns were formalized to the extent of becoming cliché. These characteristics, together with dramatic dynamic changes and expressive chromaticisms, are important characteristics of the *Empfindsamer Stil*.

Chordal structure was often the basis for melodic configuration. In fast tempos, ascending chordal patterns were often referred to as *rocket figures* (fig. 6.1).

Figure 6.1 *Symphony in G major,* including "rocket" themes

Rhythm

Classic composers most often wrote simple and constant rhythmic patterns that were clearly punctuated by rhythmic cadences. There is a tendency toward uniformity among these rhythmic patterns. Polyrhythms were no longer used as in earlier music. An important formal device of rhythm in the Classic era was the *Alberti bass,* which breaks up the triad into its components, creating broken chord figures in a repeated rhythmic pattern (fig. 6.2).

Figure 6.2 Alberti bass

Silence became an expressive rhythmic factor in the Classic era. For example, strong cadences are sometimes followed by a measure of silence in order to heighten the effect of the cadence. The tempo of movements, or sections, tended to remain constant from beginning to end.

Harmony

In music of this period, harmony is relatively simple, utilizing primary chords, their inversions, and various seventh chords (fig. 6.3). It is tonal, with harmonic rhythms that move slowly and are subordinate to the melody. This results in a predominately homophonic style (fig. 6.3). Because the bass no longer served a melodic function, the Baroque polarity between soprano and bass disappeared. Consequently, the practice of the basso continuo was discontinued.

Figure 6.3 *Piano Sonata,* K. 570, illustrating simple harmonies

W. A. Mozart

There is a formal key relationship among themes and among movements. These key relationships serve to provide contrast and interest without introducing new material. In the exposition of sonata form, the first theme is in the tonic. The second theme is in the dominant of the original, or the relative major if the first is in a minor key. The development usually contains a number of modulations away from either the tonic or dominant, with a return to the tonic. In the recapitulation, the second theme is in the tonic, thus reconciling the key relationships and enabling the movement to end with a tonic cadence. The key relations among movements are less varied. In general, all movements are in the same key with the exception of the second movement, which is in the sub-dominant, dominant, or relative minor. If the first movement is in minor, the last movement is sometimes in the parallel major.

The most commonly used cadence was the IV, V, I, with the final tonic on a strong beat (fig. 6.4).

Figure 6.4 A perfect authentic cadence (accented)

IV   V   I

The unaccented cadence was also frequently employed. This is a normal perfect authentic cadence, but with the final tonic on a weak beat (fig. 6.5).

Figure 6.5 A perfect authentic cadence (unaccented)

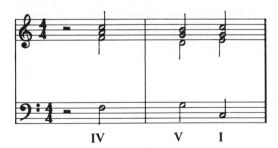

IV   V   I

Texture

The texture of Classic music is essentially homophonic, with lyric melody pre-dominating. Even when polyphonic texture is present, there is great clarity and transparency of line. In orchestral music this clarity of texture is emphasized by means of contrasting tonal coloring.

Instrumentation and Tone Color

The most popular means of musical expression in the Classic period was instrumental: the orchestra, chamber music (both strings and winds), and music for solo instruments.

The orchestra consisted of a string ensemble of approximately twenty-six, with pairs of wind instruments (e.g., flutes, oboes, clarinets, bassoons, horns, trumpets), and tympani, at the discretion of the composer. Though the harpsichord was still frequently a part of the bass line and contributed to the harmonic texture, in general its use diminished significantly toward the end of the eighteenth century.

The lute and harpsichord had been the household instruments during the Renaissance and the Baroque, but they were superceded by the piano as a chamber instrument during the late eighteenth century. Instrumental chamber music became very popular. The large number of amateur performers and the intimacy of artistocratic society supplied a suitable climate for its development. Some of the finest Classic music can be found in the literature of the string quartet, piano quintets, trios, or solo sonatas.

(Appendix 1 includes further information on instruments.)

Apart from opera, vocal music was of minor importance but remained in the form of religious music, folk songs, and the Lied. Opera was in great demand. Testimony of this can be seen in the large number of operas composed by both major and minor composers.

Performance Practice

In the printed scores of the Classic period, dynamic markings became commonplace. This was an important means of achieving contrast, but instead of changing the sonority as in the Baroque tutti and concertino, Classic composers employed crescendos and diminuendos as well as sudden, dramatic, dynamic changes. Composers gave explicit directions in dynamics, tempi, phrasing, and all other interpretive matters, leaving little to the performer's discretion.

Although ornaments were not always written out, there was a precise formula for the designation of each figure. It is in this area that Classic composers depended upon tradition, and consequently the correct interpretation of ornaments is a serious problem for performers today.

In the Classic period, composers wrote for specific instruments and combinations of instruments, such as the string quartet or woodwind ensemble. Composers designated the instrumentation to be used, in contrast to the Baroque practice of permitting the performers to choose suitable instruments.

Among the important composer-performers of the Classic period, Mozart stands out as a virtuoso pianist with numerous performances as both pianist and conductor. While Haydn was not a virtuoso performer, he was a formidable conductor, scoring great success both at the Court of Esterházy and, in his later years, in London with his Salomon symphonies. Boccherini was also a notable cellist.

IV. MUSIC FOR VOICES

Single-Movement Forms and Compositional Devices

Recitative

This is not a form, but a method of composition carried over from the Baroque period. Recitativo secco involved minimal accompaniment from the continuo forces. Both recitativo secco and recitativo accompagnato had considerable musical interest, apart from carrying the narrative portions of the drama. The accompaniment itself was often highly suggestive of the atmosphere of the text. (Ex. 6.1)

Aria

The aria in the Classic operas of Gluck and Mozart most often avoided the spectacular virtuosity of Baroque opera. The principle of the da capo aria still prevailed, but it was a much more expressive musical realization of the text. As in the accompanied recitative, the orchestra created the proper mood by means of lyric melody and tone color. (Ex. 6.2)

Choruses and Ensembles

Vocal part music was associated with music of the theater and the church. There were independent compositions written for vocal ensembles as well. Haydn, for example, wrote several such works. The Moravian church, centered in Pennsylvania and North Carolina, generated a sizeable repertory of music for various vocal combinations, usually with instrumental accompaniment. The performance of the music of this tradition continues today.

The chorus is an effective part of the drama in the operas of Gluck and Mozart. Ensembles, especially in Mozart, marvelously present subtle musical dramatization. In contrast to the homophonic texture of arias, these choruses and ensembles are usually polyphonic. Each member of the ensemble is often declaiming elements of counterplots and intrigue along with the main story. In essence, this is both musical and dramatic counterpoint. (Ex. 6.3)

Vocal Polyphony

Although homophony was the most common texture of Classic music, polyphony as a compositional device still prevailed in some forms. This was especially true in operatic ensembles and in the chorus sections of masses and oratorios. Examples can be found in the ensembles of *Le Nozze di Figaro* and *Don Giovanni* by Mozart. Haydn's *Die Schöpfung* (The Creation) and Mozart's *Requiem Mass* include examples of polyphonic texture in religious vocal music. Polyphonic forms such as the canon and the motet were still composed, and both Haydn and Mozart wrote in these forms. (Ex. 6.4, 6.5)

Lied

The Classic Lied replaced the ornamented pathos of seventeenth-century arias and songs. The Lied was characterized by simple folklike melodies and was usually strophic (the same melody and harmonic substance for each stanza of the poem). Some of the finest strophic songs were written in the late eighteenth century by Mozart and Haydn. (Ex. 6.6, 6.7)

Composite Forms

Opera

In the eighteenth century, opera underwent significant reform, moving away from the stereotypical practices of the Neapolitan school. At midcentury in Paris, partisan support for Italian opera, as opposed to French opera, resulted in a battle in the press known as the War of the Buffoons. In this verbal controversy, the merits of the languages, as well as the melody and harmony embodied in the two national styles were debated. An interesting expression of the intensity of feelings of the time was Jean-Jacques Rousseau's declaration that the French language was unsuitable for musical utterance.

The chief reforms in eighteenth-century opera were realized in the works of Gluck, who thought of himself as a reformer of opera, and by Mozart. In general, it can be said that the structure of opera in the late eighteenth century became much more fluent and subtle than that of the Baroque. The relation between music and drama was somewhat restored. No longer were singers left to their own devices in improvising dazzling vocal effects that had little to do with the story, nor was the stage mechanic more important than the composer. There was a strong emphasis upon skillful characterization of the protagonists, together with greater dramatic force. The da capo principle continued to be applied with great success in operatic arias. Each was a closed form, complete in itself. In addition to *opera seria,* there was further development of comic opera in the eighteenth century: *opera buffa* in Italy, *opéra comique* in France, *ballad opera* in England, and *Singspiel* in Germany. Each represented a national style, and all were characterized by spoken dialogue along with recitative and aria. (Ex. 6.8–6.13)

Oratorio

The oratorio continued in the tradition of the Baroque, but with emphasis on classic characteristics. For example, the instrumental forces of the oratorio were essentially those of the Classic symphony, whereas the recitative, aria, and choral components were preserved from the earlier style period. The most well-known Classic oratorios are by Haydn. *Die Schöpfung* (the Creation) was based on a text from the Book of Genesis and Milton's *Paradise Lost. Die Jahreszeiten* (the Seasons) is a secular work on poetry by the Scottish poet James Thomson, and translated into German. Both of these works have become successful concert pieces. (Ex. 6.14, 6.15)

Mass

Despite the substantial contributions to Mass literature, there was a general decline in the quality of religious music composed during the Classic era. Much of what was composed was written for liturgical use but was also appropriate for the concert hall. The Mass was the favorite of these forms and consisted of the setting of the Ordinary of the Mass with soloists, chorus, and orchestra, and was symphonic in nature. (Ex. 6.16–6.18)

A performance of Haydn's *Creation* in a palatial hall early in the nineteenth century. (Historical Pictures/Stock Montage, Inc.)

V. MUSIC FOR INSTRUMENTS

Single-Movement Forms and Structural Devices

Sonata-Allegro Form

Sonata-allegro form (first movement form) is by far the most representative single-movement form. It is almost always used as the first movement of a composite sonata or symphony, but it may also be used as a slow movement or the final movement. It was also used as the design for some single movement compositions. Derived historically from rounded binary form (ABa), its organization consists of three parts: (1) the presentation of two contrasting harmonic sections, each of which may have the same or contrasting themes or theme groups (exposition); (2) the development of these themes through harmonic and motivic exploration and transformation (development); and (3) their reconciliation harmonically, melodically, and rhythmically (recapitulation).

A stereotypical plan for the Classic sonata-allegro form follows. Two versions of the plan are shown, one for compositions in major tonalities, and one for compositions in minor tonalities. (Although the following diagrams show the interaction among themes, sonata-allegro form more accurately defines the relationships among key areas [e.g., tonic-dominant; tonic-relative major or minor].)

Sonatas in major tonalities

Exposition:
Theme I (tonic), Transition, Theme II (dominant), closing material.

Development:
Varied treatment of material from the exposition in various keys, followed by a cadence.

Recapitulation:
Theme I (tonic), Transition, Theme II (tonic), Transition, Closing Theme (tonic), Coda.

Sonatas in minor tonalities

Exposition:
Theme I (tonic), Transition, Theme II (relative major), closing material.

Development:
Varied treatment of material from the exposition in various keys, followed by a cadence.

Recapitulation:
Theme I (tonic), Transition, Theme II (tonic), Transition, Closing Theme (tonic), Coda.

Sonata-allegro form sometimes began with a slow introduction, a carry-over from the French overture. This musical device served to quiet the audience and gain attention. There was usually no connection between the musical material of the introduction and the thematic material of the sonata movement. The introductory section was most often used in the first movement of the symphony.

Many large movements in sonata-allegro form added a coda to the recapitulation. This was a section in the tonic key that strengthened the finality of the closing cadence. (Ex. 6.19–6.21)

(Because a large number of scores and recordings by numerous publishers and recording companies exist for a substantial amount of music from the Classic era to the present day, references to specific editions and recordings will be omitted from this point on. Scores may be found in the anthologies suggested in the Introduction.)

Rondo

The rondo form, with its rounded design, had its origins in the Baroque ritornello form, and was based on the principle of repetition after digression. It differs from sonata form in that it has no development section and that the principal theme is always repeated in the tonic. The typical form is as follows: A B A C A B A. In major keys, section B is usually in the key of the dominant. If section A is in a minor key, B is in the relative major. Section C, which is in the tonic, is usually a melody of minor significance or merely an episode between the repetitions of A. Late eighteenth-century composers frequently combined aspects of the sonata and rondo forms, resulting in an expansion of the middle section (C) through use of development techniques. This modification is often referred to as the "sonata-rondo form." (Ex. 6.22, 6.23)

Variation Form

In the Classic period the variation was still popular as the second movement of keyboard sonatas and also in some quartets and symphonies. The variation form was primarily homophonic in the Classic period. Variations were both harmonic and melodic, using contrasting tempi and rhythmic patterns as well as changes in tone color. (Ex. 6.24–6.26)

Three-Part Song Form

The three-part song form is in reality an instrumental form based on lyric melodies. It was often used as the second movement of a sonata. (Ex. 6.27, 6.28)

Minuet and Trio, and Other Dance Forms

Although numerous single dance forms were written specifically for ballroom dancing, the minuet, as in the *minuet* and *trio,* is practically the only one that succeeded, in stylized form, in achieving a place in the art music of the Classic period. In general the dance forms retained their two-part form of the Baroque, but with the addition of the trio, the minuet became a three-part form in Classic guise. Its plan is as follows (note that each of the sections is a three-part form):

Minuet ‖: A :‖: BA :‖
Trio ‖: C :‖: DC :‖
Minuet ‖ A ‖ BA ‖
(Ex. 6.29, 6.30)

Overture

The eighteenth-century overture possessed some characteristics of sonata form. It was associated almost exclusively with the opera and was used as an expression of mood preparatory to the first scene. In the late eighteenth century, composers began to incorporate material from the main body of the opera into the overture. (Ex. 6.31, 6.32)

Polyphonic Instrumental Music

Contrapuntal forms of the Baroque were not completely discarded during the Classic period. They were, however, most often used as musical devices rather than complete forms. For example, the first theme in sonata form was sometimes cast as a *fugato* (fugal passage). Fugal passages were also often used in the development sections of sonatas. Both Haydn and Mozart made extensive use of fugue in this manner and used polyphonic principles of construction in independent works as well as throughout complete movements in some of their multi-movement works. In contrast to the Baroque fugue, however, their subjects were usually longer and more lyrical. (Ex. 6.33, 6.34)

Composite Forms

Sonata

The most important composite form of the Classic era is the sonata, an abstract instrumental form in three or four separate movements. It was developed from the seventeenth-century dance suite and trio sonata and was influenced by the Italian operatic overture. A Classic sonata usually consisted of (1) a fast movement in sonata form; (2) a slow movement in three-part song form, variation, or sonata form; (3) a minuet and trio; and (4) a very fast movement in rondo or sonata form. On occasion this last movement was a set of variations, but always in a fast tempo. If there are only three movements, the minuet is omitted. A sonata is the name used for this composite form when written for one or two instruments. When written for more than two instruments, it takes the name of the particular ensemble, such as symphony or trio. It is the only form that is divorced from religion, drama, and to some degree the dance. It also has more universal appeal than polyphonic forms, such as the fugue, because it is less complicated intellectually. C. P. E. Bach is the composer mainly responsible for the classic sonata. (Ex. 6.35–6.38)

Symphony

The symphony is a sonata for orchestra and is normally in four movements, the first of which was often preceded by a slow introduction. The use of a larger group of instruments called for a much more extended composition. The varied tonal possibilities of the orchestra made it possible to have a greater variety of style, more extended climaxes, and a more complex development section.

There were two important "schools" of Classic symphony composers: the Mannheim school, with Stamitz as its most important representative, and the Viennese school with Haydn, Mozart, and Beethoven. (Ex. 6.39–6.42)

Concerto

The concerto is a work for solo instrument (more rarely for two or more solo instruments) and orchestra in the pattern of the sonata. The concerto generally omits the minuet and trio, thus making it a three-movement composition. In the first movement the orchestra presents an abbreviated exposition in the tonic, followed by the solo instrument's direct statement of the thematic material, a compositional practice known as the double exposition. The development follows with the solo instrument pitted against the orchestra. Following the recapitulation there is usually a brilliant cadenza—a free improvisation on the themes by the performer—although it was sometimes written out by the composer. The second and third movements follow the forms of second and third movements of sonatas, with optional cadenzas. (Ex. 6.43–6.46)

Chamber Music

All kinds of small instrumental ensembles using the forms of the sonata come under this heading. These forms were called trios, quartets, quintets, and sextets, and were for various combinations of string and wind instruments. However, the string quartet was the most common. When the piano was used in combination with string instruments, the form was designated as a piano trio, piano quartet, or piano quintet. (Ex. 6.47–6.51)

Serenades, Divertimenti, Cassations, Notturni

These works constituted a rather large body of literature usually written for specific occasions. They were related to the earlier suites and sinfonie of the Baroque, but were now based on Classic characteristics of form and style. They were written for any number of instruments, from small chamber groups to the orchestra, and in many instances they consisted of a large number of separate movements. The best-known example of a serenade from this period is Mozart's *Eine kleine Nachtmusik.* Its simple instrumentation in four voices allows it to be played by string quartet or by string orchestra. (Ex. 6.52, 6.53)

VI. COMPOSERS

Giovanni Sammartini (1701–1775) was a pioneer in the development of the Classic sonata, and was known for his chamber music in the Classic style. He was Gluck's teacher. His principal works that survive today are sonatas for chamber ensemble, especially string quartets, and symphonies. (Ex. 6.47)

Christoph Willibald Gluck (1714–1787), an opera composer, initiated many reforms that laid the foundations for later opera composers, but had little immediate effect on the composers of his time. Gluck, after writing in the traditional Italian style, finally came to the conclusion that the dramatic force of the libretto must be the most important aspect of opera. To achieve this he made the following innovations: (1) he eliminated virtuosity, substituting lyric simplicity; (2) he strove to create musical portraits of his characters and their feelings; (3) he returned to the use of plots taken from mythology—plots that avoid the complex counterplots and minor intrigues of Neapolitan opera; (4) he made the recitative more musically expressive; (5) he used the instruments of the orchestra as a tonal palette, creating the proper mood and atmosphere by tonal coloring; (6) he employed the chorus to create dramatic intensity; and (7) he made the overture an introduction to the mood and spirit of the opera. His most important works were *Orfeo ed Euridice,* 1762; *Alceste,* 1767; *Armide,* 1777; and *Iphigénie en Tauride,* 1779. (Ex. 6.2, 6.8, 6.31)

Carl Phillip Emanuel Bach (1714–1788), the son of J. S. Bach and sometimes known as the Berlin Bach, was well known as a keyboard performer as well as a composer. He was influential in establishing the form and style of Classic composition, and he is often credited with being the first to write in sonata form. There is no doubt that Haydn and Mozart were influenced by his style. He wrote more than two hundred sonatas and solo works for piano, in addition to numerous concerti and chamber music works. His sonatas show the

Franz Joseph Haydn (1732–1809) (Free Library of Philadelphia)

form of that genre, but there is little, if any, development of themes in his sonata-allegro movements. (Ex. 6.27, 6.35, 6.39)

Johann Wenzel Anton Stamitz (1717–1757), the founder of the Mannheim school, made a number of important contributions to both orchestral playing and writing for orchestra. The most important of these were: the first use of extensive dynamic shading in orchestral performance; the introduction of the clarinet into the orchestra; the introduction of the minuet into the symphony as the third movement; and the creation of what was known as the finest orchestra in all of Europe. He wrote approximately seventy-four symphonies, but these are seldom performed today. (Ex. 6.42)

Franz Joseph Haydn (1732–1809) was one of the most prolific composers of the eighteenth century. Haydn's career exemplified the patronage system functioning at its best. Born in lower Austria, he received his early training as a choirboy at St. Stephen's cathedral in Vienna. Aside from this schooling, he was largely self-taught in music, drawing heavily upon the style of such Classic composers as C. P. E. Bach. Haydn was finally given a post as assistant Kappelmeister at the Court of Prince Esterházy in 1761 and was to enjoy an ideal patronage for a period of over thirty years. His duties were to provide music requested by the prince for any and all occasions. Consequently, he was called upon to write in every contemporaneous musical form. A most important factor in the development of his orchestral music was the fact that he had an orchestra at his disposal at all times. This enabled him to experiment with various orchestral instruments and orchestral timbres. It was Haydn who brought unity to late eighteenth-century music and perfected the Classic style.

Haydn wrote a prodigious amount of music; much of it has been lost, and the remainder is only now being published in a complete edition. His more important works are the symphonies, of which 104 are published, and 82 string quartets. His main contributions to the Classic style consist of: the addition of slow introductions to the first movements of symphonies, enlarging the development section of the sonata form and developing fragments of themes, using variation form for the slow movements of symphonies and quartets, and using a more flexible orchestration that permitted melodies to be imitated in contrasting timbres. The following works are among his best known: the London Symphonies (nos. 93–104); the later quartets, especially the *Emperor, Op. 76, No. 3* and the *Lark, Op. 65, No. 5;* two oratorios, *Die Schöpfung,* (the Creation) and *Die Jahreszeiten* (the Seasons); and the piano sonatas. (Ex. 6.4, 6.7, 6.14–6.16, 6.19, 6.25, 6.26, 6.28, 6.30, 6.38, 6.41, 6.49, 6.52)

Johann Christian Bach (1735–1782), also a son of J. S. Bach, is known today as the London Bach. He lived and studied in Italy for a time after his early musical preparation in Berlin with his brother, C. P. E. Bach. He later went to England, where he became music master to the Queen of England. He was an important composer of light homophonic music that was an important source of the Classic style. He wrote numerous operas, piano sonatas, symphonies, and various kinds of chamber music. (Ex. 6.48)

Karl von Dittersdorf (1739–1799) was a successful composer of Classical symphonies, church music, and opera, although he was eclipsed by both Haydn and Mozart. His opera, *Doktor und Apotheker* (the Doctor and Pharmacist), still survives, as do numerous string quartets and a few symphonies.

Luigi Boccherini (1743–1805) was a composer and cellist who was a great admirer of Haydn's music and who copied his style. He wrote a great quantity of chamber music, including more than 100 quartets and nearly 140 quintets. His six cello sonatas and four cello concertos are still prominent in present-day cello repertory. (Ex. 6.43)

Wolfgang Amadeus Mozart (1756–1791), whose creative inventiveness and lyric genius place him among the three or four giants of music, was born in Salzburg. He showed great creativity from infancy. His youth was spent in the atmosphere of the Salzburg court, where his father was a violinist. His genius was recognized early, and his talents as a performer and as a composer were displayed to almost all of Europe through tours to the important courts and musical centers. In spite of almost ideal conditions for a successful career, and despite his superior talents, Mozart's life was one of struggle and disappointment. In contrast to Haydn, Mozart never really had a patron. He was one of the first independent composers who had to struggle for recognition and commissions without the security of a permanent post. Without patronage, Mozart was forced to write in every popular form of his day in order to interest people in his music. His death and burial in a pauper's grave came just as he was gaining some public acclaim for his opera, *Die Zauberflöte* (The Magic Flute), a recognition that might have brought him the security of a permanent position.

Sarastro's garden, from an 1815 Berlin production of Mozart's *Die Zauberflöte*. (Schinkel/AKG, London)

In style, Mozart was a conformist. He refined and polished the Classic forms, but made no major innovations over those made by Haydn. Mozart knew Haydn, and their friendship probably influenced Mozart's mature works. There are many similarities between their styles; however, Mozart is distinctive in the following ways. In general, his melodies were more lyric, more extended, and more subtle in their lyric expressiveness. He seldom repeated phrases note for note, but made changes in ornaments, rhythm, harmonic structure, or dynamics. Mozart seldom included slow introductions to his symphonies. He indulged in melodic and harmonic chromaticism, foreshadowing the Romantic style. In his chamber music especially, all parts became equally important.

Although he did not follow the devices of Gluck's reforms, his refined classic taste and his innate feeling for and love of the theater led him to write what was perhaps the happiest solution to the problems of combining pure music and extramusical ideas. Mozart's operas can be placed in three general classifications: (1) *opera buffa,* the most important of which are *Le nozze di Figaro* (Marriage of Figaro), *Cosí fan tutte,* and *Don Giovanni;* (2) the German operas (Singspiel)—*Die Zauberflöte* (The Magic Flute) and *Die Entführung aus dem Serail* (The Abduction from the Seraglio); and (3) the Italian-style operas (*opera seria)*—*La Clemenza di Tito* and *Idomeneo.*

Mozart's total output includes more than six hundred compositions. There are a few that stand out from the rest as monuments to his creative genius. At least four of his operas and many of his piano concerti are regarded as among the greatest of their genre. Mozart did not number his works chronologically by the usual opus numbers, but Ludwig von Köchel compiled a largely chronological catalog of them in the middle of the nineteenth century. This catalog was brought up to date by the late Alfred Einstein, and this numbering system is used today. (Mozart's works are designated by the letter K and the appropriate number.)

From among this genius's works, the authors would especially like to direct the reader's attention to the following:

(1) the last three symphonies, *Symphony No. 39 in E flat major* (K. 543), *Symphony No. 40 in G minor* (K. 550), *Symphony No. 41 in C major* (K. 551)

(2) the ten celebrated string quartets (Köchel numbers 387, 421, 428, 458, 464, 465, 499, 575, 589, 590)

(3) the chamber music for winds and strings, among these the *Clarinet Quintet in A major* (K. 581), *Serenade in D major for winds and strings* (K. 320), *Divertimento in D major for String quartet and 2 horns* (K. 334), and the *Sextet for String Quartet and 2 Horns* (K. 552)

(4) the violin concerti, especially those in G major (K. 216), D major (K. 218), and A major (K. 219)

(5) the twenty-five piano concertos; those most frequently performed are in C major (K. 415), B flat major (K. 450), G major (K. 453), and D minor (K. 466)

(6) the piano sonatas in C minor (K. 467), C major (K. 545), B flat major (K. 570), and D major (K. 576)

(7) the *Requiem Mass* (K. 626), his crowning achievement in sacred music. (It was left incomplete by Mozart, and his student, Süssmayr, completed the work from Mozart's sketches.) (Ex. 6.1, 6.3, 6.5, 6.10, 6.11, 6.17, 6.20, 6.22, 6.24, 6.29, 6.32–6.34, 6.36, 6.37, 6.44, 6.45, 6.50, 6.51, 6.53)

Luigi Cherubini (1760–1842) was the last important composer to show the classical restraint that identifies him as a Classic composer, even though he lived well into the nineteenth century. He was born in Italy, where he became a successful Italian opera composer. He soon made Paris his permanent home and devoted his creative life and conducting duties to the French style. His operas were influenced by Gluck's reforms but never received any great acclaim. Perhaps his best opera is *Médée,* which has been revived in recent years. His two requiem masses demonstrate the high quality of his church music and its superb counterpoint. (Ex. 6.13, 6.18)

Ludwig van Beethoven (1770–1827) must be considered both a Classicist and a Romanticist. (His work will be discussed more fully in chapter 7.) The greater portion of his compositions reveal the characteristics found in the Romantic style, but his earlier works conform to the style of the Classic. It is generally accepted that those works written before 1802 are patterned after the traditions of Haydn and, despite an occasional outburst of impatience with the harmonic and dynamic simplicity of Classicism, his acceptance of the tradition is fairly complete. The important earlier works include the piano sonatas up to Opus 53, the first three piano concerti, the string quartets of Opus 18, and the first two symphonies. (Ex. 6.21, 6.23, 6.40)

ADDITIONAL COMPOSERS

A. Austria
    F. X. Richter (1709–1789)
    Georg Christoph Wagenseil
      (1715–1777)
    Michael Haydn (1737–1806)
    Johann Nepomuk Hummel
      (1778–1837)
B. England
    Thomas Arne (1710–1788)
    William Boyce (1711–1779)
C. France
    Jean-Jacques Rousseau
      (1712–1778)
    François-Joseph Gossec
      (1734–1829)

Joseph Boulogne Saint-Georges
  (c. 1739–1799)
André Grétry (1741–1813)
D. Germany
    Johann Joachim Quantz
      (1697–1773)
    Wilhelm Friedemann Bach
      (1710–1784)
    Christian Cannabich (1731–1798)
    Johann Friedrich Peter Benda
      (1746–1813)
    Juliane Benda (1752–1783)
E. Italy
    Niccolò Jommelli (1714–1774)
    Niccolò Piccini (1728–1800)
    Domenico Cimarosa (1749–1801)
F. United States of America
    William Billings (1746–1800)

VII. HISTORIANS AND THEORISTS

Because Classicism was concerned mainly with form, there was little philosophizing about music. Most of the writers sought to formalize musical performance and consequently gave detailed instructions as to how to play instruments and interpret the various devices of musical practice. Following is a list of a few of the more important writers and their works. In most cases the writers were also creative artists, or at least performers.

Johann Joachim Quantz (1697–1773) was a composer and flutist as well as the author of *Versuch einer Anweisung, die Flöte traversiere zu spielen* (Essay on Instruction for Playing the Transverse Flute), Berlin 1752. Although the title suggests a method for flute, Quantz deals with problems and questions of the performance practice of his time.

Jean-Jacques Rousseau (1712–1778) was a French writer, philosopher, and sometime music scholar and composer. His *Dictionaire de musique* was published in 1767. This work contains many of Rousseau's articles written originally for the *Encyclopédie,* to which he was a major contributor.

Christoph Willibald Gluck (1714–1787) wrote an important treatise on opera, the *Preface to Alceste* (Vienna 1769). *Alceste* was composed in 1767, but the printed score did not appear until 1769. It was in this preface that Gluck sought to establish the aesthetics of his musical theories concerning opera. He also gave an account of what he believed to be serious abuses of the true purpose of opera in the Italian school.

Carl Phillip Emanuel Bach (1714–1788) wrote *Versuch über die wahre Art das Klavier zu spielen* (Essay on the True Art of Playing Keyboard Instruments), Berlin 1753–1762 (New York 1949). This work is still an authoritative source of information on the traditions of performance of Classic music for the keyboard. It is also valuable in the realization of Classic ornaments and embellishments.

Leopold Mozart (1719–1787) was the author of *Versuch einer grundlichen Violinschule* (Treatise on the Fundamental Principles of Violin Playing), Augsburg 1756 (London 1951). Leopold Mozart was the father of Wolfgang Amadeus and an eminent violinist and teacher. This work is one of the first written on successful methods of violin playing. Along with C. P. E. Bach and Quantz, he provided an account of the musical practice of the Classic era.

Sir John Hawkins (1719–1789) was an English music historian who wrote *A General History of the Science and Practice of Music*. It was published in London in 1776 and republished in 1875. Hawkins's history, published about the same time as Burney's, is filled with reliable information, especially about the musical scene in eighteenth-century London.

Charles Burney (1726–1814) was the most important English music historian of the eighteenth century. *A General History of Music* (London 1776, reprinted New York 1957) is the first important history of music in English. It contains many interesting comments on the contemporary musical trends that reveal the general attitudes of creative musicians and the public during Burney's time. Burney made extensive trips to the musical capitals of Europe and wrote two volumes concerning the musical scene on the continent.

Important excerpts in English from several of the foregoing works can be found in *Source Readings in Music History* by Oliver Strunk.

Paris Opera House (1861–1974). There is an opulence about this structure that reflects the tastes of the newly rich of the nineteenth-century Industrial Revolution. This opera house and others like it were the setting for Romantic operas, with their extravagant spectacles dealing with heroic and epic subjects, supernaturalism, mystery, and passion. (Victoria and Albert Museum, London. By courtesy of Board of Trustees of the Theatre Museum.)

7

⚜

Romantic
(1820–1900)

I. SOCIOCULTURAL INFLUENCES ON MUSIC

The early nineteenth century saw the rise of a style of music, literature, and art that we refer to as Romantic. The nineteenth century was a time of dramatic thought and action. It was also a time of strong contradictions between capitalism and socialism, freedom and oppression, logic and emotion, science and faith. The consequence of these contradictions was a change in the thinking of people, especially creative artists. An intellectual change took place in the minds of composers that was many-sided, complex, and often confused. Consequently it is impossible to say that there is a definite Romantic style. Other periods of the past had a core of accepted beliefs and practices that drew composers together, resulting in a similarity in their music. Romanticism, on the other hand, had the tendency to isolate creative personalities because their practices and beliefs were often in opposition and, like Romanticism itself, complex.

The revolutionary spirit that finally exploded in the French Revolution infused artists with the ideals of liberty and individualism. In terms of music, there were several Romantic results. There was a general impatience with the rules and restraints of Classicism. Just as the Revolution opposed the eighteenth-century status quo, so music demonstrated a revolt against the practices of Mozart and Haydn. To be different was the goal, and the Romantic period witnessed a great variety of musical experiments to achieve individualism. Moreover, to implement the ideals of liberty, composers sought to express their own personal convictions and to portray events and ideas as they understood them. The expression of emotion and the evocation of imagination became the primary goal of most Romantic music. In an effort to stimulate the imagination, there arose a predilection for the strange and the remote, a fascination with the mysteries of the universe.

The Industrial Revolution caused a major change in the economic and social life of common people and also gave rise to a wealthy, capitalistic middle class. There was a general leveling of society and, while composers did not write for the lower classes, their music was addressed to the masses in a far greater degree than before. The wealthy middle class was the potential patron for the composer who had all but lost aristocratic patronage because of the increasing decline in the power and influence of the court. Literature and the visual arts were quick to use the injustices of the Industrial Revolution, the exploitation of the workers, the low standards of living, and the social abuses of the lower classes as subjects for their works. Music, however, when presented in its absolute form, could not address these pressing problems. Instead composers expressed the emotional extremes of the human spirit, often in ways that seemed to seek an escape from reality.

The development of the business of music was also an important influence on the direction composers took in their writing. In order to cultivate the patronage of a wider and unorganized public, composers, together with publishers and concert managers, had to sell music. Publication was on a different basis than it had been. In the effort to capture audiences, a dynamic and colorful personality came to be an important asset, as can be noted in such individuals as Liszt, Berlioz, and Wagner. The concert manager, or impresario, was also an important figure in the business of music. Another important person behind the scenes of music was the music critic, who was a sort of liaison between the public and the composer. In this role, critics served not only to interpret the composer to the public, but also to set standards of musical taste. Needless to say, the composer was usually in conflict with most of the critics, but the critic was still often responsible for the acceptance or rejection of a composer's works.

The revolutionary spirit had its origin in France, but it was in Germany and Austria that Romanticism had its strongest manifestation. The French almost abandoned the Romantic ideal because of their affinity for the classic. Germany and Austria, however, were younger; they had never known the kind of oppression generated by a strong, central absolutism. There seemed to be a conscious emphasis on folklore and historical epics in their desire to achieve a cultural heritage equal to the older countries. Whatever the reasons, the seeds of musical romanticism were to fall upon very fertile ground, particularly in Vienna.

II. FUNCTION OF MUSIC

Romantic music still served a sophisticated and aristocratic society, as had Classic music. Aristocratic patronage was considerably reduced from what it had been in the eighteenth century, and there were practically no opportunities for the kind of patronage enjoyed by Haydn. The intimacy of the exclusive salon was still an ideal setting for chamber music and solo forms. Performance was no longer exclusively by amateurs, however, for Romantic music was often too demanding technically for unskilled performers.

Outside the patronage of the exclusive salon was a large, but unorganized and unsophisticated, concert-going public that loved music. Romantic composers were constantly striving to gain the recognition of this vast audience, and in an effort to win acceptance, they were very sensitive to the likes and dislikes of these music lovers. These middle-class listeners searched for new excitement or diversion from everyday life in music. The function of composers was to create music that evoked and explored human feelings. There were several types of music that appealed to these patrons—especially symphonic music, the extravagant spectacle of opera and ballet, and virtuosic music of all kinds.

Performers, as well as composers, wanted to be accepted, and to dazzle audiences. Composers like Liszt and Paganini, who were often also extraordinary performers themselves, wrote a large number of virtuoso pieces to thrill the public with technical display. In fact, virtuoso performers and their agents, the impresarios, were central to nineteenth-century concert life.

Because Romantic composers expressed personal feelings and convictions, much music was written without benefit of patronage. They expressed themselves in personal documents of art. These were sometimes experimental and uncompromising, with no concern for public taste. The last piano sonatas and string quartets of Beethoven, and many songs by Schumann and Wolf, are examples of this kind of expression.

Social dancing by all segments of society gave composers a large market for dance music. The great popularity of the waltz led to fame and fortune for composers like Johann Strauss and his son of the same name, and in addition aroused the envy of many who may have been artistic successes but never gained public favor.

In the Romantic period, the church was no longer a patron of music to any significant extent. The small amount of sacred music written during this time contained the personal religious feelings and convictions of the composer, expressed in music, largely for the concert hall.

The teaching of music became an established profession. Many fine conservatories and schools of music were founded for the education of performing and creative musicians. Research in music history and theory was introduced into the programs of many universities by the end of the nineteenth century. A great number of prominent composers and performers such as Liszt, Mendelssohn, Rimsky-Korsakov, and Schumann achieved wide recognition as teachers. To meet pressing needs for pedagogical material, composers wrote études and other short pieces for teaching purposes. Many of these works, like the *Études* of Chopin, are of a very high level of artistry and form an important segment of the repertory for the piano.

Research at universities led to the beginning of complete editions of composers' works, including Bach, Mozart, and Beethoven, to name but three, as well as large anthologies or collected editions, such as the *Denkmäler der Tonkunst in Oesterreich,* and the *Quellenlexikon der Musiker und Musikgelehrten* of Robert Eitner.

III. STYLE AND PERFORMANCE PRACTICE

Because Romanticism is so personal and so filled with contrasting concepts of music, not all characteristics of style are present in all forms. There are contradictions in style among groups of composers and even the works of individual composers. There were Romantic idealists or absolutists who insisted that music must exist for its own sake without extramusical associations. In contrast, increasing numbers of composers experimented with music that told stories (program music) imitated sounds of nature, or illustrated scenes aurally. This music may be in single-movement form, such as Richard Strauss's *Till Eulenspiegels lustige Streiche,* or in the multimovement form of the symphony, as represented by Hector Berlioz's *Symphonie fantastique*. Whereas some examples of descriptive music incorporate a program (a prose description), others indicate their descriptive nature by their titles and the expressive content of the music.

In Romantic arts there was a dualism between virtuosity and intimacy. Some Romantic composers excelled in spectacular virtuosity, which was expressed by brilliant technical performances and often by the resources of a vast number of performers. On the other hand, there were those who emphasized the intimacy of miniature forms and delicate textures expressing their personal feelings in solo songs, chamber music, and lyric piano works. Solo songs enjoyed considerable attention during the Romantic era, as composers became involved with literary forms for their texts.

There was also a contrast between nationalism and internationalism. There were composers whose aim was to extol national characteristics and evoke patriotic feelings by using folklore, folk songs, and dances. They often used realistic devices to evoke expressiveness associated with national or ethnic subjects. Nationalism became strong in such countries as Russia, Poland, and Bohemia. In Russia a group called the "Russian Five," or "Mighty Five," whose members were César Cui, Mily Balakirev, Modest Mussorgsky, Alexander Borodin, and Nikolai Rimsky-Korsakov, made a special effort to break away from the dominance of the Italian and Germanic traditions. There were also Romanticists who avoided nationalistic devices in the search for a universal musical language. In general these composers believed that music should express itself and nothing else.

One common goal of Romantic composers was the evocation of emotion as a primary function of music. The goal was based on the premise that a feeling of musical tension is necessary to achieve a corresponding intensification of emotional response. All Romantic music, therefore, concerns itself with the problem of achieving this tension. Most Romanticists revolted against the restraints and formalism of the Classic era. However, some Romantics, such as Schubert, Mendelssohn, and Brahms, cast their Romantic expressions in molds of Classic forms.

Formal Organization

Musical form continued to be based on contrasting melodies in homophonic style, and the sonata was the most important type of formal organization. Rather than two contrasting melodies, there were often contrasting theme groups and sometimes only motives pitted against each other.

In addition to the Classic forms that were still in use, there were sectional forms, such as the ballade, nocturne, and fantasy. These were most common in piano music. The free forms, however, were still based on contrasting themes, but usually without development sections. Sometimes, in the very short preludes or études, only one theme or melody might be used, with changes in harmony or rhythm for contrast.

Forms were not as precise and clear as in the Classic period, and their sections were often overlapping, vague, and without strong cadences. Sections and even movements of longer works often merged into one another by means of subtle and mild harmonic and rhythmic cadential effects. There was a proliferation of hybrid forms and a freedom from the constraints of form that pervaded the Classic period.

It was common practice, especially in larger forms, to use some of the same thematic material in each movement as a means of maintaining a constant expressive character. This is referred to as *cyclic construction.*

Forms were not always symmetrical or balanced. Within a musical composition, phrases and periods were often of uneven lengths. Development sections in sonata forms were frequently extended, where composers could use imagination and ingenuity to best advantage.

Folk melodies, or at least folk-style melodies, were frequently included in Romantic music. This was especially true in nationalistic music, but was also a common practice in the music of the Romantic idealists. Folklore was especially popular in Romantic opera, where it was, no doubt, aimed at arousing enthusiasm among the general public.

Melody

Melody was characterized by an intensity of personal feelings. Dynamic climaxes and frequent changes in dynamics served to build the tension necessary for its expression. Frequent chromaticism helped to create harmonic tension.

Melodic themes were of varying length and were frequently fragmentary, with rhythmic interruptions and irregular phrases. They could be extremely long, with many avoided and deceptive cadences, giving a feeling of continuous "spinning out." There was also a tendency to write many rising and falling melodic curves.

Rhythm

In the early Romantic period, the element of rhythm remained much as it had in the Classic era. From about the middle of the century, however, rhythm became more irregular, complex, and interesting, often with changes in the number of beats in a measure, cross-rhythms, and syncopations (fig. 7.1).

Folk dance contributed to the rhythmic vigor and rhapsodic character of romantic music, especially that of nationalism. It sometimes avoided strong stresses in order to increase the sense of tension, especially in slower movements. Tempo in Romantic music was not always constant. There were frequent changes in tempo, and many occasions for rubato and accelerando.

Harmony

Romantic harmony was still tonal, but the sense of key center was eroded in the music of the nineteenth century. Chromaticism, nonharmonic tones, altered

Figure 7.1 *Nocturne in F♯ major,* illustrating complex rhythmic relationships

Chopin

soto voce

Figure 7.2 Prelude to *Tristan und Isolde,* exhibiting dissonance, chromaticism, and harmonic tension

Wagner

chords, and extensive use of ninth and thirteenth chords built harmonic tension and weakened the sense of tonal center (fig. 7.2). In fact, almost all the characteristics of harmony during this period show a gradual disintegration of the major-minor system.

Tonality was weakened by the fusion of major and minor modes, using chords typical of one mode in the other. Key relationships were less formalized than in Baroque and Classic music. Modulations to distant keys, including the mediant and submediant, and sudden moving in and out of keys for short periods of time added to tension and weakened the strong feeling for a particular key. Strong formal cadences sometimes were avoided, with numerous deceptive cadences that give a harmonic sense of tension. Modal harmonization of folk melodies, especially in nationalistic music, served to open new avenues of harmonic expressiveness.

Texture

The texture of Romantic music mixed vertical and horizontal elements. Polyphonic texture was not pervasive and occurred more as a device than a style. An accompanied lyric line was one important stylistic feature of the Romantic era, most particularly evident in the German Lied. The texture also can be described as heavy, in contrast with the lighter and transparent quality of the Classic. Even in works for solo voice, the accompaniment provided a sonority and tonal fabric that served to blend the voice with the instrument.

In orchestral works, the larger complement of instruments yielded a rich texture. In addition, the texture was made even more sonorous by more subdivisions of instruments, increasing the number of independent parts. Wagner, for example, sometimes divided the first violin section into as many as four different parts.

Instrumentation and Tone Color

The piano became the most popular instrument of the Romantic period because it could run the gamut of all ranges of sound and because it could be played by one person. It became almost a musical symbol of Romanticism. Moreover, the piano was enlarged to give it a wider range and more tonal power. The instrument reached such heights of popularity that it became the favorite household instrument.

Tone color became an integral part of melodic and harmonic texture. Melodies were created in terms of timbre, with their musical expressiveness identified with specific instruments. Harmonic texture was also influenced by orchestral innovations that created new and unusual combinations of instruments.

The Romantic orchestra grew to be the favorite large ensemble of the century. It featured great size and varied color, capable of exploring the widest variety of dynamics and human feelings. It was expanded from the Classic orchestra by the addition of instruments such as the English horn and clarinet, and also by the addition of more brass and percussion instruments. Moreover, technical refinement of already-existing instruments, especially brasses and woodwinds, increased the virtuosity of the orchestra. Among the major contributors to the expressive orchestra were Berlioz and Wagner.

(Appendix 1 includes further information on instruments.)

The solo song with piano accompaniment (*Piano Lied* and *mélodie*) was another favorite medium of Romantic expression. The voice was also a personalized instrument, for it combined with the literary elements of Romanticism to give an added intensity to the poetic text. The piano assumed an increasingly important and independent role in nineteenth-century song.

Opera was an important musical medium in the Romantic era. Combining, as it does, drama, poetry, and the visual experience of action, along with music, it is able to make a powerful impression on the emotions of an audience. Its popularity and importance are evident in the large number of Romantic operas that are still in the repertory today.

The operetta, a light form of musical drama, made its appearance in the nineteenth century as a development of the forms of comic opera of the eighteenth century. With its farcical or sentimental plot and its alternation of light songs and spoken dialogue, the operetta gives expression to romanticism in popular form.

Performance Practice

Written dynamic indications became more explicit than in the music of the Classic period. Subtle shadings of timbre and minute gradations of loudness were indicated by more specific terminology, and tempi were more accurately designated by the use of metronome markings.

Because the orchestra was enlarged to become one of the more important vehicles of Romantic expression, the orchestral conductor emerged as a virtuoso performer. The use of the baton took the conductor from the keyboard to the podium. Weber, Mendelssohn, Berlioz, Liszt, Wagner, and Mahler were among the many composers who achieved fame as conductors. Although they were not great composers, Hans von Bülow and Hans Richter also became well known for their conducting skills.

It was an era of massive festival performances. Because of the fondness for sonority and power, an enormous number of participants were often used. Sometimes, as in the case of the works of Berlioz, the large orchestra and chorus constituted an essential part of the composer's style. At other times the usual number of performers were greatly augmented to suit the public's taste for massed effects. Large festival orchestras and choruses appeared in all countries, and are still very popular. There are instances in which more than a thousand performers took part in the performance of a single work.

The love of the middle class for music making led to the establishment of choral societies. Folk music, political songs, and popular melodies provided the musical fare, but the artistic level ranged from the shallow to the musically excellent. Some of these societies made presentations of Handel and Haydn oratorios, and, especially in Germany and Austria, they prompted new compositions by Schubert, Schumann, and Brahms.

The art of improvisation was of diminished importance in the practice of Romantic music, due to the complexity of its composition and the precise directions for performance. A few individuals, like Chopin and Liszt, continued to make brilliant use of it, but in concerto writing, most cadenzas were written in a manner to give the effect of improvisation.

Because of the emphasis on individualism and the spectacular, it follows there would be a number of virtuoso performers during the Romantic era. Beethoven, until deafness curtailed his performances, was a pianist of exceptional virtuosity. His early triumphs in Vienna were probably due to his pianistic artistry as much as to his compositions.

Franz Liszt was the most successful Romantic virtuoso pianist. His personality and theatrical effects, coupled with his spectacular performances, made him almost a legend in his own time. His virtuosity had a marked influence on piano performance for all time. Frédéric Chopin was another pianist whose music and performance was so personal, refined, and brilliant that he has become almost a symbol of the Romantic spirit. In addition, Carl Czerny, Anton Rubinstein, and Robert and Clara Schumann were pianists and composers.

Paganini. Caricature of the renowned violinist's playing.

Niccolò Paganini developed the technique of the violin to its present state. His dazzling performances of double stops, harmonics, runs, and trills are still a challenge to violinists. His fame as a performer was widespread and influenced many composers, including Liszt and Berlioz. Joseph Joachim, another Romantic violinist, had an important influence on the music of Brahms.

Because instrumental virtuosi were usually composers as well, their technical exploits were notated in their scores. This was not true, however, for operatic singers. Theirs was usually a spontaneous realization of the ideas of the composer. It was not until the development of the recording industry that reliable examples of singers' technical skills became available.

IV. MUSIC FOR VOICES

Single-Movement Forms and Structural Devices

Art Song

The solo song occupied an important place in Romantic music. Romantic poetry was set for the voice and piano in a highly personal and subjective manner. The two basic types of formal organization in these works were strophic (songs in which all stanzas were sung to the same music) and

Ein Schubertabend, an unfinished oil painting by Moritz von Schwind, showing Schubert at the keyboard with his patron, Josef Ritter von Spaun. (Erich Lessing/Art Resource, NY)

through-composed. The latter had more possibilities for the Romantic idiom because it allowed every poetic nuance to have its own musical expression. The piano created and sustained the mood of each poem and was an equal partner with the singer. German composers of *Lieder* set poems by such writers as Heine, Schiller, and Goethe—poets who epitomized the Romantic spirit. Songs with related texts were often grouped into cycles. These song cycles were frequently settings of one poet, and were related by a central idea, or theme. Schubert, Schumann, Brahms, Wolf, and Richard Strauss were the most important composers of the German Lied. The venue for Lieder performances was primarily the homes of patrons. While the German Lied held the prominent place in song literature, both the French and the Russians also fostered art song literature of high quality. The French especially were helped by the French Romantic poets to create songs of exceptional lyric beauty, commonly referred to as *mélodie.* (Ex. 7.1–7.3)

Choral Music

Very little music was written for liturgical purposes in the Romantic period. However, composers combined voices with instruments, emphasizing the symphonic, rather than the vocal ideal. These were heard most often in the concert hall, and when used in a church they served a nonliturgical purpose. (Ex. 7.4–7.6)

A great wealth of secular choral music was written in the nineteenth century; however, only a few important works have survived, and most of these are for voices and orchestra. Some composers, such as Beethoven, Liszt, and Mahler, used the chorus as a part of the symphonic form. The *part songs* of Schubert, Schumann, Mendelssohn, and Brahms, to name but four composers, may have been conceived for one voice on each part, though today they are often treated and performed as choral works. (Ex. 7.7–7.8)

Composite Forms

Opera

Opera provided the best opportunities for all aspects of Romantic music to be combined into a single form. Romantic operas can be described as extravagant spectacles with a tendency toward heroic and epic subjects, supernaturalism, mystery, and passion. Eighteenth-century opera was dominated by the Italian style, with its multiplicity of closed forms, but in the nineteenth century, Italy, France, and Germany continued to develop their own styles, with special qualities that were indigenous to each. Therefore, it becomes necessary to describe briefly the form of opera in each of these countries.

Italian opera. Early Romantic opera in Italy retained a series of recitatives, arias, duets, and choruses, with little dramatic continuity. Later in the century, mainly under the influence of Verdi, it showed greater dramatic unity, better-developed characters, and more credible plots. These plots were often quasidramatic, but there was a general improvement in quality. The recitative and aria were still the principal closed forms, with melody in the popular bel canto style and an emphasis on virtuosity. There was also greater balance among voices and instruments, but the orchestra still served as accompaniment.

Another development in Italian Romantic opera was the style embraced by Leoncavallo, Mascagni, and Puccini, known as *verismo,* or realism. Realism was not limited to music. It was also shown in the choice of libretti that presented subjects from everyday life and depicted people in familiar situations. (Ex. 7.9–7.13)

French opera. Opera in nineteenth-century France showed some characteristics that were different from the Italian. French grand opera treated historical subjects and was an art form of excess. The stage sets were grandiose, casts were very large, and the libretti were generally of great length. The entire text was sung. The chorus and ballet were extensively used as in earlier French opera. Meyerbeer, a German, was the most important composer in this form. During the early part of the century there was a marked distinction between grand opera and *opéra comique,* but as Romanticism matured, the two styles merged into one. Opéra comique was generally distinguished from grand opera by use of some spoken dialogue instead of a continuous musical texture. Generally it was simpler in musical expressiveness, used fewer characters, and compared with earlier French opera, relied very little on the chorus. In the

French lyric opera the theatrical aspect and the simpler forms of opéra comique were combined with the virtuosity and drama of the grand opera. A particular trait in all French opera was the ballet, and it became even more important during the Romantic era. There was unity of dramatic action with the music that was seldom found in the Italian style. There was also less virtuosity with more emphasis on the lyric quality of melody. Moreover, French Romantic opera rarely displayed the intensity and passion of either the Italian or the German but was more conservative in its music and in its dramatic content. (Ex. 7.14, 7.15)

German opera. Opera in Germany presented two significant styles: German Romantic opera and music drama, the latter conceived and developed by Richard Wagner. In German Romantic opera, the libretti were often based on German legends and folklore, with the mystery of nature and supernatural forces serving to intensify dramatic expression. The recitatives and arias in German Romantic operas were distinct forms and were sometimes based on folk song or melodies in folk style. *Melodrama* (instrumentally accompanied speech), sometimes an independent form, was used for special effects. Two other traits of the music drama were exhibited to some degree in the German Romantic opera. The orchestra became a powerful instrument in creating atmosphere, moods, and even bits of realism. There was also a prototype of the music drama's *leitmotif,* in which particular instruments and melodies are used to identify and characterize individuals. (Ex. 7.16)

The ideal of music-drama, or the art of the future as it was called by Wagner, was that of an art form in which all the arts were woven into one cohesive and continuous line of dramatic expression. Wagner continued the German tradition but developed his own stories, drawing heavily upon German myths and folklore. His libretti were filled with romantic mysticism and supernaturalism, and almost all were concerned with the concept of redemption through love. There were few closed forms, such as recitative and aria. The vocal line became a continuous melody rising out of an orchestral fabric that was also continuous, without usual cadences. The leitmotif unified the sonorous and tension-filled musical texture. The Wagnerian leitmotif was a musical figure that was associated with a particular idea, person, object, mood, or situation. Because Wagner used the orchestra as the main source of dramatic expression, his operas are symphonic in nature. Consequently, it has been possible to have successful concert performances of much of his music without staging or vocal parts. (Ex. 7.17, 7.18)

Nationalistic opera. In addition to Italian, French, and German operas, there were operatic developments in those countries where nationalism was strong, especially in Russia and Bohemia. These operas were also based on folklore or upon events of national significance with nationally important personages. Composers such as Mussorgsky in Russia created works that are highly original, with great dramatic power but without using the closed forms of the Italians and without imitating Wagner. (Ex. 7.19, 7.20)

Large Sacred Choral Works

In the first half of the nineteenth century, important masses continued to be written, notably by Beethoven and Schubert. Earlier, requiem masses were created for performance in services for the dead. During the course of the nineteenth century, the purposes for requiem masses became separated from their earlier liturgical function. Those by Berlioz, Verdi, Cherubini, and Brahms are masterpieces of this later genre, and each, for different reasons, would not be appropriate in liturgical services.

The Romantic oratorio followed the choral tradition of Handel in the works of Mendelssohn, who added the melodic, harmonic, and sonorous qualities of Romantic style. Although there were very few who wrote for the Protestant church, many composers set quasi-religious stories of mysticism and Catholic symbolism to music in the manner of the oratorio. Some of these works are not easily classified because they are neither operas, oratorios, nor cantatas (e.g., Gounod, *La Rédemption*). The orchestra generally plays a more important role than in earlier oratorios, with the chorus and soloists bringing texts to what were conceived largely as symphonic works. Mendelssohn, Liszt, and Berlioz wrote compositions in this fashion for performance in the concert hall. (Ex. 7.21–7.22)

V. MUSIC FOR INSTRUMENTS

Single-Movement Forms and Structural Devices

Sonata Form

The Romantic sonata form was still based on the organizational principles of the Classic sonata. There was, however, a notable expansion of both the melodic and harmonic substance. Instead of two contrasting themes, composers often used groups of themes in the exposition. In such cases, different theme groups were frequently presented in different, often remote keys, extending the harmonic range. In order to develop this melodic and harmonic material, the development was often much longer than in the Classic era. To reconcile the key changes and to reestablish the tonic, a long coda was sometimes added. (Ex. 7.23–7.25)

Two-Part and Three-Part Song Forms

Varied descriptive titles that suggested moods or revealed the personal feelings of the composer were attached to short forms. These were often referred to as *character pieces*. They were usually in two-part or three-part forms, but sometimes were short enough to have only one section. These forms bore such titles as *nocturnes, preludes, caprices, serenades, bagatelles, impromptus,* and so forth. *Ballades* were usually longer works that suggested the possible moods of stories without defining a particular sequence of events. In addition, titles suggestive of personalities, scenes, or ideas were often applied to these shorter pieces. There was no formal distinctiveness, except mood and atmosphere, to differentiate one from another. (Ex. 7.26–7.29)

Variations

The variation form was sometimes used as a movement of a sonata or symphony, but it was also important as an independent form for both orchestra and piano solo. Variations were created on preexisting themes or on specially composed melodies. Occasionally, variations were made to suggest particular moods or ideas suggested by the theme. (Ex. 7.30–7.31)

Dance Movements

The nineteenth century saw the rise in importance of stylized dance movements for the orchestra and solo instruments, especially the piano. Dances of a national character, such as the *polonaise, mazurka,* and *jota,* were set by many composers. Moreover, general national types—Hungarian, Spanish, and Slavonic—formed the bases of many works. These were usually expanded, idealized concert versions, not social dances. Sometimes dance movements that symbolized ideas or events, such as *Danse Macabre* by Saint-Saëns and Liszt's *Mephisto Waltz,* gave Romantic composers the opportunity to use realistic devices to intensify the mood or atmosphere. (Ex. 7.32–7.34)

Rhapsody

Rhapsody was a term often used in Romantic music to designate a free fantasy on themes of a national or epic character. It was a single movement form with the usual contrasts and Romantic tensions. It appeared in orchestral and piano literature, and sometimes for a solo instrument combined with orchestra. (Ex. 7.35–7.37)

Études

Originally *études* were study pieces designed for solo instruments and for perfection of technique. It was expanded as a concert work with emphasis on a display of virtuosity. Even when it became a concert piece, however, it never lost its function as a study piece. Each étude usually emphasized some particular technical problem. They were in binary or three-part form, with the usual tension of contrast and repetition. (Ex. 7.38, 7.39)

Concert Overture

The concert overture was a symphonic work in the manner of an overture that was not associated with an opera. In general, the concert overture did not attempt to tell a story but created a mood that can be associated with a literary theme, a place, or an event. Many works of this nature adhere closely to the principle of the sonata form. (Ex. 7.40, 7.41)

Programmatic Symphonies and Symphonic Poems

Two typical forms of orchestral program music in the Romantic era were the programmatic symphony and the symphonic poem. The structural elements of the programmatic symphony were largely free of classic predictability. Its programmatic content could vary from a simple extramusical title to an elaborate verbal description. The symphonic poem was the invention of Franz Liszt and was sometimes called a tone poem, especially when it was based on a poetic idea. The form comprises one continuous movement and is usually based on the principle of variations on a theme, or contrasting themes, that are inspired by a program or a literary idea. It is a transformation of themes in which they retain their identity through various stages and forms. (Ex. 7.42–7.44)

Composite Forms

Sonata and Symphony

The Romantic sonata and symphony, like sonata form itself, were based on Classic patterns. Some composers, such as Beethoven and Schubert, adhered rather closely to Classic style, but others, including Berlioz, Mahler, Bruckner, and Tchaikovsky, made significant departures from it. During the early years of the Romantic era the piano sonata retained its popularity, along with sonatas for violin or cello and piano. As the century progressed the symphony became the most important composite instrumental form. Composers enriched its sonorities and combined it with literary ideas because of its new sonorous possibilities for realism. There was greater contrast among the themes of the Romantic symphony than in the Classic, especially contrast between a vigorous first theme or theme group and a more lyric second theme or theme group. Modulations were more varied, often without the usual preparation. Because there was less emphasis on balance and logic, a more sectional scheme of organization resulted. Unity among movements was often achieved by the cyclic principle; that is, using the same themes, or portions of them, in each movement. While the emphasis in the Classic sonata or symphony was on the first movement, the Romantic symphony often placed its emphasis on the last movement. This is especially true when such works were cast in cyclic form in which the climax, or culmination of the thematic material, occurred during the last movement. A number of composers included solo and choral writing in their symphonies in the desire to emphasize the climax of the last movement. The minuet was usually replaced by a scherzo, a movement quicker in tempo that provided more contrast to the second and last movements. The variation form was frequently used as either the second or last movement. Some composers used five movements in their symphonies, in contrast with the usual four-movement Classic symphony. (Ex. 7.45–7.53)

Concerto

The Romantic concerto became more symphonic than its eighteenth-century counterpart, and technical demands made the solo parts more spectacular. To a large degree the musical development of the Romantic concerto was dependent on the orchestra rather than on the solo instrument. The double exposition of the Classic concerto was usually abandoned. The Romantic predilection for cyclic form was also apparent in the solo concerto. (Ex. 7.54–7.57)

Chamber Music

The forms of music for chamber ensembles generally followed the forms of the Romantic symphony and sonata. The instrumentation, however, remained much the same as in the Classic period. There was an increased emphasis on virtuosity, which demanded a higher degree of professional skill for performance than in the chamber music of Haydn and Mozart. (Ex. 7.58–7.61)

Ballet

The ballet had been a part of opera in the seventeenth and eighteenth centuries, especially in France. It continued its important role in the nineteenth century, but in the Romantic era ballet achieved consideration by composers as a unified dramatic form independent of opera. This was accomplished with great success by the Frenchman, Delibes and the Russian, Tchaikovsky. Dramatic expression was achieved by the music and its corresponding dance, which was performed by soloists and ensembles, serving the same purpose as the vocal solo and chorus in opera. (Ex. 7.62, 7.63)

Symphonic Suite and Incidental Music

The suite was revived in about the middle of the nineteenth century. However, instead of the traditional scheme of dances as written during the Baroque era, it presented a free succession of contrasting movements, usually national dances or ballet movements. It was sometimes a series of extracts from a ballet, or incidental music to a play, such as Felix Mendelssohn's *A Midsummer Night's Dream*. This work is perhaps the best example of the genre. Incidental music often suggested a series of scenes, sometimes from a story. It was usually for orchestra but also appeared in the literature for piano. (Ex. 7.64, 7.65)

VI. COMPOSERS

Ludwig van Beethoven (1770–1827) was named earlier among the composers of the Classic style, but it is as a Romanticist that his greatest compositions were conceived. Born in Bonn, Germany, Beethoven displayed strong musical gifts as a child. He suffered at the hands of his father, who hoped he could mold the young talent into a prodigy like Mozart. The incompetence of his father as a manager finally caused Beethoven to become the sole support of his family. His gifts as a pianist, organist, violinist, and composer won him an official position at the Bonn Court. He remained there until 1792, when he left for Vienna, where he was to live the rest of his life. He was first known in Vienna as a brilliant pianist, but a slowly developing deafness caused him to abandon performance for composition. He was the first composer in history to develop a large degree of independence from the patronage of the aristocracy or the church.

Beethoven's life is generally viewed in three periods. The first, during which time he was a pianist and composer, ends about 1802. Compositions

Beethoven conducting.

from this period hold the seeds of Romanticism but are still cast in the molds of the Classic tradition of Mozart and Haydn. The second period ends about 1814 and reveals him coming to maturity a complete Romanticist. The third and last period is somewhat enigmatic. In it Beethoven seemed to be stretching the bounds of Romanticism by becoming more introspective, more profoundly spiritual, more improvisational, recalling the contrapuntal style of the Baroque.

Beethoven was largely responsible for freeing music from the harmonic, rhythmic, and formal restraints of Classicism and for leading the way to individualism and subjective feeling in music. He made important contributions to the literature of every musical genre, especially the symphony and the string quartet. His works became models for his contemporaries as well as later composers. Almost all of the Romanticists found justification in Beethoven for their individual styles. Beethoven's major contributions can be summarized as follows: (1) he showed a remarkable economy of material in the sonata form that led the way to the cyclic type of multiple forms; (2) his themes were often constructed from short motives that were gradually built up and expanded into full-length lyric melodies; (3) he raised the piano to a new level of importance and Romantic expression; (4) he expanded the use of polyphonic procedures in thematic development; (5) he used dissonance as a functional part of his

Manuscript page from Beethoven's *Piano sonata in E♭* Opus 81a. (Historical Pictures/Stock Montage, Inc.)

harmonic structure; (6) he achieved a new fluency in modulation that opened new possibilities of harmonic contrast and interest; (7) he expanded the traditional forms of the sonata and symphony to accommodate thematic materials and expressive purposes, rather than making the materials fit the forms; and (8) he wrote idiomatic compositions for ideal performers.

Beethoven's compositions exerted an important influence on nearly all subsequent composers. Among his many important compositions, are the following:

(1) nine symphonies, among which *Symphony No. 3 in E flat major*, Op. 55 (Eroica); *Symphony No. 5 in C minor,* Op. 67; and *Symphony No. 9 in D minor,* Op. 125 (Choral) are the best known;

(2) instrumental concertos, including five for piano and one for violin;

(3) thirty-two piano sonatas, including the *Sonata in C minor,* Op. 13 (Pathétique), and *Sonata in F minor,* Op. 57 (Appassionata);

(4) a prodigious amount of chamber music, of which the sixteen string quartets are justly renowned; and

(5) large works for voices and orchestra, including one opera, *Fidelio,* Op. 72b; an oratorio, *Christus am Oelberg,* Op. 85; and the *Missa Solemnis,* Op. 123. (Ex. 7.7, 7.23, 7.24, 7.31, 7.45, 7.48, 7.58, 7.62)

Niccoló Paganini (1782–1840) was the first great instrumental virtuoso of the nineteenth century. An Italian violinist, he developed a spectacular technique, demonstrated in his *caprices,* that enabled him to dazzle audiences. In addition, his innate showmanship gave him an almost hypnotic power over his listeners. His compositions include many virtuoso works for violin. He had a profound effect on many Romantic composers, especially Schumann and Liszt, who tried to adapt Paganini's concepts of virtuosity to the piano. (Ex. 7.27)

Carl Maria von Weber (1786–1826) was the founder of the German Romantic school of opera. His father was an amateur musician and also the director of a traveling theatrical group. No doubt this environment helped to stimulate young Weber's imagination as a dramatic composer. He was some-thing of a child prodigy, learning the piano and violin at an early age. His first piano works were published when he was twelve years old. His most impor-tant posts as a mature musician were as Kapellmeister at Prague and as Director of the Opera at Dresden. In addition to his fame as a composer, he was well known as a brilliant pianist and conductor, and was among the first to use a baton, which he grasped in the middle. Although he composed in almost every medium, his best works are for piano or the stage. The piano works are brilliant concert pieces with emphasis on virtuosity but, with the exception of the *Invitation to the Dance,* are seldom performed today. His opera *Der Freischütz* is based on a German folk tale that dwells on supernat-ural phenomena and reveals the sentimentality of the middle class. Although Weber broke with the Italian operatic tradition, he still used arias in the Italian manner. It was the chorus effects, the orchestral coloring, and the stories that made the operas typically German. His music includes motifs that predate the leitmotifs of Wagner. These motifs are associated with specific moods and ideas. For Weber, the overture was a collection of the most important melodies in each opera, serving as a sort of preview of what was to come. His most important operas are *Der Freischütz, Euryanthe,* and *Oberon.* The latter was first produced in England a few months before his death in 1826. (Ex. 7.16)

Gioacchino Rossini (1792–1868) was one of the most brilliant early Italian Romantic opera composers. His music exhibited a remarkable flow of melody in the bel canto tradition. This, combined with brilliant orchestration, dynamic rhythms, and clear-cut phrases, made his operas popular throughout Europe. One of his notable devices of orchestration was the use of crescendo through numerous repetitions of phrases, adding instruments and increasing the degree of loudness with each repetition. Rossini was at his best in *opera buffa,* and his principal works in this form are *La gazza ladra* (The Thieving Magpie), *L'italiana in Algeri,* and *Il Barbiere di Siviglia.* The latter became his most popular opera and was produced in almost every opera house of Europe. *Guillaume Tell,* his last opera, was written for the Parisian opera audience. Its misfortune is that the overture is far better known than the opera. (Ex. 7.9)

Franz Schubert (1797–1828) was one of the few Viennese composers to claim that city as his birthplace. His early musical training was as a singer in the Vienna court and as a student in the Konvict, a training school for singers. Here he learned to play the violin and studied theory, as well as singing until his voice changed. For three years he held a post as an elementary school teacher. After this brief period of teaching, Schubert's life was illustrative of a kind of Bohemianism often associated with the Romantic spirit. He was one of the few Romantic composers to live in poverty. He never held a position as a musician in either an institution or in an aristocratic household. Moreover, he did not even have the security of benevolent patronage or a steady income from the sale of his works. He eked out a precarious existence as a private tutor, sold a few compositions to publishers, and had a few commissions. His early death at the age of thirty-one was unquestionably hastened by poverty. While Schubert's piano, chamber, and orchestral works are significant contributions to the literature of music, it is in art songs that his expression of Romanticism reaches its height. Among the outstanding qualities of his music are its lyric melodies and harmonic coloring. Moreover, in his lieder there is a musical sensitivity to the poetic expression that makes Schubert's songs among the finest in all vocal literature. His piano works, chamber music, and orchestral works are generally classic in their formal organization. The Romantic element lies in the substance of melody and harmony.

Schubert composed more than six hundred songs, nine symphonies, twenty-two piano sonatas, seventeen operas, six masses, about thirty-five chamber music works, and numerous occasional pieces for orchestra and solo instruments. It is only Schubert's operas that have failed to gain recognition. Some of his best songs can be found in the two song cycles, *Die Schöne Müllerin,* and *Die Winterreise.* Of his symphonies the *Symphony No. 8 in B minor* (the Unfinished) and the *Symphony No. 9 in C major* are the most well known. The *String Quartet in D minor* (Death and the Maiden), the *Quintet in A major* (The Trout), and the *Piano Trio in B flat major* each hold a high place in the literature for chamber music. The piano sonatas in C minor and B flat major are among the finest works for this instrument. His works have been catalogued by Otto Erich Deutsch and frequently bear the letter *D* before the number Deutsch assigned to each composition. (Ex. 7.2)

Gaetano Donizetti (1797–1848) was one of the most prolific Italian opera composers. His music is notable for its remarkable melodies, with which he expressed the full range of emotions. Actually, his harmony, rhythm, and orchestration are at times repetitive, but it is his talent for melody and stagecraft that caught the public's favor and has served to keep many of his works popular to this day. He wrote instrumental music, cantatas, and church music, but only his operas receive frequent performances. The best of these are *Lucia di Lammermoor* and the comic operas *La Fille du régiment* (The Daughter of the Regiment), *L'elisir d'amore* (the Elixer of Love), and *Don Pasquale.* (Ex. 7.10)

Vincenzo Bellini (1801–1835), like so many Italian opera composers, is remembered for his gift of melody. More reserved in expressive range than Donizetti, Bellini was exceedingly adept at psychological characterization. His sentimental melodies express the Romantic ideal. All of his operas were

Berlioz conducting. (Art and History Archive, Berlin)

based on serious subjects. The more important works are *Norma, La sonnam-bula* (The Sleepwalker) and *I Puritani* (The Puritans).

Hector Berlioz (1803–1869) was one of the first recognized composers who did not come from a musical family, or at least a strong musical back-ground. His father was a doctor, and young Berlioz was destined for a medical career. However, his interest in music caused him to desert his medical studies in Paris in favor of composition. Berlioz never became a proficient performer on any instrument. His only musical post was as a music librarian at the Paris Conservatory. In effect he was a freelance composer-conductor, writing music and then arranging concerts for its performance. He wrote mainly in the larger forms of the overture, symphony, and opera, composing virtually nothing for solo instruments or chamber music.

Berlioz was a pioneer in the area of symphonic program music. He devel-oped the *idée fixe,* a recurring melody or theme that identifies programmatic ideas and persons in a purely musical manner. His most famous programmatic work is the *Symphonie Fantastique.* In it, Berlioz shows his mastery of orchestration, bringing new colors and even new sounds into the orchestral fabric. He also enlarged the orchestra enormously, even planning a work for an orchestra of 465 performers. His technique of orchestration and instrumentation was set forth in his book, *Grand traité d'instrumentation et d'orchestration modernes* (Treatise on Instrumentation and Orchestration), published in 1844, which served as a source book of orchestration well into the twentieth century. Berlioz was also a musical journalist, enabling him to campaign actively on behalf of Romantic ideals in opposition to the conservatism of Classicism.

His important works, in addition to the *Symphonie Fantastique,* are *Harold in Italy,* for solo viola and orchestra; *Roméo et Juliette,* for solo voices, chorus, and orchestra; *The Damnation of Faust,* a concert opera; a *Requiem Mass; L'enfance du Christ* (The Childhood of Christ), for solo voices, chorus, and orchestra; and the opera *Les Troyens* (The Trojans). In addition he wrote a number of concert overtures, of which the *Roman Carnival,* and *Benvenuto Cellini* are still frequently performed. (Ex. 7.22, 7.51)

Fanny Mendelssohn-Hensel (1805–1847) was the daughter of a wealthy Jewish banker and the granddaughter of a famous philosopher. When the family embraced Christianity, their family name was changed to Mendelssohn-Bartholdy. She is best known today to singers of lieder as the composer of over two hundred songs, several of which were formerly attributed to her younger brother, Felix. Her compositional style is easily confused with his. In addition to her importance as a composer, she was an accomplished pianist. Her diaries provide important information on the life of her brother.

Felix Mendelssohn (1809–1847) was fortunate to be surrounded with the finest opportunities for becoming a musician, for he had the wealth for unlimited study and a highly cultivated cultural and social environment. He became a proficient concert pianist as well as an illustrious composer. His most important positions were Director of the Royal Conservatory in Leipzig, which he founded, and Conductor of the Gewandhaus Orchestra, also in Leipzig. He was widely traveled, and his music became very popular in many countries, especially in England. Among his other accomplishments, Mendelssohn was largely responsible for the revival of interest in the works of J. S. Bach. Mendelssohn's music is closely allied to the Classic traditions in form; the Romantic spirit appears in his melodies and imaginative orchestral coloring. His music has little of the passion and violence of Romanticism but almost always expresses a serenity and sentimentality that achieved wide audience appeal.

Mendelssohn wrote copiously during his short life, but his fame rests largely on works for piano, orchestra, and two oratorios, *Elijah,* Op. 70, perhaps the finest Romantic oratorio, written especially for performance in England, and *St. Paul,* Op. 36. Among his orchestral works the most often performed are *Overture to a Midsummer Night's Dream,* Op. 21; *Hebrides Overture,* Op. 26; *Symphony No. 3 in A minor,* Op. 56 (the Scottish); and *Symphony No. 4 in A Major,* Op. 90 (the Italian). The *Violin Concerto in E minor,* Op. 64, has remained a classic in violin literature. His finest large work

Manuscript page form Mendelssohn's *The Hebrides* (Fingal's Cave), Opus 26

for piano is the *Variations sérieuses in D minor,* Op. 54. However, he more characteristically wrote small piano pieces, as in the *Lieder ohne Worte* (Songs Without Words). (Ex. 7.21, 7.40)

Frédéric Chopin (1810–1849) was born in Zelazowa Wola, near Warsaw, Poland, but left his native land at the age of twenty and spent the rest of his short but creative life in Paris. His music is often associated with Polish nationalism. Frequent settings of the *polonaise* and *mazurka* illustrate this facet of his creative output. He composed almost exclusively for the piano and was most successful in shorter forms such as the *étude, nocturne, impromptu, mazurka,* and *polonaise.* He generally eschewed larger forms but wrote two piano concertos, as well as several scherzos and ballades.

Chopin exploited the technical possibilities of the piano to a greater degree than previous composers. He concentrated on melody, which he decorated with delicate and graceful, often virtuosic passages. He also made daring harmonic innovations with enharmonic modulations and new dissonances, which often prolonged harmonic tension far beyond that of his contemporaries. Moreover, Chopin enhanced the harmonic texture of piano music by skillful use of the pedal to increase the number of tones in a chord. He was also responsible for the development of the left-hand figuration based upon tenths rather than the fifth and octave of the Alberti bass. In addition to the short forms mentioned above, his twenty-four *preludes,* the *waltzes, ballades,* and *sonatas,* most often hold the interest of present-day pianists and their audiences. (Ex. 7.26, 7.28, 7.32, 7.38)

Robert Schumann (1810–1856) was the son of a bookseller, a circumstance that brought him into close contact with the writings of the new Romantic movement during his formative years. After a period of law study and an unsuccessful attempt to become a concert pianist, he turned his efforts toward composition and musical journalism. He founded and became editor of

Clara (1819–1896) and Robert (1810–1856) Schumann both were gifted composers and performers. Recently Clara Schumann has begun to receive the acclaim that her works and performing career deserve. (Art and History Archive, Berlin)

the *Neue Zeitschrift für Musik,* a journal devoted to musical criticism. He also taught for a time at the Leipzig Conservatory and was Municipal Musical Director at Düsseldorf. However, organized musical activity was not congenial to his nature, and he devoted most of his time to writing, composing, and going on concert tours with his wife, Clara Wieck. Schumann suffered from a mental disorder and, after attempting suicide, was confined to an asylum, where he died in 1856.

Schumann, more than any other composer, represented the revolt against Classicism and championed revolutionary tendencies in music. In addition, he became the ardent supporter of such men as Chopin and Brahms, and it was through his writing that much of their music became known to the concert world. Although his compositional efforts extend from opera and symphony through piano works and solo song, it is in the smaller forms that he is most successful. The symphonies, piano concerto, and some chamber works are still retained in the repertory, but it is generally agreed that Schumann's craftsmanship was less successful in the larger forms. Schumann's music can be identified by its lyric melodies, its vague and imaginative formal structures, and its remarkable range of expression, from the most tender to the most heightened passion. He showed interest in Bach by using contrapuntal devices within the framework of Romantic harmony. His piano music is idiomatic, making full use of the harmonic and tonal possibilities of the instrument. He had a Romantic predilection for suggesting poetic titles for many of his piano and orchestral works, but he admitted that the music was always composed before the title was attached. In his lieder, many of which were written in 1840, the year of his marriage to Clara, the piano was of almost equal importance with the voice, interacting with the vocal melody, suggesting and sustaining the mood of the poem. In some of his lieder, the piano plays an extended prologue or epilogue. His major works include a large number of songs, of which the love songs are perhaps the best. The cycle *Dichterliebe,* Op. 48, on poems by Heine, represents the finest of these songs. The piano music includes the *Concerto in A minor,* Op. 54; *Carnival,* Op. 9; *Kreisleriana,* Op. 16; *Papillons,* Op. 2; the *Symphonic Études,* Op. 13; and many other short works. The four symphonies and numerous works of chamber music are also important. (Ex. 7.1, 7.54, 7.59)

Franz Liszt (1811–1886) was one of the most fascinating Romantic personalities. As a virtuoso pianist-composer, he left the imprint of his virtuosity and sentimental Romanticism on almost all subsequent pianists. Born in Hungary, he studied in Vienna and then in Paris, where he became known as a concert pianist. He later settled in Weimar, Germany. There he devoted most of his energies to composing and teaching, with only an occasional concert tour. Liszt was deeply impressed by the virtuosity of the great Italian violinist Paganini and tried to do for piano technique what Paganini had done for the violin. In addition, Liszt inaugurated the recital as a popular form of musical presentation. He was also a popularizer of music and made innumerable transcriptions for the piano of all sorts of music, from Beethoven symphonies to Schubert lieder. As a Romantic realist, Liszt was a champion of program music and was responsible for the creation of the symphonic poem. His orchestral music gives the effect of an extravagant theatrical style with a wide range of emotion, from tender sentimentality to intense passion. To gain these effects he used a large orchestra and followed the lead of Berlioz in colorful orchestration.

Liszt's piano music contains brilliant technical passages, dense chromaticism, and sentimental melodies, all set with loose organization. The outstanding piano works by Liszt include the *Concerto in E flat major; Sonata in B minor; Mephisto Waltz, No. 1; Transcendental Études;* the *Hungarian Rhapsodies;* and numerous short virtuoso pieces. Liszt's orchestral music has less appeal today than in the nineteenth century; however, the symphonic poems, *Lés preludes, Mazeppa,* and his programmatic symphonies (*"Dante"* and *"Faust"*) are often performed by present-day orchestras. (Ex. 7.33, 7.35, 7.39, 7.42)

Richard Wagner (1813–1883), one of the most controversial figures in music history, was the arch Romanticist of the nineteenth century. Raised in a theatrical atmosphere by his stepfather, who was an actor and playwright, young Wagner's musical training was rather desultory. However, his ambition to be a conductor and a theatrical composer finally brought him conducting posts with provincial orchestras. Filled with ambition, he went to Paris, where he hoped to rival the success of Meyerbeer. After a disastrous three years in Paris, he finally returned to Germany. The Paris years, however, saw the completion of the operas *Rienzi* and *Der fliegende Holländer* (The Flying Dutchman), both of which were finally produced in Dresden. But Wagner became embroiled in the revolutionary movements of the time and was forced to flee Germany.

He spent the next twelve years in exile, during which time he wrote *Tannhäuser* and *Lohengrin.* It was during these years that he formulated his theories about opera, writing essays on aesthetics, the most important of which was *Oper und Drama.* In this essay he set forth the idea that the ideal art form would be equal portions of music, drama, poetry, and stagecraft. He called this art form *Gesamtkunstwerk* (unified art work), the art of the future. One of the important results of his new theories was the beginning of *Der Ring des Nibelungen,* a gigantic saga of four operas to be given on successive nights: *Das Rheingold, Die Walküre, Siegfried,* and *Götterdämmerung.* Drawing heavily on German and Norse mythology and based on the idea of redemption through love, the "Ring" is the longest and most complicated dramatic work ever to be successfully staged. The whole cycle took more than twenty years to complete.

In 1864 young King Ludwig II of Bavaria invited Wagner to Munich, and it was there that *Tristan und Isolde* was first produced. Wagner's expensive tastes drained the Bavarian treasury, and he was forced to leave the country. He then moved again to Lucerne, Switzerland, where he completed *Die Meistersinger.* The "Ring" was completed in 1874. Wagner had long dreamed of a theater especially constructed for his own works, and finally in Bayreuth, northern Bavaria, such a theater was built with a revolving stage, sunken orchestra pit, and every device of stage mechanics possible at that time. In 1876 the first performance of the "Ring" took place in this theater, which has since become a mecca for lovers of Wagnerian opera. His last opera was *Parsifal,* a quasi-religious drama based on the story of the Holy Grail. Wagner died in Venice in 1883.

Critics of Wagner were usually either violently opposed to his theories and music or were ardent supporters in his struggle for recognition. He was a supreme egotist. As one writer has put it: "Wagner thought of himself as the world's greatest composer, poet, dramatist, philosopher, and politician, and remarkably, he was very nearly all of these."

Wagner's musical style reveals the Romantic ideal at its greatest intensity. A few of the most important devices he used to achieve Romantic expressiveness are discussed here. Wagner used leitmotifs to identify people, objects, ideas, and emotions in his music-dramas. In addition to serving as a unifying device, they also convince the listener of the reality of his Romantic illusions. Wagner's music-dramas were through-composed rather than a series of recitatives and arias. He carried the dissolution of tonality to the very edge of atonality by using dense chromatic harmonies and vague cadences. This practice is especially prevalent in *Tristan und Isolde.* The orchestra carries the burden of dramatic expression, thus making his operas predominantly symphonic. Consequently, he enlarged the orchestra by adding instruments and subdividing the normal sections, resulting in a range of sonorities that made it possible to reach new heights of orchestral tension. (Ex. 7.17, 7.18)

Giuseppe Verdi (1813–1901) is the greatest figure in the history of Italian opera. He was not a revolutionary like Wagner, for he never departed completely from the traditions of the closed forms of recitative and aria. He enriched the long-established forms with superb melodies, dramatic scenes, and an instinctive sensitivity for the theater. Some of his earlier works were rooted in nationalism and succeeded in stirring up the patriotism of Italians who yearned for their freedom and unity as a nation. Verdi's position as a nationalist was further enhanced by a brief period as an elected member of the Italian Parliament. His operas cover a wide range of subjects, from the Egyptian story of *Aida* through the dramas of Shakespeare. With the exception of the *Messa da Requiem,* his nontheatrical works are of lesser importance. Verdi's more important operas are *Rigoletto, Il trovatore* (The Troubadour), *La traviata* (The Wayward Woman), *Un ballo in maschera* (A Masked Ball), *La forza del destino* (The Force of Destiny), *Don Carlos, Aida, Otello,* and *Falstaff.* All of these works are still prominent in the repertory of opera companies. (Ex. 7.4, 7.11)

Charles Gounod (1818–1893) was a French composer who is best known for several operas and Romantic sacred music in the Catholic tradition. His most famous operas, *Faust* and *Roméo et Juliette,* remain in the opera repertory today. *Faust* was first composed as a lyric opera with spoken dialogue and was later reworked in its present form with sung recitatives. Gounod's music abounds in sentimental lyricism and a type of mild Romanticism that was imitated by many lesser talents of his time.

Clara Wieck Schumann (1819–1896), the first prominent woman concert pianist, was more honored in her lifetime for her piano virtuosity than for her compositions. After the death of her husband, Robert, she toured regularly throughout Europe and England. Liszt and Chopin were among her professional admirers, and Brahms was her intimate friend. Her compositions include a piano concerto, chamber music, lieder, and part songs.

César Franck (1822–1880), a French Romanticist, was a Belgian by birth. He lived in Paris, where he was an organist, choirmaster, and teacher of such composers as d'Indy and Chausson. His compositions reveal polyphonic treatment of Romantic melodies and harmonic substance comparable to that of Wagner. There is an air of Romantic mysticism in almost all of his works. He was one of the few Romantics to write extensively for the organ, but his greatest religious music is the oratorio, *Les béatitudes.* He is best known for the *Symphony in D minor,* the *Violin Sonata in A major,* and a number of works for piano, including the *Symphonic Variations for Piano and Orchestra.*

Bedřich Smetana (1824–1884) is considered the father of Czech music. An ardent nationalist, he wrote a long orchestral work called *Ma vlast* (My Fatherland), consisting of six symphonic poems depicting scenes from the life and history of Bohemia. *Vltava* (The Moldau) is the most successful of this cycle. Smetana was a disciple of Liszt, and his symphonic poems are modeled after those of Liszt. A *Quartet in E minor* (From My Life) and an opera, *The Bartered Bride,* are two of his best-known works. (Ex. 7.43)

Anton Bruckner (1824–1896), an Austrian composer, developed a symphonic style, serious and profound, that permeated everything he wrote. An organist and a deeply religious man, Bruckner wrote a number of religious works for the Roman Catholic Church, including a *Te Deum* and three masses. His nine symphonies make up his major works and are marked by their great length and massive, sonorous structures. There is also religious mysticism embodied in all of his works, especially in the slow movements. He used songlike themes as bases for symphonic forms and achieved great climaxes by using the orchestra in a manner that suggests the sound of a full organ. Bruckner is regarded as a nationalist in his native Austria. (Ex. 7.6)

Alexander Borodin (1833–1887) was a member of the "Russian Five," a group that was dedicated to the development of an indigenous Russian style in music. Professionally, Borodin was a teacher of chemistry. However, his intense interest in music resulted in a number of notable compositions. His music reveals Russian orientalism that was based on Caucasian and central Asian coloring. His main works are an opera, *Prince Igor;* a symphonic poem, *In Central Asia;* three symphonies; two string quartets; songs; and numerous other small works. (Ex. 7.61)

Johannes Brahms (1833–1897) was born in Hamburg, Germany, and began studying the piano at age eight. By the time he was thirteen he was playing the piano in taverns to help supplement the meager income of his family. After a period of teaching and concertizing, he moved to Vienna in 1863, where he remained until his death in 1897. He held minor positions as director of various choral societies, but he was never interested in a permanent position, preferring to remain an independent, freelance composer.

It was Schumann who called attention to Brahms's genius as a composer in an essay in the *Neue Zeitschrift für Musik.* Stylistically, Brahms's music is Romantic in its emotional expressiveness but more Classic in formal

Brahms playing the piano. (The Bettmann Archive)

organization. He is sometimes referred to as a neoclassicist because of his devotion to the principles of the Classic sonata and the polyphonic treatment of his musical materials. He was an absolutist, writing no program music in the Romantic sense of the term. Brahms often used a single motif as the basis for an entire movement. His orchestration is always full, giving a massive musical sound. Rhythmically, Brahms's music is exceedingly complex, using cross-rhythms with numerous shifting accents and metric patterns. He is best known for his four symphonies. Other important works are the *Violin Concerto in D major,* Op. 77; the *Piano Concerto in B flat major,* Op. 83; and a substantial amount of solo piano and chamber music. His writing for voices includes *Ein deutsches Requiem,* Op. 45; *Schicksalslied,* Op. 54 (Song of Destiny); the *Alto Rhapsody,* for alto, men's chorus, and orchestra; and over two hundred songs. (Ex. 7.5, 7.8, 7.25, 7.29, 7.30, 7.36, 7.41, 7.46, 7.55, 7.60)

Georges Bizet (1838–1875) was one of the first French composers to be influenced by Wagner. Perhaps this influence was responsible for the failure of his earlier works, for the French generally were not sympathetic toward the Wagnerian style. Bizet's fame rests almost solely on the opera *Carmen,* which was a failure when it was first performed in 1875. In *Carmen,* Bizet introduced realism into French opera. Wagnerian influences are apparent in such devices as the "death motive," but Bizet shows originality in the vivacity of the music and its psychological characterizations. *Carmen* has become the most popular opera of all time. Bizet also achieved some success with incidental music to *L'arlésienne,* a composition for orchestra based on a play by Daudet, but most of his music gained popularity only after his death. (Ex. 7.15)

Modest Mussorgsky (1839–1881), an ardent Russian nationalist, was probably the most talented and important member of the "Five." He was untutored in the basic theory of music but possessed a great genius for creative expression. Mussorgsky never held a musical post but spent most of his life as a government clerk. His early death was probably hastened by malnutrition and alcoholism. His greatest works are in the medium of song and opera, although his orchestral suite *Pictures at an Exhibition,* originally for piano, and *A Night on Bald Mountain,* both programmatic works, have retained their popularity. His greatest gift was his ability to translate the inflection of speech into dramatic, passionate, and poetic melody. His most famous opera is *Boris Godunov,* in which he created a nationalistic music-drama. Divorced from the Italian operatic tradition, yet not imitative of Wagner, *Boris Godunov* is truly an original work that had great influence on many non-Russian composers. Because Mussorgsky was unskilled as an orchestrator, his operas and orchestral music were revised and orchestrated by Nikolai Rimsky-Korsakov, and in this form they were first introduced to European audiences. (Ex. 7.3, 7.19)

Piotr Ilyitch Tchaikovsky (1840–1893) embarked on a course of law study and entered government service, but he gave it up at the age of twenty-three and turned to music. After only two years of intensive study, he was appointed professor of composition at the Moscow Conservatory. Although Tchaikovsky is associated with the Russian spirit in music, and emotionally was a nationalist, he was not a member of the "Five." He wrote in the style of Schumann and Berlioz. His melodies are lyric, with a tinge of Slavic modal harmonies that identify them with Russian folk song. His music is often sentimental, but it has a directness and a range of emotional expression that has wide appeal to all audiences. He is best known for his fourth, fifth, and sixth Symphonies; the concert overture, *Romeo and Juliet;* the ballets, *Swan Lake,* and *The Nutcracker;* and the *Piano Concerto No. 1 in B flat minor. Eugene Onegin,* one of two operas, is still in the operatic repertory. (Ex. 7.50, 7.56, 7.63, 7.64)

Antonin Dvořák (1841–1904), a Czech nationalist, first gained recognition through his Slavonic orchestral dances. He later turned to symphonies and chamber music. His style bears some relationship to that of Brahms, and usually exhibits his national roots. His best-known work is the *Symphony No. 9 in E minor,* better known as the "New World Symphony," written during a sojourn in the United States, where he had come to be the Artistic Director of the National Conservatory in New York. For decades it has been claimed that the "New World" was based on themes derived from Negro and Indian folk tunes, but more recent opinion attributes the origins to his Bohemian heritage. Among his other well-known works that remain alive in music literature are a number of symphonies, the *Slavonic Dances,* Op. 46 and Op. 72; the *Concerto for Cello,* Op. 104; the *String Quartet in F major,* Op. 96; *Stabat Mater,* Op. 58; and songs. (Ex. 7.52, 7.57)

Edvard Grieg (1843–1907) was a Norwegian nationalist who wrote in the traditional style of the German Romantics. He was trained under the influence of Mendelssohn and Schumann; however, he was successful in adapting the German style to the modal melodies and harmonies of Norwegian folk song and dances. The result was music of lyricism with freshness and charm. Grieg's important large works include an orchestral suite derived from incidental music he wrote for Ibsen's drama *Peer Gynt,* a play about a Norse folk hero, and the famous *Piano Concerto in A minor,* Op. 16. The special charm of his music, however, is found in the shorter works—songs, dances, and the many *Lyric Pieces* for the piano. (Ex. 7.65)

Nikolai Rimsky-Korsakov (1844–1908) was a member of the Russian "Five" and has been credited with writing the first Russian symphony. He was a naval officer and a self-taught musician. In spite of his lack of formal training, he was appointed Professor of Instrumentation and Composition at the St. Petersburg Conservatory, a position he held until his death. His music utilizes the true Russian folk idiom and oriental melodic patterns. His musical output is not large, mainly because he gave a great deal of his time to revising and orchestrating the works of his friends, especially Mussorgsky. Rimsky-Korsakov's best operas are *The Maid of Pskov, The Snow Maiden,* and *Le Coq d'or* (The Golden Cockerel). His orchestral works include *Scheherazade* and *Sadko,* the first Russian tone poem. Rimsky-Korsakov is also the author of a textbook, *Foundations of Orchestration,* and an autobiography, *The Chronicle of My Musical Life.*

Gabriel Fauré (1845–1924), one of the later Romantic composers, remained outside the influence of Wagner and Brahms. He developed an almost impressionistic style that evolved from the use of modal scales and transient harmonies. He is best known for his *Mélodies,* but his *Messe de Requiem, Violin Sonata in A major,* and the *Piano Quintet No. 1* have remained popular.

Giacomo Puccini (1858–1924) was the most famous and successful Italian opera composer after Verdi. His operas include, among others, works in "verismo" style, which dealt with realistic subjects from everyday life and used melodramatic recitative with less emphasis on traditional subjects and forms. He was skillful in the technique of the theater, and his operas contain enough Romantic sentimentality that they rivaled Verdi's in popularity. Puccini's most successful operas are *Gianni Schicchi, La Bohème, Tosca, Madama Butterfly,* and *Turandot.* (Ex. 7.12)

Hugo Wolf (1860–1903), an Austrian composer, represents the Wagnerian influence on the lied. Their complex contrapuntal textures and chromatic harmonies give his songs a tension and expressiveness not unlike the music of *Tristan und Isolde.* Moreover, Wolf had the capacity for deep insight into the poetic spirit of the text. On hearing his lieder, one sometimes feels the text is the dominant element, with the music subordinate. Unlike Wagner's music, his compositions are usually succinct. He used the piano to intensify the dramatic element and not as a mere accompaniment. Although he wrote an opera and some instrumental works, it is for his more than three hundred lieder that he is remembered.

Gustav Mahler (1860–1911), the last great composer of the Viennese Romantic style, held various positions as conductor, including the directorship of the Vienna Court Opera, the Metropolitan Opera of New York, and the New York Philharmonic Society. Mahler's nine symphonies are dramatically conceived, colossal tone paintings. His scores call for enormous orchestral resources comparable to those of Berlioz. Mahler was also a skillful and imaginative orchestrator, devising new sounds and even special tunings for strings to achieve dramatic effects. Using song as melodic material with solo voice and choral groups, his symphonies were sometimes expanded into choral works symphonically conceived. He frequently attached programmatic notes or poetic quotations to his scores to suggest a feeling or a mood. Mahler's most important works are *Symphony No. 1 in D major; Symphony No. 2 in C minor* (the "Resurrection"); *Symphony No. 8 in E flat major,* called the "Symphony of a Thousand" because of its great number of participants; *Das Lied von der Erde* (The Song of the Earth) for tenor, contralto, and orchestra; and *Des Knaben Wunderhorn* (The Youth's Magic Horn), a cycle of ten songs with orchestra. (Ex. 7.49)

Richard Strauss (1864–1949), one of the last of the Romantic realists, was also distinguished as a conductor in opera and in the concert hall. As a composer, however, he made his greatest musical impact, for he was one of the virtuosi of orchestral writing. Together, these activities made him extremely wealthy. Strauss was a disciple of Liszt, Berlioz, and Wagner, adapting their methods to his own uses. After a few early works in the forms of the sonata, quartet, and symphony, he turned to program music for his expression. His realism was sometimes subjective. He attached states of feeling to melodic and harmonic ideas as in the symphonic poem, *Tod und Verklärung* (Death and Transfiguration), for which he had Ritter compose a poem to illustrate the music. On the other hand, he used realism in a descriptive manner by suggesting scenes, não

movements and actual sounds of life and nature, as in the *Alpine Symphony,* in which he employs a wind machine and a thunder machine to portray a storm scene. Strauss's realism covered a wide range of subjects, from the humorous to the hysterical.

His music was brilliantly orchestrated, with dramatic and sweeping sonorities that are marked by strong harmonic dissonances and sharp contrasts in tonal coloring. He made use of parallel chord progressions and arbitrary dissonances that obscure tonality but do not deny it. Moreover, he used a contrapuntal fabric that ignored the traditional intervallic relationships among the moving parts and pushed relentlessly to climactic conclusions.

Strauss's earlier works were mainly symphonic poems; however, he also made an imposing contribution to opera. His first important opera was *Salome,* based on a text by Oscar Wilde, an opera that shocked the public of the 1900s more by its subject than its music. *Elektra,* on the other hand, used sharp dissonances and strong tonal color to characterize the decadent story of hate and sordid revenge. *Der Rosenkavalier,* a comic opera written in 1911, is more Classic in its form but is still infused with the lyric sentimentality of Romanticism. While he lived almost to the middle of the twentieth century, his period of creative greatness peaked with *Der Rosenkavalier.* The best of his symphonic poems are *Don Juan, Till Eulenspiegels lustige Streiche* (Till Eulenspiegel's Merry Pranks), *Tod und Verklärung* (Death and Transfiguration), *Ein Heldenleben* (A Hero's Life), *Also sprach Zarathustra* (Thus Spoke Zarathustra), and *Don Quixote* (variations for solo viola, violoncello, and orchestra). In spite of Strauss's seeming preoccupation with the larger forms of program music, his fine songs comprise a distinct contribution to song literature. (Ex. 7.44)

Jean Sibelius (1865–1957) was the most important Finnish composer of the late nineteenth and early twentieth centuries. His style remained deeply rooted in the nineteenth-century Romantic tradition. He consciously carried out a program of nationalistic musical expression, basing much of his thematic material on the Finnish folk-song idiom, though never employing the folk melodies literally. Most of his works are for orchestra. In addition to seven symphonies, his orchestral compositions are typically based on Finnish legends, history, and landscapes. Among his best-known works in this genre are the tone poems *Finlandia,* Op. 26, No. 7; *En Saga,* Op. 9; and *The Swan of Tuonella,* Op. 22, No. 3. (Ex. 7.53)

ADDITIONAL COMPOSERS

A. Austria
    Johann Hummel (1778–1837)
    Carl Czerny (1791–1857)
    Johann Strauss (Sr.) (1804–1849)
    Johann Strauss (Jr.) (1825–1899)

B. Denmark
    Niels Gade (1817–1890)

C. England
    Sir Arthur Sullivan (1842–1900)
    Sir Charles Hubert Hastings Parry
      (1848–1918)

Sir Charles Villiers Stanford
(1852–1924)
Sir Edward Elgar (1857–1934)
Samuel Coleridge-Taylor
(1875–1912)
D. France
François-Adrein Boieldieu
(1775–1834)
Daniel-François-Esprit Auber
(1782–1871)
Jacques Offenbach (1819–1880)
Henri Vieuxtemps (1820–1881)
Pauline Viardot-Garcia (1821–1910)
Édouard Lalo (1823–1892)
Camille Saint-Saëns (1835–1921)
Léo Delibes (1836–1891)
Emmanuel Chabrier (1841–1894)
Jules Massenet (1842–1912)
Vincent d'Indy (1851–1931)
Ernest Chausson (1855–1899)
Cécile Chaminade (1857–1944)
Gustave Charpentier (1860–1956)
Paul Dukas (1865–1935)
E. Germany
E. T. A. Hoffman (1776–1822)
Louise Reichardt (1779–1826)
Ludwig Spohr (1784–1859)
Giacomo Meyerbeer (1791–1864)
Heinrich Marschner (1795–1861)
Carl Loewe (1796–1869)
Albert Lortzing (1801–1851)
Otto Nicolai (1810–1849)
Robert Franz (1815–1892)
Engelbert Humperdinck
(1854–1921)
Max Reger (1873–1916)

F. Hungary
Ferenc Erkel (1810–1893)
G. Ireland
John Field (1782–1837)
H. Italy
Muzio Clementi (1752–1832)
Gasparo Spontini (1774–1851)
Arrigo Boito (1842–1918)
Ruggiero Leoncavallo (1857–1919)
Pietro Mascagni (1863–1945)
Ferrucio Busoni (1866–1924)
Ermanno Wolf-Ferrari
(1876–1948)
I. Poland
Henryk Wieniawski (1835–1880)
Ignace Paderewski (1860–1941)
J. Russia
Mikhail Glinka (1804–1857)
Alexander Serov (1820–1871)
Anton Rubinstein (1829–1894)
César Cui (1835–1918)
Mily Balakirev (1837–1910)
Alexander Scriabin (1872–1915)
Sergei Rachmaninoff (1873–1943)
K. Spain
Isaac Albeniz (1860–1909)
Enrique Granados (1867–1916)
L. Sweden
Franz Berwald (1796–1868)
M. United States
Louis Gottschalk (1829–1869)
John Knowles Paine (1839–1906)
Arthur Foote (1853–1937)
George Chadwick (1854–1931)
Edward MacDowell (1860–1908)
Daniel Gregory Mason
(1873–1953)

VII. HISTORIANS AND THEORISTS

The wide variety of writings on musical subjects in the nineteenth century can be placed in the following categories: (1) music theory, (2) criticism, (3) history and biography, and (4) aesthetics.

The teaching of music outgrew the old apprenticeship method, partly because of the large number of nonprofessionals who became interested in the processes and techniques of musical composition. Moreover, it was in conservatory and university classes that much of music theory was taught. To meet the growing demand for a systematic approach to theory, manuals of harmony, counterpoint, form, composition, and orchestration were written.

The scholarly study of music, its history, and theory began to be formalized in the nineteenth century. At first primarily an enterprise of German-speaking countries, it began to be practiced in France, Italy, and England as well. This systematic study of music, which was to become known as musicology, gave rise to a number of monumental musical collections. Among these in German-speaking countries were the *Denkmäler der Tonkunst* (Monuments of Music, Bergedorf 1869–1871); *Denkmäler Deutscher Tonkunst* (Monuments of German Music, Leipzig, begun in 1892); and *Denkmäler der Tonkunst in Oesterreich* (Monuments of Austrian Music, begun in 1894). Other early works included Expert's *Les maîtres musiciens de la renaissance française* (Master Musicians of the French Renaissance, Paris, 1894) and Torchi's *L'arte musicale in Italia* (The Art of Music in Italy, Milano, 1898?).

Music criticism won the attention of many writers, including composers themselves. With less sophisticated audiences than in the eighteenth century, there was an interest in, and a need for, interpretations and evaluations of musical works and their performances. Such evaluations were made not only of contemporary composers but also of composers of the past. In addition, the rise of virtuoso performers made performances noteworthy, and reviews of these performances had a profound effect on box-office appeal.

The most famous journals that served as sounding boards for critical writings were the *Allgemeine Musikalische Zeitung* published in Leipzig, the *Neue Zeitschrift für Musik* founded by Schumann in 1834 in Leipzig, and the *Gazette Musicale,* published in Paris.

With the study of history becoming more systematic and with the romantic cult of personality, history and biography became important areas of literary effort. The practice of musicology led to authoritative editions of older composers and definitive biographies of composers and performers.

The Romantic period, as we have seen, was a time of conflicting theories and ideas about what music could and should express. Writers on aesthetics argued the pros and cons of various opinions regarding music and its perception. This was especially true of the conflict between program music and absolute music and the new theories of opera.

Ernst Theodor Amadeus Hoffmann (1776–1822) was a German writer and composer who espoused the Romantic ideal of the union of the arts. He wrote poetic and romantic appraisals of such composers as Mozart and Beethoven, using the pen name of Johannes Kreisler (made famous by Schumann's *Kreisleriana*). His critical writings were published in the *Allgemeine Musikalische Zeitung.*

François Fétis (1784–1871) was a Belgian music theorist and historian. He wrote a number of theoretical treatises, but his most famous work is the monumental *Biographie universelle des musiciens et bibliographie générale de la musique* in eight volumes (Paris, 1833–1844). This was the first fairly complete dictionary of musicians and still serves as a prime source of information concerning some composers.

Hector Berlioz (1803–1869) wrote the first important treatise on orchestration, *Traité d'instrumentation et orchestration modernes,* published in Paris in 1844. (*Treatise on instrumentation and orchestration,* a modern edition, was published in New York in 1948.) In addition, Berlioz frequently contributed critical essays to the *Gazette Musicale,* and he published a book of essays on orchestral music, *Les Soirées de l'orchestre,* Paris, 1853 (Evenings in the Orchestra, New York, 1956).

Charles-Edmond-Henri de Coussemaker (1805–1876) was a French music historian who wrote a number of important works on early music. His interest in ancient documents led to a number of valuable collections of early music. His major work, *Scriptorum de musica medii* (Writings of Medieval Music) was published in Paris between 1864 and 1876.

As mentioned earlier, *Robert Schumann* (1810–1856) was the founder and editor of the *Neue Zeitschrift für Musik,* published in Leipzig. His writings were militant essays propagandizing the new Romantic ideals. In the imaginary *Davidsbündlertänze* (Society of David), the different facets of his own romantic personality were represented by the characters of Florestan and Eusebius, names he often used in signing his essays. Schumann was also the first composer to recognize the genius of Chopin and Brahms, writing enthusiastic critiques of their music.

Franz Liszt (1811–1886) made numerous contributions to musical literature as a critic, as a commentator on the current musical scene, and as a champion of the "modern" style of his day. He wrote a series of articles, *Zur Stellung des Künstlers* (On the Position of Artists, 1835), in which he discussed the social consciousness of composers and performers. He also wrote on church music, calling for a return to the function of music as a spiritual force.

Richard Wagner (1813–1883) was the most prolific writer on the aesthetics and criticism of music among the Romantic composers. In addition to being the author of libretti for his own operas, Wagner wrote essays and pamphlets on a variety of musical subjects. Of special significance were his writings on the problems of opera. *Oper und Drama* (Leipzig, 1851) outlined his theories of the artwork of the future. His autobiography set forth his ideas on the union of the arts and his thoughts on almost everything from music to politics. He also wrote an important essay, *Religion und Kunst,* that was related to his opera *Parsifal.*

August Wilhelm Ambros (1816–1876) was an eminent German historian and musicologist. His *Geschichte der Musik* (Leipzig, 1862) was one of the first music histories that tried to draw parallels between developments in music and the developments in the visual arts.

Sir George Grove (1820–1900) was an English historian, musicologist, and biblical scholar whose fame as a writer on music was achieved with the *Dictionary of Music and Musicians* (four vols., London, 1879–1889), a work that has gone through many editions and revisions. The latest edition, titled *The New Grove Dictionary of Music and Musicians* (1980), was expanded to twenty volumes and utilized the latest in research techniques and computer technology.

Herman von Helmholz (1821–1894) was a German scientist and an expert on acoustics. His *Lehre von den Tonempfindungen als physiologische Grundlage für die Theorie der Musik* (On the Sensations of Tone as a Physiological Basis for the Theory of Music, New York, 1948), was first published in Braunschweig in 1863. It laid the foundation for modern research in the physical and physiological aspects of musical sound and perception. He based his work on experimentation but drew heavily upon the research of Rameau and Tartini.

Eduard Hanslick (1825–1904) was the most famous of the Romantic critics and aestheticians in the field of music. Born in Prague, he lived most of his life in Vienna. Hanslick was a champion of absolutism in music. He published *Vom Musikalisch-Schönen: Ein Beitrage zur Revision der Aesthetik der Tonkunst* (On the Beautiful in Music: A Contribution to the Revision of Musical Aesthetics, New York, 1957) in Leipzig in 1854. In this work Hanslick argued that the beauty of a musical composition lay wholly in the music itself, without extramusical ideas. The fact that the book has been translated into many languages, including English, demonstrates its importance. His opposition to the new school of Romantic realism led to his criticism of Wagner, Liszt, Berlioz, and the other programmatic composers. In retaliation, Wagner caricatured Hanslick in the character of Beckmesser in *Die Meistersinger,* a distinction that led to an undeserved lack of appreciation of Hanslick's writings. He opposed the Wagnerian group, but he wrote glowing accounts of Schumann and Brahms, who represented the more classic facets of Romanticism.

Karl Franz Chrysander (1826–1901) was a German music historian and critic. He shared in the editing of the monumental collection of music, *Denkmäler der Tonkunst,* Leipzig, 1869–1871. Subsequent additions to this collection have expanded its size considerably. Chrysander is best known, however, for his writings on the life and works of Handel. He started the *Deutsche Händelgesellschaft* (German Handel Society) and wrote a definitive biography of Handel that was published in Leipzig between 1858 and 1867. He likewise assumed responsibility for the first collected edition of the works of Handel.

Ebenezer Prout (1835–1909) was an English theorist and teacher. He was the author of textbooks on theory, including harmony counterpoint, fugue, and musical form. His text on orchestration went through many editions and was used as a handbook of instrumentation until well into the twentieth century.

Hugo Riemann (1849–1919) systematized the discipline of musicology. He led the way in a stylistic study of types and periods of music, a specialization that has resulted in a wealth of authoritative studies by contemporary musicologists. The list of Riemann's writings is long, but most significant is the *Musik-Lexikon,* (Leipzig, 1882), a work that has gone through many editions and is recognized as a standard reference in music.

Vincent d'Indy (1851–1931) was one of the few successful composers to write a text on the art of musical composition, *Cours de Composition musi cales* (Course of Musical Composition, Paris, 1903–1933). A student of César Franck, d'Indy also wrote an authoritative biography of the Belgian master.

Henry Expert (1863–1952), a French musicologist, was committed to the study of vocal music of the French Renaissance. He prepared editions of music of most of the important composers of that era. As a corollary, he formed choirs in Paris to bring this music to a wider public. Together with Brunold, he prepared the *Anthologie des maître français du clavecin des XVIIe et XVIIIe siècles* (Anthology of 17th and 18th century French Masters of the Keyboard, Paris, 1913–1921).

Aaron Copland, Virgil Thomson, Nadia Boulanger, and Walter Piston. The famous French teacher, Boulanger, with three of her important American students. (From the Fred and Rose Plaut Archives, Music Library of Yale University)

8

Early Twentieth Century (1900–1945)

CHRONOLOGY

1854	*Leoš Janáček* (1854–1928)
1856	Sigmund Freud (1856–1939)
1857	*Edward Elgar* (1857–1934)
1862	*Claude Debussy* (1862–1918)
1866	*Erik Satie* (1866–1925)
1867	*Mrs. H. H. A. Beach* (1867–1944)
1872	*Ralph Vaughan Williams* (1872–1958)
1874	*Arnold Schoenberg* (1874–1951)
	Charles Ives (1874–1954)
	Winston Churchill (1874–1965)
1875	*Maurice Ravel* (1875–1937)
1876	*Manuel de Falla* (1876–1946)
1879	Josef Stalin (1879–1953)
1880	*Ernest Bloch* (1880–1959)
1881	*Béla Bartók* (1881–1945)
1882	Franklin Delano Roosevelt (1882–1945)
	Igor Stravinsky (1882–1971)
1883	*Anton Webern* (1883–1945)
	Edgar Varèse (1883–1965)
1884	Harry S. Truman (1884–1972)
1885	*Alban Berg* (1885–1935)
1887	*Heitor Villa-Lobos* (1887–1959)
	Nadia Boulanger (1887–1979)
1889	Adolf Hitler (1889–1945)
1890	Charles DeGaulle (1890–1970)
1891	*Sergei Prokofiev* (1891–1953)
1892	*Arthur Honneger* (1892–1955)
	Darius Milhaud (1892–1974)
1893	*Lili Boulanger* (1893–1918)
1895	*Paul Hindemith* (1895–1963)
	William Grant Still (1895–1978)
1896	*Roger Sessions* (1896–1985)
1898	*George Gershwin* (1898–1937)
1899	*Carlos Chávez* (1899–1978)
1900	*Aaron Copland* (1900–1990)
	Ernst Krenek (1900–1991)
1901	*Ruth Porter Crawford (Seeger)* (1901–1953)
1903	Wright brothers first airplane flight
1906	*Dmitri Shostakovitch* (1906–1975)
1914	The First World War began
1915	Panama Canal opened
1917	First printed use of the term Russian Revolution
1918	First World War ended
1939	Second World War began
	Television developed
1945	Atomic bomb destroyed Hiroshima and Nagasaki
	Second World War ended

History is that branch of knowledge that relates and analyzes past events. Music history, as set forth in many texts, deals with the description and analysis of past musical creativity, often disregarding more recent and contemporary events. This is not a criticism of historical reporting. It is, rather, the recognition that there is a need for perspective in assessing the importance of events, which ones deserve relating, what should be analyzed, and for what purpose.

For example, in the first half of the eighteenth century J. S. Bach was little known beyond his immediate sphere of activity, whereas Georg Phillip Telemann was an international figure. Until almost one hundred years after his death, Bach's music was practically unknown. With very few exceptions, none of it was even available in published form until the nineteenth century. In the opinions of his contemporaries, Telemann was by far the more highly regarded. Bach was third choice, after Telemann and Graupner, for the post of cantor at St. Thomas Church in Leipzig. Only the insight gained from historical perspective revealed the relative importance of these composers. The importance of this historical perspective is corroborated by one of the twentieth century's most influential composers, Arnold Schoenberg, who said in *Style and Idea* (1941), "Contemporaries are not the final judges, but are generally overruled by history."

The diversity of musical styles and the frenetic artistic activity of the twentieth century make it necessary to divide the study of this century into two major historical segments. The dropping of the atomic bomb on Hiroshima, concluding the Second World War, provides a convenient watershed date for the division of the century and for the study of its musical history. Technological developments after World War II make such a division logical. Musical evolution following these technological developments will be discussed in chapter 9. Those composers who flourished during midcentury may be mentioned in both chapters 8 and 9.

I. SOCIOCULTURAL INFLUENCES ON MUSIC

The transition from nineteenth-century Romanticism to twentieth-century "modernism" was as far-reaching as the transition from the ars antiqua to the ars nova, or from the Renaissance to the Baroque. As in the earlier transitions, the seeds of the new are already to be found in the dissolution of the old. Although at the time these changes seemed almost revolutionary, historical perspective has revealed that these changes had a logic and order not immediately apparent.

Because the speed of twentieth-century attainments in so many areas was accelerated, music moved from one new practice to another with such rapidity that no previous era can be compared with the diversity and extremes of its expressions. The search for originality on the part of every composer led to great variety of expression—reversion to past historical styles, neoclassicism, neoromanticism, serial composition, microtonal music, and *musique concrète.* The insistence on originality was so compelling that its end results often appear questionable.

The scientific research already begun in the nineteenth century continued in the twentieth and led to a number of discoveries and inventions that influenced human relationships beyond all previous imagination. The invention of rapid sound communications, such as the telephone and telegraph in the nineteenth century, led to the further development of sound transmission and resulted in the invention of the phonograph and radio. By the middle of the twentieth century, radio and phonograph recordings had made music available to most of the world.

Parallel scientific investigations of the human psyche were conducted by Freud, Jung, Adler, and others. They attempted to provide scientific explanations for what was being explored intuitively by artists and composers of the same generation. This artistic activity is represented by Schoenberg's *Pierrot Lunaire,* Berg's *Wozzeck,* and his later opera, *Lulu.*

Two great political movements, communism and fascism, made deep impressions on musical compositions in the first half of the twentieth century. Fascism in Italy and its Nazi counterpart in Germany were comparatively short-lived. In their most virulent forms, Nazism and fascism condemned all nontraditional creativity as decadent and typical of the weaknesses of Western democratic society. For almost twenty years, much of the creativity of Germany and Italy was carried on only by exiled composers who fled their native lands, mainly to the United States.

In the first years of the Soviet Union, following the First World War, there was a brief period in which the most advanced contemporary musical expression found performance and creative encouragement. This ended with the rise of Josef Stalin as a dominant figure, and until after his death Russia was cut off from mainstream twentieth-century Western musical thought. A strong emphasis on traditional, nationalistic trends of the nineteenth century prevailed for the most part.

The other European countries had scarcely recovered their economic and artistic equilibrium after the First World War before the impending cataclysm of the great economic depression of the thirties and the disaster of the Second World War overtook them.

II. FUNCTION OF MUSIC

The commercial aspects of music distribution, along with new means of musical communication, led to great changes in the function of music. Organized concert series in large and small urban centers were largely a twentieth-century phenomenon. The availability of performing artists in comparatively remote areas encouraged large audiences for a season of musical performances.

Composers were more and more at the mercy of performers who, through managerial pressure, felt the necessity of emphasizing traditional works to satisfy large but often undiscriminating audiences. Such concerts undoubtedly raised the musical taste of the general public, but performances were likely to contain a preponderance of standard literature.

One twentieth-century outlet for composers was in music for motion pictures. Nowhere was the effect of the mass audience more clearly discernible than in this field. The early decades of the film industry resulted in only a few film scores that were artistically distinguished. Even those films that won distinction, and for which competent composers wrote successful scores, indicate that, for the most part, film music was on the periphery of the musical mainstream. Ironically, however, in one sense, the ideal of Wagner's thesis that music and drama should be a synthesis is more nearly achieved in the best motion pictures than in the musical dramas of Wagner, where music dominated. One positive aspect of this new musical genre was that film audiences were occasionally introduced to new and different musical idioms.

Beginning in the first half of the twentieth century, a great part of the world's population began to be bombarded with musical sounds from recordings and radio: at home, the market, the office, the factory, the playground, and even the sports field. These venues, however, provided no outlet to serious composers. In fact, such music serves a largely psychological function, providing an antidote for the multifarious sounds that surround humans at all times. The kind of music played has no intent to raise or lower taste. It induces the hearer to pay little or no direct attention, and thereby cultivates less discriminating listeners.

During this period, the church was not significantly involved with the music of its time. There are notable exceptions, most especially in countries where there is a state church. There, composers of stature were commissioned by the church to write such works as Te Deums, Magnificats, anthems, and masses for their liturgical services. Parish choir directors, however, found much twentieth-century religious music too difficult for their choirs to perform. Movements in the Christian church to raise the quality of the music used in the services resulted primarily in the revival of much fine music of the past, especially the sacred repertoires of the Baroque and Renaissance.

Opera continued to function as an important means of reaching a large public; its activity varied greatly from country to country. Whereas central Europe had an active opera life, opera in the United States was restricted to a few cities and to short seasons. Some of the subjects most attractive to composers of opera pertained to social issues. Examples of such works were Gershwin's *Porgy and Bess* (1935) and Weill's *Die Dreigroschenoper* (1928). The latter opera was imported to the United States a few years later in an English translation titled *Three Penny Opera* by the American composer Marc Blitzstein.

III. STYLE AND PERFORMANCE PRACTICE

Many composers continued to write in a style closely akin to the Romantic, often referred to as post-Romanticism. However, a break with the nineteenth century was felt as a compelling necessity by other twentieth-century composers. Musical techniques employed to achieve the realistic and nationalistic ends of the previous century had been explored about as far as possible. Composers found it necessary to devise new ways to say new things. This meant that the elements of music and compositional style had to be reassessed.

The first attempts at new modes of composition in any age need to be tried in the fires of experimental creativity. Those less effective are discarded, and new modes are established that help determine which musical innovations best give expression to the musical imagination of the period.

One new compositional style, Impressionism, was a response to Romanticism by writers, painters, and composers. It emerged at the close of the nineteenth century and was the connecting link between Romanticism and the experimentalism of the early twentieth century. It was a style whose artistic language included suggestive colors, lines, words, melodies, and harmonies. The listener, viewer, and reader were called upon to supply the details and complete the images. The movement was strongly influenced by the painters Manet and Monet and by the symbolic imagery of the poets Verlaine and Mallarmé, among others. Led by Debussy, composers denied both the objectivity of programmatic composers and the pathos of the Romantic idealists. Impressionistic music was a music of coloristic effects, of vague harmonies, and loosely knit forms.

Two other manifestations of the composers' search for new stylistic expression presented themselves: the use of more tonal material than the twelve semitones of the octave, and the development of new principles of construction with the old material. The first gives rise to attempts at splitting the octave into smaller intervals than the twelve half steps. This device, *microtonality,* attempted by a few composers, used newly constructed instruments— quarter-tone pianos—or took advantage of those instruments that could play intervals smaller than the semitone—the violin family, the trombone, or the human voice. The second, finding new principles of construction, resulted in the *twelve-tone technique,* as developed originally by Arnold Schoenberg. Subsequently, that technique was embraced by most of the composers of the twentieth century. Their styles placed great emphasis on timbre and rhythmic complexity, which rivaled pitch in importance.

Formal Organization

The most important new means of formal organization in the twentieth century was the *twelve-tone,* or *dodecaphonic,* method of composition. This system evolved from Schoenberg's earlier *free atonalism* and used the twelve chromatic tones as independent entities without reference to a tonal center. Dodeca-phonic composition was based on a set pattern of the twelve tones, called the tone row, repeated continuously throughout the work in many varied forms. In this music, the basic row may be subjected to the various forms of contrapun-tal treatment traditionally used to secure variety in imitation: inversion, retro-grade (cancrizans), retrograde inversion, augmentation, and diminution. More-over, the tone row can be transposed to any of the twelve levels of the chromatic scale. Later, the term *serialism* was used indicating that the series might consist of fewer than twelve tones, and might even be a rhythmic or tonal pattern. The basic device of serial technique is, of course, nothing more than a construction of a tonal pattern (of twelve or fewer notes) and the con-tinuous variation of this construction. In Schoenberg's *Variations for Orches-tra* (fig. 8.1), the cello part (measures 34–40) presents the original twelve-tone set in transposition.

Figure 8.1 Twelve-tone technique in *Variations for Orchestra* (Used by permission of Belmont Music Publishers, Pacific Palisades, California.)

One of the significant characteristics of early twentieth-century formal organization was the variation principle. True repetition and contrast were used less frequently than before. Literal repetition was used for expressive pur-poses, not for formal organization. Repetition actually became variation.

There was a tendency toward brevity in all new musical composition. The expansive thematic structures of the Romantic gave way to short musical ele-ments. Long, spun-out themes were displaced by short, pithy motives. In such musical constructions all elements were tightly organized. The desire for brevity eliminated or at least shortened such formal structures as bridge pas-sages, modulatory sections, and closing sections.

Melody

Whole-tone scales were sometimes used by Impressionists. These scales, which do not have the perfect fourth, fifth, or leading tone, deny a sense of tonic, or center, thus permitting each tone to move without creating tension to any other tone of the scale (fig. 8.2).

Figure 8.2 *Piano Prelude: Voiles,* illustrating whole-tone writing

In the music of the early twentieth century the melodic line, whether for voices or instruments, may include wide intervallic leaps and a high degree of rhythmic complexity. In addition, it was often placed in extreme ranges in order to make use of varied tone qualities.

Phrases and periods were no longer symmetrical. There was a tendency to form melodies from short, motivic fragments. In dodecaphonic music, consecutive notes of a melodic line were often sounded over several octaves and assigned to different instruments rather than contained within the range of a single instrument. Additionally, the general tendency to write in a contrapuntal style lessened the importance of melody as a dominating vehicle in music. Even in works for solo voices or instruments, the solo part became one of the lines of the contrapuntal fabric rather than a dominating melodic line.

Vocal melody was subjected to contours that were expressive of the text even to the extent of losing specific tonal designation, as in the technique of *Sprechstimme.* This term is literally translated as "speech voice" or "speech intonation." A similar technique was apparent in the presentation of popular music in which the singer did not confine the textual rendition to a well-defined melody, but exaggerated and stressed the actual pitches according to the intensity of emotional expression conveyed by the words. In the following example, the vocalist is instructed to avoid the absolute pitches of the notes that are designated by the crosses on the stems (fig. 8.3).

Figure 8.3 Sprechstimme from *Pierrot Lunaire*

Rhythm

Traditional metric units continued to be used in twentieth-century music. However, many compositions emerge that employ irregular and asymmetrical measures and phrases. Much use is made of odd-numbered metric patterns—five, seven, eleven. Such rhythmic irregularity may be simultaneous, as in the case of polyrhythms, or more generally consecutive, as in Stravinsky's *Le Sacre du printemps,* where successive measures of 4/8, 5/16, 7/16, and 4/8 yield great rhythmic energy (fig. 8.4).

Figure 8.4 Rhythmically complex excerpt from *Le Sacre du printemps*

Harmony

Early twentieth-century harmony was much more dissonant than that of previous eras. Those intervals that were considered dissonant in the harmonic practice of the eighteenth and nineteenth centuries were used with great freedom in the twentieth. In music that still adhered to traditional tonality, dissonant harmonies, while much more freely used, were still recognized as dissonant and were eventually resolved, even if delayed.

Music that did not adhere to the tradition of tonality is often referred to as *atonal.* In this style, the distinction between dissonance and consonance theoretically ceased to exist. Harmony was recognized as a relationship of all the tones to one another rather than the relationship of all the tones to a single central one. Under such circumstances, all relationships were possible and usable.

The use of dissonance was extended in traditional harmony through bitonality and eventually polytonality, the use of two or more tonal centers at the same time (fig. 8.5).

Sometimes traditional harmonic constructions were based on nontraditional scale patterns. Such scale patterns were derived from medieval modes, folk scales, or non-Western scales.

Figure 8.5 Polytonality in piano reduction of *Psalm 67* (Copyright © 1939 (Renewed) by Associated Music Publishers, Inc. (BMI) International Copyright Secured. All Rights Reserved. Reprinted by Permission.)

Texture

Contrapuntal texture was frequently employed by twentieth-century composers, especially the twelve-tone composers who exploited thin, almost ephemeral, contrapuntal textures in which notated silences tended to play as important a part as the notated sounds.

Contrapuntal practice was not restricted to a counterpoint of individual melodic lines but often extended in ensemble and orchestral works to a counterpoint of rhythms in which several rhythmic patterns were used simultaneously. Likewise, a counterpoint of timbres might have been employed in which various groupings of instruments and sound sources were pitted against one another.

With those composers who wrote in a neoromantic style, the texture—both harmonic and contrapuntal—was inclined to be very thick and heavy. Full, rich, chordal structures were derived from the use of dissonance and counterpoint.

Instrumentation and Tone Color

Although compositions using large forces were still written, there was a marked tendency to use small ensembles in which unusual combinations were specified. A kind of heterophony of color was achieved by the contrast of widely differing timbres in combination. There was a tendency to combine wind instruments and string instruments in more nearly equal numbers, and wind instruments were used more often for solos and in choirs in the orchestra. The voice was often combined with instruments as an integral part of an ensemble and was exploited to give a greater variety of tonal color.

Performance Practice

At times, notational and dynamic differences were increasingly specific, but there was also the opposite tendency in some compositions to leave greater freedom to the performer by calling for purely improvisational passages. Many of the directions were found in the vernacular rather than in traditional Italian, and indicated the attempt to communicate even more clearly than before.

The high standard of instrumental and vocal performance demanded by the recording industry made such technical considerations as purity of tone, accurate intonation, and clarity important criteria in the evaluation of musical performance. Virtuosity was expected of all concert performers and as such was taken for granted.

In most cases a high degree of musical specialization resulted in the separation of composing and performing. In the past, composers were often virtuoso performers, whereas in the twentieth century the expectation of technical perfection in performance, live and recorded, made demands on the performer that usually excluded creative activity. Pianists such as Ignace Paderewski, Arthur Rubinstein, Vladimir Horowitz, Rudolph Serkin, Artur Schnabel, and many others became notable performers of music from Bach to the present. A few pianists, such as Sergei Rachmaninoff, Ferruccio Busoni, and Sergei Prokofiev, gained reputations as pianists and composers. Fritz Kreisler, Jascha Heifitz, Joseph Szigeti, and Nathan Milstein were violinists who performed all styles of music. The list of singers who gained extraordinary reputations as performers in concert and opera is almost endless, partly because of the nature of the human voice, which limited the number of years available to them as performers. Among the great voices of the first half of the century were Feodor Chaliapin, Enrico Caruso, Lauritz Melchior, Kirsten Flagstad, Rosa Ponselle, and Mary Garden.

Orchestral conducting demanded the same virtuoso performance. Richard Strauss, Arturo Toscanini, Leopold Stokowski, Serge Koussevitzky, Wilhelm Furtwängler, Bruno Walter, and others brought remarkable and definitive performances to millions in the concert hall, on radio, and recordings.

IV. MUSIC FOR VOICES

In general, the vocal forms used in the early twentieth century were those found in earlier periods. Dating as far back as the Romanesque, they were adapted to contemporary contrapuntal and harmonic practices. The voice in solo and choral compositions was treated more as an instrument than previously. Vocal ranges were expanded, and intervallic skips, which are not technically difficult for instruments, were demanded of the voice. Vocalists were confronted with technical demands of production that seemed at times insurmountable.

Single-Movement Forms

Art Song

The art song continued to be a popular vehicle for composers. While some composers continued in the tradition of the late Romantics, others sought new and widely varied means of expression. In the songs of the experimental composers such as Berg and Webern a more angular melodic treatment was given to the voice and greater emphasis was given to the accompaniment. "Accompaniment" inaccurately designates the instrumental part of most twentieth-century vocal compositions, because the voice and associated instruments form an ensemble rather than a vocal line with instrumental background. In many instances composers turned to folk melodies and set them in a modern idiom, settings that were not governed by the lush harmonic textures of Romantic music. Such works often involved instrumental chamber groups instead of the piano.

One modern phenomenon of song writing has been the disintegration of the melodic line into a highly inflected declamatory part. The device known as *Sprechstimme* was used in combination with small instrumental groups by a number of the twelve-tone writers as well as other composers. In these cases the vocal part was almost pure declamation, without exact tonal designation but with rhythmic notation and general inflection indicated. (Ex. 8.1–8.5)

Choral Works

A great demand developed for choral music for church, amateur and professional choirs, and for secondary schools and universities as well. This demand gave rise to many shorter choral works, usually of one movement. These were settings of significant poems or prose texts of historical or timely interest. They were usually unaccompanied but often used the piano or organ in support of the voices. The treatment of these texts was often contrapuntal, with independent lines and free rhythms.

During the first half of the century, one of the major areas of sociological and academic study was the collection and recording of indigenous folk music of Europe, Australia, and North America. Composers such as Kodály, Bartók, Vaughan Williams, Holst, and Grainger created numerous and effective choral settings of these folk tunes. (Ex. 8.6–8.8)

Composite Forms

Opera and Music Theater

Some twentieth-century operas retained the symphonic character of the Wagnerian tradition. In others the preference for economy of material made dramatic presentation much more concise and intense. In some there was a return to set forms of aria and chorus, reverting to the simplicity of Classical opera. Some operas, such as Berg's *Wozzeck,* were written in large symphonic forms in which several scenes were treated as movements or sections of abstract music, such as the sonata or the variation form. Dramatic expression was achieved in some operas through the twelve-tone method of composition, or through highly dissonant chromaticism. Other composers reverted to the ballad opera of the seventeenth century with its simple forms, such as the popular street song and folk song. These examples of stylistic diversity indicate the enormous variety in operatic music of the twentieth century.

The musical theater came close to a revival of the ballad opera, with some harmonic and melodic parallels to the nineteenth-century tradition. Rhythmically it had much of the freedom of twentieth-century jazz, and its general mood reflected a freedom of expression typically American. Several of these compositions have established themselves in the repertoires of opera houses in many countries.

Despite the variety represented in these dramatic works, an economy of treatment, realism, expressionism, dramatic intensity, some degree of dissonant harmony, and irregularity of rhythm characterized all the twentieth-century musical dramas. The twentieth-century musical theater was a descendant of the opéra comique and the operetta, but with a distinctive flavor. It was usually romantic, with spoken lines, choreography, choruses, and music related to popular song and jazz. It has commanded attention in many world centers, even in the European opera houses of long-established tradition. The fact that many of its productions were transferred to motion pictures enhanced the popularity of musical theater. (Ex. 8.9–8.18)

Oratorio/Choral Works with Orchestra

The oratorio in the twentieth century remained almost as dormant as it had in the latter half of the nineteenth century. Those that were written generally employed the traditional plan of this form, albeit in a style that was in keeping with the twentieth century. Composers set poetic and prose texts of a less dramatic nature in works of several movements. Sometimes they were only for chorus and orchestra; in others soloists were added. Composers experimented with instrumentation and tone color. In most of these works the instrumental ensemble was more than a mere accompaniment, and the vocalists were something less than featured soloists. Such choral works tend to be cast in forms dictated by the texts. (Ex. 8.19–8.24)

Liturgical Music

Early in the twentieth century, there was little music written for purely liturgical purposes. Some settings of the Mass for the Roman Catholic Church were written using the twelve-tone system, but these were rare, and their performance as liturgical music is even rarer. Likewise, some able composers wrote music for the Protestant church and the Jewish synagogue. (Ex. 8.25, 8.26)

V. MUSIC FOR INSTRUMENTS

No form is unique to the twentieth century. As a result, composers of instrumental music returned to the classic form of the sonata as an ideal for their compositions. The sonata changed substantially in the hands of modern composers. The old symmetry of phrase, period, and section gave way to a balance that was based on other principles. While most composers retained the traditional terminology of the Classic era, new schemes of formal organization, melody, harmony, rhythm, texture, and tone quality gave them new meaning.

Single-Movement Forms

Overture and Symphonic Poems

The overture continued as a single-movement form quite apart from its original purpose as a prelude to a dramatic work. Most overtures in the twentieth century were short symphonic poems, often of dramatic expressive quality. Dramatic musical works rarely employed an overture in the traditional sense, so there were few overtures of this kind in the repertory of the twentieth century. (Ex. 8.27, 8.28)

Variation

While modern composers were generally concerned with problems of construction, variation form regained its popularity. However, the traditional techniques of variation gave way to such devices as variations on a tone row, on tonal coloring, and on rhythmic patterns. (Ex. 8.29–8.31)

Short Forms: Dances, Poetic Pieces

Many short works were written in modern or exotic dance forms, or in simple two-part or three-part song forms. Most of these works were written for piano, though solo instruments combined with piano and small ensembles, or even orchestral compositions, were sometimes cast in these forms. (Ex. 8.32–8.34)

Composite Forms

Sonata, Chamber Music, and Symphony

These multimovement forms presented modern composers with the principal vehicle for extended instrumental composition, whether for solo instrument, chamber ensemble (e.g., string quartet), or orchestra. Typical of contemporary style, these pieces were characterized by brevity, achieved by reducing the recapitulation section of the sonata-form, using fragmentary motives rather than extended themes, avoiding most repetition, omitting transitions and bridge passages between motivic statements, and reducing the instrumentation. Often the whole sonata was presented in a reduced number of movements, if not in a single movement, with several related sections in differing tempos and moods. In some instances the juxtaposition of movements or of sections of the sonata were used to achieve new formal constructions.

The strict harmonic relationship of tonic and dominant of the classical sonata was no longer valid, but formal structures were realized in a multitude of ways outside the harmonic realm, and twentieth-century composers experimented with such devices.

Early twentieth-century sonatas embraced the many neoclassical instrumental works for piano as well as those for a single melodic instrument with keyboard. The idiom and style varied from composer to composer. The technical difficulties posed for the performer also varied greatly—from works called *Gebrauchsmusik* to those that obviously are meant exclusively for concert performance. The former were written with the amateur and student musician in mind, whereas the latter require proficiency of the highest order.

Chamber music afforded early twentieth-century composers one of the prime areas of musical expression. Composers of chamber music went far in using newly conceived combinations of instruments and voices in their works. The traditional string quartet was still employed, as well as several other classical combinations, but many compositions were written for two to fifteen performers in which not only the standard instruments of all families were combined, but rarely used instruments were often incorporated. Percussion instruments of all kinds, especially those with tuned bars, were used. The inclusion of the voice in small ensembles was especially characteristic of modern chamber music. The use of these instruments was more than mere exploitation of new and unusual media; it was the use of tone color as a means of formal organization.

The symphony continued as the principal large form for instrumental composition. In the case of some writers, particularly those whose style still favored the Romantic, this form was likely to be extended with colorful orchestration and it often combined voices with the orchestra. At the other extreme were those symphonic writers who reduced the symphony to a mere shadow of its classical self. Serial composers made the most use of this treatment, although a large number of composers wrote music that lay between these extremes and employed many devices to rejuvenate the classical symphonic form. (Ex. 8.35–8.43)

Concerto

In the twentieth century, the frequent return to ideas of earlier music was reflected in the revival of the concerto grosso. Solo concertos were also frequently written. The orchestral concerto, in which many of the instruments act as soloists or in which groups of instruments are pitted one against the other, was typical of the return to earlier forms but with twentieth-century idioms. In the solo concerto, composers handled their material in much the same way as in the symphony. The solo instrument was no longer exploited only for virtuoso effects, although virtuoso techniques were required for performance. The tendency to exhibit solo instruments at the expense of the orchestra was abandoned in favor of a kind of composition in which the soloist and orchestra exploited the musical material together. Cadenzas were employed primarily as means of developing the musical material. (Ex. 8.44–8.48)

Suite

The twentieth-century suite was usually a selection of scenes or sections from a larger work, such as a ballet, incidental music to a drama or motion picture, or a series of pieces connected rather loosely by thematic relationship, mood, or extramusical idea. Only in a few instances was the suite based on the tradition of the dance suite. As a consequence, it was often the product of the more romantically inclined composers because of its connection with extramusical purpose. The title "suite" was used for compositions of this character for various solo instruments and ensembles. (Ex. 8.49–8.53)

Ballet-Modern Dance

Instrumental music written for the ballet continued into the twentieth century in a form that was much more concise than its predecessors, and in a form that was much more abstract than the set of closed dances that made up the classical ballet. Most of the ballets of the twentieth century were in one act, with one or more scenes. The music rarely consisted of set dances but was rather in the form of a highly rhythmic symphonic poem, interpreted by the dancers in appropriate pantomime and dance gestures. In modern dance the stylized figures of the dancers of the classical tradition gave way to free gestures and movements, symbolizing the drama in collaboration with the musical symbolism of the orchestral score. Dance was one of the most successful vehicles for presenting modern music to a receptive public. In the United States it was the most successful form of dramatic music. Dance music constituted one of the most frequently heard forms in orchestral concert programs because the music could be presented in its entirety or in suites made up of selected scenes from the score. (Ex. 8.54–8.58)

Incidental Music for Film and Drama

Most music written for film and drama in the early twentieth century was merely "background music"; however, some had artistic merit and appeared later in concert form. This was more generally the case with incidental music to staged drama than with music for the motion picture. When written by competent composers, however, this music was so carefully integrated with the film that it could only rarely have an independent existence. (Ex. 8.59–8.62)

VI. COMPOSERS

It is impossible to state with any authority which composers of the early twentieth century will achieve a permanent position among the great composers. Lack of perspective denies to us the luxury of making such judgments. Some composers wrote predominantly in one style, but the majority, as often in the past, composed in several styles, often with equal success. Consequently, the authors have not placed the following composers under stylistic headings but rather have mentioned the important stylistic characteristics in the description of each composer.

Leoš Janáček (1854–1928) was a renowned Czech composer. Although he lived the greater portion of his life in the nineteenth century, most of his significant works were composed during the last decade of his life. His operas, *Kát'a Kabanová* (1921) and *From the House of the Dead* (1928); the *Glagolitic Mass* (1926); the *Sinfonietta* (1926); and the *Concertino for Piano and Chamber Orchestra* (1925), are examples of his late work. His musical expression was terse and economical, based on motivic construction that was derived from a study of speech inflection. *Janáček* wrote chamber music and orchestral works, but it was his operas that first brought him international recognition and are finding special favor again, more than sixty years after his death.

Edward Elgar (1857–1934) was one of the greatest English composers since Henry Purcell, and the first of a line of outstanding modern English composers. His birth, religion, and education placed him somewhat outside the mainstream of English music. Around the turn of the century his oratorio, *The Dream of Gerontius,* and the *Enigma Variations* firmly established his position in the English musical scene. He is best known for his *Pomp and Circumstance* marches, the first of which has long been associated with English royalty. (Ex. 8.29)

Claude Debussy (1862–1918), a French composer, was the leading figure of the impressionistic movement in music, the most influential development of late nineteenth- and early twentieth-century French music. Impressionism was an antirealistic movement that originated first in painting and poetry. In addition to being antirealistic, it was anticlassical; even its Romantic qualities were milder, and it avoided the violence and passion of the earlier Romanticists. It was concerned with vague and transitory suggestions, subtle moods and atmosphere. Debussy's music was directly influenced by literature and painting; he was greatly stimulated by the symbolist poetry of Verlaine and the paintings of Monet, and he tried to suggest the same kind of feeling as these colleagues. Debussy sought to express the shimmering effects of light and shade in painting by tone color and chordal structure in music, sacrificing lyric melody, traditional forms, and polyphonic complexities for suggestive harmonic progressions. In order to achieve a more luminous harmonic coloring, he destroyed the traditional function of the successive scale steps by the use of the whole-tone scale, in which each note has a subtle character all its own. Debussy also added to the sense of vagueness by weakening cadences with parallel chordal progressions and unresolved dissonances.

Debussy's nontraditional practices aroused much controversy, even in his early works, such as the *Prélude à l'après-midi d'un faune* (Prelude to the Afternoon of a Faun), the *Nocturnes,* and *La Mer.* His opera *Pelléas et Mélisande* is a music drama with restrained musical expression that captures the emotional atmosphere of Maeterlinck's drama. A string quartet and a number of pieces for piano, including the *Twenty Four Preludes,* are among his works written before 1910. The very late compositions written during the last year of his life, the violin and cello sonatas, and the two books of études place Debussy in the forefront as an innovative composer, bridging the Romanticism of the nineteenth century to the style of the twentieth century. (Ex. 8.1, 8.9, 8.19)

Erik Satie (1866–1925) was a French composer whose importance lies more in the personal influence he had on his contemporaries than in his few compositions. He was the counselor, before the First World War, of the group of young composers in France who came to be known as "Les Six," a group which comprised Darius Milhaud, Arthur Honneger, Francis Poulenc, Georges Auric, Germaine Tailleferre, and Louis Durey.

Satie's style can be characterized as one of complete simplicity. He used the simplest harmonies, melodies, polyphonic textures, and formal structures. There was no attempt to be profound. This trend toward simplicity was the forerunner of the break with Romanticism and Impressionism and the gradual turn toward neoclassicism. His utter disdain for the sentimental and pretentious was reflected in the titles he attached to many of his works. These include *Cold Pieces, Airs to Make One Flee,* and *Three Pieces in the Shape of a Pear.* These, and *Gymnopédies* and *Gnossiennes,* are among the best known of his works. (Ex. 8.32)

Mrs. H. H. A. Beach (1867–1944), an American pianist and composer premiered her *Romantic Piano Concerto* with the Boston Symphony. She toured Europe, performing her own works to great acclaim. Mrs. Beach was the first American woman to write in the European classical style successfully. She wrote many songs, as well as music for piano, chamber ensemble, and orchestra.

Ralph Vaughan Williams (1872–1958), an English composer, consciously and ardently allied himself with the great English folk-song revival centered around Cecil Sharp. For a number of years he participated actively in the search for and study of English folk songs. Williams quoted folk songs in his early works, but he rarely used actual folk melodies after World War I. Most of his works are, however, infused with the spirit of the English folk song. He never developed a style that was at the same time national and twentieth century, but the idiom of English folk song scarcely allowed such a combination. Although his works are characterized by modal polyphonic treatment, he was essentially a melodist and used chromaticism and dissonance sparingly. He wrote in virtually all the musical genres, though his symphonic works and vocal compositions are the more frequently performed. Among the nine symphonies, the best known are *A London Symphony* (No. 2), the *Pastoral Symphony* (No. 3), and the *Symphony in F minor* (No. 4). *On Wenlock Edge* for tenor, string quartet, and piano, and a number of sacred compositions, including the *Mass in G minor,* were written in the first quarter of this century. Vaughan Williams is also remembered as a Professor of Music at the Royal College of Music and as the editor of *The English Hymnal* and the original *Oxford Book of Carols.* (Ex. 8.42)

Arnold Schoenberg (1874–1951) was an Austrian composer most widely known as the founder of the twelve-tone compositional technique. Schoenberg's earliest compositions were in the Romantic tradition of Wagner. However, his later preoccupation with sonorities that avoided functional harmony placed him in the forefront of those radical composers often referred to as twelve-tone composers or *expressionists.* Exploitation of new relationships among pitch materials began as early as 1914 and continued in the *Five Piano Pieces,* Op. 23.

The *Suite for Piano,* Op. 25, by Schoenberg was the first composition to be built exclusively on the principle of twelve-tone composition. Schoenberg

Arnold Schoenberg (1874–1951) (The Bettmann Archive)

contended that his new system was not revolutionary, but evolutionary, a natural outcome of the tradition of western European music. A group of disciples who had already gathered about him in the early years of the century adopted his techniques and, along with Schoenberg himself, laid the foundations of the twelve-tone style.

Schoenberg's influence as a practicing teacher continued throughout his long life, from his early years in Vienna, where he was later engaged as a professor of composition at the Vienna Academy, through a professorship at the Prussian Academy of Arts in Berlin, which had to be relinquished with the advent of the Nazi regime in 1933. From 1933 until his death he resided in the United States, where he was a member of the faculties of the University of Southern California and the University of California, Los Angeles.

Schoenberg was influential in the stylistic development of a large number of pupils and followers. Among the most important of these are Berg, Webern, Krenek, Dallapiccola, and Kirchner, who adopted some or all of the principles of their teacher. Even Igor Stravinsky in his seventies began to use serial techniques, showing the influence of Schoenberg.

Among the most widely heard works of Schoenberg are those of his early period, *Verklärte Nacht* (Transfigured Night), originally a string sextet and later transcribed for string orchestra; the *Gurre-Lieder*, for chorus, soloists,

Charles Ives (1874–1954) (Art and
History Archive, Berlin)

and orchestra; a number of chamber music works, such as the string quartets
nos. 1 and 2, *Pierrot Lunaire,* and a large number of songs. The most outstanding of the works in the twelve-tone system are the *Piano Concerto; Violin Concerto,* Op. 36; string quartets nos. 3 and 4; as well as chamber music
for unusual instrumental combinations. An incomplete opera, *Moses und Aron,*
first performed posthumously, has enjoyed some success. (Ex. 8.5, 8.12, 8.30,
8.41, 8.44, 8.53)

   Charles Ives (1874–1954) was one of the most unusual American composers. Trained as a musician, he hesitated to subject his creative talents to the
demands of others, knowing that he would be dependent on their musical
tastes for his livelihood. As a consequence he entered the business world and
became a very successful insurance broker, leaving his composition free from
all remunerative considerations. This double life led to a physical breakdown
in 1918 that ended his compositional career. Almost all of his works were written in the years between 1896 and 1918.

   In some respects he foreshadowed many of the practices of later twentieth-
century composers, such as Schoenberg and Stravinsky. His use of polytonality, polyrhythms, and contrapuntal methods are also part of the serial
composer's technique. Inversion, retrograde, augmentation, and diminution
are all characteristic of Ives's music. Although his works are frequently constructed on a tonal basis, he achieved a considerable degree of dissonance, in
some cases almost a feeling of atonality, with these devices. Despite all the

characteristics of modern music, Ives's musical ideas were deeply rooted in the folk and religious music of New England, with themes from folk songs and New England hymns. Strangely, almost none of his compositions were performed until the 1940s. The *Symphony No. 3,* which received a Pulitzer Prize, was performed in 1947, almost forty years after it was written. *Symphony No. 2* was given its first performance exactly fifty years after it was written. Their influence on American composers was not felt until a few years before his death. His output was devoted mainly to orchestral, chamber, piano, and song literature. Among his most important compositions are the four symphonies; several symphonic poems, including *Three Places in New England, Central Park in the Dark,* and *The Unanswered Question;* over one hundred songs, among which *General Booth Enters Heaven* is representative; choral works; and many piano pieces, including the *Concord Sonata.* (Ex. 8.2)

Maurice Ravel (1875–1937), a French composer, mixed impressionistic style with classical clarity. He was not a pupil of Debussy but stood in close relation to him. He extended the practice of unresolved dissonances but rarely came to the point of atonality. In many respects he remained closer to the Romanticists than to those who came to be considered radical twentieth-century composers. Ravel's love of the exotic in music was revealed not only in his use of rhythms and scale constructions derived from his Basque heritage, but also in his predilection for expression in other exotic idioms. His settings of *Deux mélodies hébraïques* (Two Hebrew Melodies), *Cinq mélodies populaires grecques* (Five Popular Greek Melodies), and the *Chansons madécasses* (Songs of Madagascar), as well as his occupation with oriental themes in a number of compositions, such as *Schéhérazade,* demonstrate this affinity. Likewise, he was influenced by medieval as well as unusual folk tonal systems. His *Rapsodie espagnole, Pavane pour une infante défunte* (Pavane for a Dead Infanta), and *Tsigane* represent these interests. Even in those compositions in which he exhibited a decided neoclassic tendency, the harmonic idiom, as well as the instrumentation, reflected Ravel's deep interest in old and unusual modes and tone colors. Among his neoclassic works are *Le Tombeau de Couperin;* the *Ma mère l'Oye* (Mother Goose Suite); *String Quartet in F major;* Two Piano Concertos; and a number of piano works, an area in which Ravel was outstanding—*Gaspard de la nuit, Jeux d'eau* (Fountains), and *Sonatine.* Ravel also wrote a few stage works, among them the operas *L'Heure espagnole, L'Enfant et les Sortilèges* (The Boy and the Sorceries), and the ballets *Daphnis et Chloé, La Valse,* and *Boléro.* A careful listening to any of the above compositions will confirm Ravel as the prime orchestrator among twentieth-century French composers. (Ex. 8.3, 8.40)

Manuel de Falla (1876–1946) was the most important Spanish composer since the Renaissance. His style was essentially that of the French impressionists, but he combined impressionism with a conscious Spanish nationalism in *Nights in the Gardens of Spain.* He was aware, however, of twentieth-century stylistic advances, and combined these with a musical expression that has a genuine Spanish authenticity. He left Spain when it fell to the anti-Republicans, and lived his last years in Argentina. His most successful works were ballets, among which are *El amor brujo* (Love, the Magician) and *El sombrero de tres picos* (The Three Cornered Hat). A *Concerto for Harpsichord, Flute, Oboe, Clarinet, Violin, and Cello* is representative of his interest in abstract forms as well. (Ex. 8.54)

Ernest Bloch (1880–1959) was a Swiss composer who lived much of his productive life as composer, conductor, and teacher in the United States. Bloch was an intensely expressive writer, first in a neoromantic, and later in a somewhat more neoclassic style. His influence as a teacher of twentieth-century American composers was widespread, including Roger Sessions, George Antheil, and Leon Kirchner, among others. Representative examples of his major works include *Schelomo, Trois poèmes juifs* (Three Jewish Poems), and *America.* His neoclassicism is expressed in the concerti grossi nos. 1 and 2. He wrote chamber music, including five string quartets, piano music with orchestra, and solo works for various instruments. His *Sacred Service (Avodath Hakodesh for Baritone, Chorus, and Orchestra)* has been very successful, and the opera *Macbeth* has gained some attention. (Ex. 8.25)

Béla Bartók (1881–1945) was the most distinguished Hungarian composer of the twentieth century. *Bartók*'s music reflected the twentieth-century character of freely combined sonorities. His music is essentially tonal, but he made extensive use of nonharmonic tones. His harmonic, rhythmic, and melodic styles were derived from an intense commitment to primitive folk music. The use of exotic scales derived from this source gave rise to melodic and harmonic practices that conformed generally to the twentieth-century abandonment of the tonal practice. *Bartók* also made extensive use of polytonality, a device that resulted in a kind of controlled dissonance.

Folk music for *Bartók* was not a means of romantic nationalistic expression, but rather a source of expressive material, universally applicable. His scholarly interest in folk music extended beyond his own national culture and included the music of all Balkan peoples and North Africa. His music not only reflects an interest in the rhythmic, melodic, and harmonic aspects of primitive

Béla Bartók (1881–1945) (Music Division/New York Public Library for Performing Arts. Astor, Lenox and Tilden Foundations)

folk music, but it applied the impulse of the primitive to instruments, in particular to the piano, which is treated as a percussive instrument.

In his earliest works *Bartók* was obviously influenced by the impressionism of Debussy. This influence never completely disappeared and is found in many of the slow movements of his later works. The most distinctive design employed by Bartók is the arch form, a symmetrical balance of movements within the composite form of the sonata.

His compositions, which succeeded in finding wide acceptance only after his death in New York in 1945, have since become extremely popular. Among the most distinguished are the three piano concertos; the *Violin Concerto;* six string quartets; the ballet *The Miraculous Mandarin;* the opera *Bluebeard's Castle;* the *Mikrokosmos,* a series of instructional pieces for piano in the modern idiom; the *Concerto for Orchestra,* and many songs. (Ex. 8.33, 8.35, 8.39, 8.48, 8.52)

Igor Stravinsky (1882–1971), a Russian by birth, lived most of his creative life in Paris and Hollywood. Although his style was one of the principal influences on other composers in the twentieth century, particularly the French and those schooled in France, he was never attached to any institution or academy and only occasionally lectured on the aesthetics of music. He had no pupils as such. With the composition of his ballet *Le Sacre du printemps* (The Rite of Spring) in 1913, Stravinsky adopted a dissonant harmonic style. His exploration of bitonality, polytonality and use of free dissonances and nonharmonic tones showed an expansion of the complex chromaticism of the nineteenth century, though never completely denying tonal centers.

Stravinsky's style was characterized by its harmonic innovations and perhaps even more by its primitive and brutal rhythmic patterns. The resulting complexities included the consecutive use of widely varying metric patterns and polyphony of widely differing rhythmic strata. The syncopations of jazz rhythms were often imitated. In many instances, rhythm constituted the single most important element in Stravinsky's musical fabric.

Stravinsky, following the model of his mentor Rimsky-Korsakov, exploited tone color to its utmost in both large and small instrumental combinations. Typical examples of his unusual scoring include the elimination of all the violins, violas, and clarinets in the orchestra for the *Symphony of Psalms,* or the accompaniment of four pianos and percussion in *Les Noces* (The Wedding).

Stravinsky was at various times a post-Romantic, a primitivist, a neoclassicist, a neoromantic, an abstractionist, an expressionist, a constructionist, and a surrealist, though throughout he maintained a personal idiom that marks all of his compositions.

Few other twentieth-century composers exhibited as many diverse styles as Stravinsky, who composed prolifically over a period of fifty years. His rich output, dating from 1908, when he was studying with Rimsky-Korsakov, never abated. The list of well-known and often-heard works made him the one twentieth-century composer whose recognition was comparatively immediate

Stravinsky rehearsing *Le Sacre du printemps.* (Historical Pictures/Stock Montage, Inc.)

and universal. This was due in part to the great number of stage works, principally ballets, which made the introduction of his music to the general public easier than if his compositions had been more predominantly in the form of abstract orchestral or chamber music.

Some of his important works written before World War II are the ballets—*The Firebird, Pétrouchka, Rite of Spring, L'Histoire du Soldat,* and *Jeux de cartes* (Game of Cards); works for orchestra, including several suites taken from the ballets, *Fireworks, Concerto for Piano and Wind Instruments, Symphony in C,* and *Concerto "Dumbarton Oaks";* chamber music, including *Octet for Wind Instruments;* choral works, including *Symphony of Psalms;* and works for piano, including *Capriccio for Piano and Orchestra* and the *Sonata for Two Pianos.* (Ex. 8.21, 8.55)

Anton Webern (1883–1945), with Alban Berg and several other Viennese composers, was a pupil and disciple of Arnold Schoenberg. Webern adapted the twelve-tone method to his pointillistic technique, which resulted in an extremely economical use of musical material. In it, every aspect of musical expression was reduced to its barest minimum, with thematic material often replaced by compressed motives. The polyphonic texture was varied by placing successive notes of the contrapuntal lines in different octaves and by changing the tone quality of each successive note by using different instruments. His compositions were of extreme brevity, an entire symphony lasting only a few minutes. The ensemble consisted of very few instruments, and they were used only sparingly.

Such techniques applied a term from the visual arts, *pointillism,* to describe the writing of Webern. He wrote many works, but their brevity reduced his total output to something less than three or four hours length in performance, a remarkable fact when compared with the total output of other composers. His influence among the serial and electronic composers later in the century is especially significant. His most important works are *Symphony,* Op. 21; *Variations* for piano solo, Op. 27; *String Quartet,* Op. 28; and the cantatas, Op. 29 and 31. (Ex. 8.31, 8.43)

Edgard Varèse (1883–1965), a French composer who lived most of his active musical life in America, was a significant innovator of the twentieth century. His better-known works exhibited an engagement with sounds for their own sake, a characteristic that finally led him to the exploration of electronic sounds. Although he was a contemporary of Debussy, he felt a closer affinity for early music than the music of his own generation. In his search for timbral richness he exploited the tone qualities of all kinds of unusual instruments and instrumental combinations, particularly percussion instruments and percussive effects generated by more conventional instruments. His most frequently performed work are *Hyperprism,* scored for two woodwind, seven brass, and sixteen percussion instruments; *Ionisation,* written for thirteen performers on thirty different percussion and friction instruments; *Octandre,* a chamber work for eight performers; and *Density 21.5,* for solo flute. (The specific gravity of platinum, the metal of which some flutes are made, is 21.5.)

Alban Berg (1885–1935), an Austrian composer and pupil of Schoenberg, was one of the most expressive composers in twelve-tone technique. As with Schoenberg, his early compositions showed a marked influence of Wagner and Mahler. In his masterpiece, the opera *Wozzeck,* Berg organized his music drama into abstract forms such as rhapsody, suite, and theme and variations (passacaglia). The opera caused great protest when first performed in the 1920s but has since established itself as one of the great repertoire pieces of the twentieth century. Another incomplete opera, *Lulu,* a number of songs, as well as some orchestral and chamber music, represent his short productive life. Among the instrumental works that are frequently played are the *String Quartet, Lyric Suite, Violin Concerto,* and the *Chamber Concerto for Piano, Violin, and Thirteen Wind Instruments.* (Ex. 8.10, 8.45, 8.49)

Heitor Villa-Lobos (1887–1959), one of the foremost South American composers, was a native of Brazil who was eventually engaged as superintendent of musical and artistic education in Rio de Janeiro. Villa-Lobos's idiom was highly influenced by the folk music of Brazil and sometimes was actually based on folk-song themes. He was interested in fusing the peculiarities of Brazilian music with the tradition of western Europe. An example of this style is *Bachianas Brasileiras,* a set of nine suites in which the Brazilian folk-music idiom was combined with Bachian counterpoint. A more typically original Brazilian form was *Choros.* In a series of fourteen of these works, Villa-Lobos combined the many elements of Brazilian folk, popular, and Indian music into compositions that used quite unusual instrumental and vocal forces. The most popular among these two groups of compositions are the *Bachianas Brasileiras Nos. 1* and *5,* and the *Choros Nos. 1* and *7.*

Sergei Prokofiev (1891–1953) was one of Russia's outstanding composers of the twentieth century. He listed the following as the four elements of his style: (1) Classicism (neoclassicism); (2) innovation, which at first was represented in an individual harmonic style, later as an expression of strong emotions; (3) the motoric element; and (4) lyricism. He regarded another element, the grotesque, as an outgrowth of the others. Much of his music is flavored by a certain puckishness or humor.

Prokofiev was widely known as a concert pianist in his early years. Having located in Paris in 1920, he remained there until 1933, and then returned to Russia. His connection with the modern compositional practices of western Europe often brought him criticism at home, and in some instances caused him to adopt the official Soviet aesthetic doctrine, Socialist Realism. Nonetheless, he remained a highly revered composer and undoubtedly influenced the younger composers of the Soviet Union.

His musical output was extensive. The total number of works that eventually found concert performance was, perhaps, second only to Stravinsky among modern composers. His compositions embraced every genre, with the exception of sacred music. Among the best known are his seven symphonies, written between 1916 and 1951; the *Third Piano Concerto;* two violin concertos; *Peter and the Wolf;* an orchestral suite, *Lieutenant Kije;* ten piano sonatas; and many short piano works, including *Sarcasms.* (Ex. 8.34, 8.46, 8.51, 8.58)

Arthur Honneger (1892–1955), a Swiss composer, was closely allied with the French trends of the twentieth century by his inclusion in the group known as "Les Six." Although his early descriptive tone poem, *Pacific 231,* was looked upon as representative of the new machine age, Honneger turned from realistic writing to a neoclassic style. His dramatic oratorios, *Jeanne d'Arc au bûcher* (Joan of Arc at the Stake) and *Le roi David* (King David), are two of the great choral works of the twentieth century. Among a large number of orchestral compositions his five symphonies are worthy of note, but a more significant achievement was the large number of film scores he wrote between 1923 and 1951. Honneger also wrote music for piano, voice, and chamber ensemble.

Darius Milhaud (1892–1974) was one of the French composers who pioneered the modern idiom in the early part of the twentieth century. He was prolific, with works in every genre, and was active as a teacher for many years in the United States. He experimented with jazz, polytonality, and eventually electronic devices. He did not subscribe to any form of atonality, though his use of dissonance in combination with lively melodic lines gave his works an individual style. His ballets, *La Création du monde* (The Creation of the World) and *Le Boeuf sur le toit* (The Cow on the Roof), are representative of his concern with jazz. Other works illustrate his preoccupation with the melodies of his native Provence, such as the *Suite provençale*. Concertos, sonatas, symphonies, and many pieces of chamber music are among his large list of compositions that date from the first half of the century. (Ex. 8.56)

Paul Hindemith (1895–1963), composer, performer, conductor, and teacher, including thirteen years at Yale University, was a significant musical force in the twentieth century. He employed several styles of composition. In his early works he was openly rebellious toward tradition. His music included free counterpoint that made use of dissonance. Hindemith was also occupied with the idea of music for use in common life, reflected in his production of *Gebrauchsmusik* (Music for Use). Later he preferred to call this music *Sing-und Spielmusik* (Music for Singing and Playing). This work was intended to introduce the young and the amateur to modern musical style through school and home performance. A neoclassic turn is evident in much of Hindemith's music of the 1930s. Further study of early music led Hindemith to polyphonic writing, which, while modern in harmonic idiom, is reminiscent of thirteenth- to sixteenth-century practices. Even the lack of bar lines and metric signs, a characteristic of music before 1600, was imitated.

Hindemith was a prolific composer who wrote in every conceivable genre of musical composition. He wrote solo works for almost every instrument but was not as interested in the exploitation of tone color as were his contemporaries. Construction rather than emotional expression characterizes his works.

Among his important works are a song cycle, *Das Marienleben* (The Life of Mary); an opera, *Mathis der Maler* (Mathis, the Painter); *Wir bauen eine Stadt* (We Build a City), for children performers; *Ludis Tonalis,* for piano; *Symphonic Metamorphosis on Themes of Weber;* and *The Four Temperaments,* for piano and strings. (Ex. 8.4, 8.11, 8.37)

William Grant Still (1895–1978) studied composition with Varèse and Chadwick. One of the pioneers of African American symphonic music in America, he composed for the stage and symphonic band as well as the orchestra. Still's *Symphony No. 1* (Afro-American) was premiered in 1931 by Howard Hanson and the Rochester Philharmonic. His list of recorded music is extensive. These works reflect his commitment to African American music and culture.

Carl Orff (1895–1982), whose stage works have won international recognition, was perhaps one of the most conservative of twentieth-century composers. Despite this, he represents a number of trends that were typical of the first half of the century. In contrast to nineteenth-century musicians, who regarded harmony as the principal shaping force, Orff, typical of the twentieth century, placed rhythm in this role. His rhythmic force was drawn from word rhythms, especially from ancient and folk speech, folk dances, and folk songs. He treated these rhythms with a kind of repetitious primitiveness that makes for intense dramatic feeling. Structurally his music is very simple. He avoids contrapuntal practice for the most part, resorting to simple, harmonized melodic lines, with rather rare instances of clashing dissonances resulting from the use of nonharmonic tones. Percussion instruments appear abundantly in all his orchestrations. His best-known works are the dramatic cantatas *Carmina Burana* (based on a collection of thirteenth-century Goliard songs) and *Catulli Carmina,* along with several operas, among which *Der Mond* (The Moon), *Die Kluge* (The Wise Woman), and *Antigonae* are the most popular. In addition, Orff wrote *Schulwerk,* a series of five books (called Music for Children, in English), which has done much to revolutionize music education. (Ex. 8.24)

Roger Sessions (1896–1985) was one of America's foremost composers. A pupil of Ernest Bloch, his early works tended toward the Romantic. He soon turned, however, toward a very complex counterpoint that contained much dissonance. He eventually came under the influence of Schoenberg and wrote music that approached the twelve-tone system and its atonal results, but he never adopted this style of composition. Sessions defies any label such as neoromantic, neoclassic, or expressionistic, though he took part in each of these to some degree. He was not a prolific composer and made his greatest contribution in orchestral, chamber, and piano music. Among the four symphonies, the *First Symphony* represents his early neoclassic style. Other important works are the *Piano Sonata No. 2,* the *Second String Quartet,* and *The Black Maskers,* an early work for orchestra, written as incidental music to a play.

George Gershwin (1898–1937) was the first and most successful American composer to incorporate the popular jazz rhythms of the 1920s in classical

George Gershwin (1898–1937) (The Bettmann Archive)

Manuscript page from Gershwin's *Porgy and Bess.* (Art and History Archive, Berlin)

forms. His success as a composer of popular songs and musicals was already well established when he turned to other types of expression. In these, his melodic gift and rhythmic genius gained him success as a composer. In addition to numerous Broadway hits, such as *Of Thee I Sing, Let 'em Eat Cake,* and *Girl Crazy,* other popular works are *Rhapsody in Blue, An American in Paris, Piano Concerto in F major,* and the opera, *Porgy and Bess.* (Ex. 8.14)

   Carlos Chávez (1899–1978) wrote in a style heavily influenced by Mexican folk music, though he infrequently incorporated actual folk tunes. The revolutionary spirit of Mexico led him to develop a musical style different from the inherited European model. His success as a conductor and an advocate of Mexican music is of special importance.

   Aaron Copland (1900–1990) was a pupil of Nadia Boulanger and is perhaps the most widely known American composer of his generation. He experimented with numerous styles and techniques such as jazz and modified twelve-tone technique, while preserving a strong sense of tonality. His most successful works reflected the American scene through symphonic poems, ballets, and operas, as well as numerous works for radio and motion picture, some of which have been performed as concert music. Copland also wrote more abstract music: symphonies, chamber music, and piano music. Among his best-known compositions are the ballets, *Appalachian Spring, Billy the Kid,* and *Rodeo;* the orchestral works, *El Salon Mexico, Outdoor Overture, Lincoln Portrait,* and the *Third Symphony;* and the piano works, *Passacaglia, Piano Variations,* and his *Piano Sonata.* (Ex. 8.27, 8.36, 8.50, 8.59, 8.60)

   Ernst Krenek (1900–1991) was born in Vienna but spent much of his creative life in the United States. His music shows the influence of almost all the stylistic experiments of the early twentieth century. An early opera (1927), *Jonny spielt auf,* utilized jazz idioms and had great success both in Europe and America. After many experiments, Krenek finally embraced a modified twelve-tone style. A prolific composer, he composed eleven operas, three ballets, incidental music for seven plays, a large number of choral works, five symphonies, four piano concertos, six piano sonatas, and eight string quartets. He is also the author of several books, including *Music Here and Now.*

   Ruth Porter Crawford (Seeger) (1901–1953), an American composer and teacher, wrote in a style considered experimental by her contemporaries because of its dissonance and occasional reliance on devised numerical systems. She was known primarily during her lifetime, however, as an arranger and compiler of American folk music.

   Dmitri Shostakovitch (1906–1975) was a leading composer of midcentury Russia. His *Symphony No. 1,* written as a graduation piece when he was eighteen years old, brought him immediate fame. He was under severe official criticism for incorporating the techniques and dissonances of modern western European music in such works as the opera *Lady Macbeth of Mtzensk.* Obediently, he turned to the traditional forms and styles of the Classic and Romantic periods, with tremendous success within Soviet Russia. Six of his fifteen string quartets and a *Piano Quintet* are among his best-known chamber music.

He wrote fifteen symphonies, of which the fifth has been the most popular. Several ballets and operas, including a well-known opera, *The Nose,* and many film compositions are numbered among his works. (Ex. 8.57)

ADDITIONAL COMPOSERS

A. Austria
   Egon Wellesz (1885–1974)
   Ernst Toch (1887–1964)
B. Belgium
   Marcel Poot (1901–1988)
C. Canada
   Healey Willan (1880–1968)
   Ernest Campbell MacMillan
   (1893–1973)
D. Chile
   Domingo Santa Cruz
   (1899–1987)
E. Czechoslovakia
   Bohuslav Martinů (1890–1959)
   Alois Habá (1893–1975)
F. Denmark
   Carl Nielsen (1865–1931)
G. England
   Frederick Delius (1862–1934)
   Gustav Theodore Holst
   (1874–1934)
   Havergail Brian (1876–1972)
   John Ireland (1879–1962)
   Arnold Bax (1883–1953)
   Gerald Finzi (1901–1956)
   William Walton (1902–1983)
   Constant Lambert (1905–1951)
H. France
   Albert Roussel (1869–1937)
   Florent Schmitt (1870–1958)
   Charles Koechlin (1876–1950)
   Nadia Boulanger, renowned teacher
   of composers (1887–1979)
   Jacques Ibert (1890–1962)
   Germaine Tailleferre
   (1892–1983)
   Lili Boulanger (1893–1918)

Francis Poulenc (1899–1963)
Georges Auric (1899–1983)
I. Germany
   Hans Pfitzner (1869–1949)
   Max Reger (1873–1916)
   Hans Eisler (1898–1962)
   Kurt Weill (1900–1950)
   Hugo Distler (1908–1942)
   Bernd Alois Zimmerman
   (1918–1970)
J. Greece
   Nikos Skalkottas (1904–1949)
K. Hungary
   Ernst von Dohnányi (1877–1961)
   Zoltán Kodály (1882–1967)
L. Italy
   Ferruccio Benvenuto Busoni
   (1866–1924)
   Ottorino Respighi (1879–1936)
   Ildebrando Pizzetti (1880–1968)
   Gian Francesco Malipiero
   (1882–1973)
   Riccardo Zandonai (1883–1944)
   Alfredo Casella (1883–1947)
   Mario Castelnuovo-Tedesco
   (1895–1968)
   Goffredo Petrassi (1904–)
M. Japan
   Yoritsuné Matsudaira (1907–)
N. Mexico
   Julian Carrillo (1875–1965)
   Silvestre Revueltas (1899–1940)
O. Netherlands
   Daniel Ruyneman (1886–1963)
   Willem Pijper (1894–1947)
P. Norway
   Fartein Valen (1887–1952)
Q. Poland
   Karol Szymanowski (1882–1937)
   Grazyna Bacewicz (1913–1969)

R. Russia
    Nikolai Miaskovsky (1881–1950)
    Aram Khachaturian (1903–1978)
    Dmitri Kabelevsky (1904–1987)
S. Spain
    Joaquin Turina (1882–1949)
T. Switzerland
    Othmar Schoeck (1886–1957)
    Frank Martin (1890–1974)
    Willy Burkhard (1900–1955)
    Rolf Liebermann (1910–)
U. United States of America
    Charles Martin Loeffler
    (1861–1935)
    Carl Ruggles (1876–1971)

Charles Tomlinson Griffes
    (1884–1920)
Wallingford Riegger (1885–1961)
Marion Bauer (1887–1955)
Florence Price (1888–1953)
Douglas Moore (1893–1969)
Walter Piston (1894–1976)
Leo Sowerby (1895–1968)
Howard Hanson (1896–1981)
Virgil Thomson (1896–1989)
Henry Cowell (1897–1965)
Quincy Porter (1897–1966)
George Antheil (1900–1959)
Marc Blitzstein (1905–1964)

VII. HISTORIANS AND THEORISTS

The growth of musicological research during the first half of the century resulted in the publication of a large number of books by eminent scholars dealing with all phases of music. Many scholarly works dealing with musicological research in the past are therefore readily available. Only the most important of those published (many of which have been translated into English) are listed here.

Guido Adler (1855–1941), Austrian musicologist, led the development of the science of musical research. Among his many publications is the *Denkmäler der Tonkunst in Oesterreich* (Monuments of Austrian Composition), which reached eighty-three volumes from its inception in 1894 to its completion in 1938, near the time of his death. Many volumes have been added to this series more recently. The DTO served as a scientific research model for many subsequent collections and anthologies of music history.

Ferruccio Benvenuto Busoni (1866–1924), an Italian composer and piano virtuoso, championed new music at the turn of the twentieth century. His book, *Entwurf einer neuen Aesthetik der Tonkunst,* Trieste, 1907 (Sketch of a New Aesthetic of Composition, translated by Dr. Theodore Baker, New York, 1911), was a general encouragement for the "modern" composer of that time. Another important work, available in an English translation by Rosamond Ley, is *The Essence of Music and Other Papers* (London, 1957).

Heinrich Schenker (1868–1935) was an Austrian theorist whose system of analysis has been influential in theory and composition. Schenker himself was concerned principally with compositions of the eighteenth and nineteenth centuries, but his disciples, such as Felix Salzer, have extended his theories to twentieth-century styles. His works, all published in German, cover a period from 1906 to 1935. *Structural Hearing* (1952), by Salzer, is one of a number of English publications dealing with Schenker's theories.

Donald Francis Tovey (1875–1940) was an eminent English scholar and critic. His *Essays in Musical Analysis* (1935–1939), published in six volumes, are among the finest in English musical criticism. *A Companion to Beethoven's Piano Sonatas* (1948) continues to be of value to performers and scholars.

Alfred Einstein (1880–1952) wrote biographies of Gluck, Mozart, and Schubert in addition to many other books on music history. Perhaps his strongest contribution to musicology was his monumental three-volume work, *The Italian Madrigal* (Princeton, 1949).

Ernst Toch (1887–1964), a Viennese by birth, lived in the United States from 1935 until his death. He was active as a teacher during much of his career in Europe and America. His *Melodielehre* (Berlin, 1923) was one of the few books dealing with the nature of melody. An English book, *The Shaping Forces in Music* (New York, 1948), considered general theory and aesthetics of music both past and present.

Joseph Yasser (1893–1981), of Polish birth, fled Russia in the 1920s and lived in the United States since that time. His most important work, among many others, is *A Theory of Evolving Tonality.* In this work he offered a hypothesis not only for the origin of the pentatonic and heptatonic scales but for a future scale which he envisaged as being implied in the work of the twelve-tone composers.

Willi Apel (1893–1988), a German-American musicologist, made a substantial contribution to the understanding of early music through his many publications. Among these are *The Notation of Polyphonic Music, 900–1600* (Cambridge, Mass., rev. 1961), and *Gregorian Chant* (Bloomington, Ind., 1958). Many generations of American music students have relied on *The Harvard Dictionary of Music* (Cambridge, Mass., rev. 1969) and the two-volume *Historical Anthology of Music* (Cambridge, Mass. 1946, 1950). This latter publication was a collaboration with Archibald T. Davison.

Paul Hindemith (1895–1963) always interested himself in the teaching of music. His compositions in the 1920s, which he called *Gebrauchsmusik,* were evidence of this interest at an early age. From 1940 to 1949 he held the post of professor of the theory of music at Yale University in the United States. Among a large number of books that he wrote, two stand out as particularly pertinent to twentieth-century theory and composition—*The Craft of Musical Composition* (New York, revised 1945), and *A Composer's World: Horizons and Limitations* (Cambridge, 1952). They state the individual theory of Hindemith's composing technique as well as his aesthetic concepts concerning music of the twentieth century.

Aaron Copland (1900–1990) is known as a writer and teacher as well as a composer. Three books dealing with music in general, but of great importance to the understanding of modern music, have come from his pen. *What to Listen for in Music* (New York, 1939), *Our New Music* (New York, 1941), and *Music and Imagination* (Cambridge, 1952) constitute a valuable addition to the writings on contemporary music.

Ernst Krenek (1900–1991) was active as a teacher and writer, as well as a composer. In his book, *Music Here and Now* (New York, 1939), he wrote about the contemporary music scene, about which he had extensive personal knowledge.

Portrait of Sergei Prokofiev (1934) by P. P. Konchalovsky. (Art and History Archive, Berlīn)

9

Music Since World War II

I. SOCIOCULTURAL INFLUENCES ON MUSIC

History reveals countless discrepancies between the views of past scholars and the public concerning their musical contemporaries, and the views of later scholars and the public who view the past with the added advantage of perspective. Any discussion of music since World War II lacks such perspective. That does not mean that the assessment of recent music is necessarily invalid, but what may look important and permanent at one time may soon diminish in importance. Furthermore, the speed of communication and the rapidity of change are so great that students of music need to make special efforts to be informed about the musical activities of the present, yet recognize that their judgments regarding that music may later need revision.

In addition to the general sociocultural influences of the first part of the twentieth century, the application of new technological and scientific discoveries is one of the greatest influences on musical creativity and production today. Some of those developments have resulted in a world that is not only more thoroughly informed about events elsewhere, but is also developing similarities of taste that are more uniform than before. This can be illustrated by the extensive effects on concert and popular music of such musical genres as Latin American dances, African American call-and-response settings, and microtonal melodies of Asian music.

After the war, scientific developments were put to commercial and social use with great vigor. Not only was the speed of communication in all its aspects increased, but all phases of communication were made generally available. Some of the post-1950 developments include television, solid-state physics (transistors), rocket propulsion (space satellites, interstellar exploration), laser beams, computers, microchips, and the internet. Each of these contributes in important ways to the musical scene of the late twentieth century.

The development of long-playing records, tapes, and compact discs enabled recordings of large works with minimal interruption. The transistor radio, cassette recorder, and other relatively inexpensive and readily available machines now make music accessible at any location, and at any time. For the first time in history, music from the banal to the most esoteric and from all historical periods became easily accessible through sound recordings. In the past, such an abundance of music was never at the bidding of even the wealthiest patron, secular or religious.

Since 1950, electronic instruments of many kinds have engaged composers in experimentation with an entirely new field of sound. Rhythmic complexities beyond the possibility of human realization are comparatively easy to achieve on electronic instruments. Sound generators and synthesizers are commonly used in musical composition. They have opened new vistas of tone color and pitch manipulation. In addition, composers use computers for musical composition itself. Recent technology has also made available a standardized Musical Instrument Digital Interface (MIDI) to connect microcomputers to various synthesizers. This enables both the professional composer and the layperson to play and write music more easily than before. Finally, the urge to achieve uniqueness has led to multimedia experiments with music, dance, lights, and other effects, especially in commercially produced, mixed-media entertainments for television such as Music Television (MTV).

A subtle environmental factor of the twentieth century has also made its influence felt on musical composition. We live in an environment that is more acoustically disturbing than at any time in the past. The noise of modern life has increased enormously with sounds of the mechanized world. This heightened sound level has affected music as well. Orchestras and ensembles are not necessarily larger, but the decibel level of individual instruments, and the quality of tone called for, often tends to be strident and piercing. This is especially true in rock music, in which a high decibel level is an essential part of the music.

Composers today recognize that it is through recorded music that they have the greatest opportunity to reach large audiences. Consequently, they compose with recordings in mind. This leads to the manipulation of the recording devices that control and change the original sound as part of the compositional process.

To some people, listening to recorded music is more satisfying than listening to live concerts. For many people, listening to recorded music is also more convenient. As a result, there are many avid music lovers who rarely hear live music. Moreover, recordings are capable of almost perfect technical performance because all mistakes can be erased and repaired. This allows composers to expect perfect recorded performances, which has had a salutary effect on the expectations of live performances.

Following World War II, those countries that became part of the Communist bloc, such as Poland, Czechoslovakia, Hungary, Bulgaria, Rumania, and East Germany, were cut off from the leading musical trends of the second half of the century. This continued until the death of Stalin, after which some of the restrictions on artistic creativity were removed. The music of Western Europe, avant-garde and popular, was then introduced to Eastern Europe and was widely performed by east European artists. The composers of these countries, notably Poland, Rumania, and Czechoslovakia, became as representative of late twentieth-century Western music as the composers of Western Europe. The recent dissolution of the USSR and the Soviet bloc will inevitably affect musical developments throughout the Western world.

Another political change that has had an effect on music is the dissolution of great overseas empires, especially those of the British, Dutch, and French. As new nations acquired their own national identities, they began to cultivate their indigenous music and art. One outcome of this has been that the music of Africa and Asia has spread worldwide and exerts an influence on composers in many parts of the world. This new interest in diverse musical cultures resulted in a revival of many exotic musical practices, as well as a resurgence of interest in heretofore obsolete musical instruments, especially those of the Renaissance and Eastern cultures.

One final sociological development affecting music is the worldwide emphasis on teaching music in public schools, colleges, and universities. Creative and performing musicians have been appointed to their faculties, offering, in a way, creative artists and performers the patronage that musicians in the seventeenth and eighteenth centuries received from the church and the aristocracy. Among the composer-teachers of this period whose students in turn became noteworthy composers are the following. (The teachers' names are followed by their students' names in parentheses.)

Arnold Schoenberg (Alban Berg, Anton Webern)

Paul Hindemith (Norman Dello Joio, Ulysses Kay, Lukas Foss)

Olivier Messiaen (Pierre Boulez)

Nadia Boulanger (Louise Talma, Walter Piston, Elliott Carter, Aaron Copland, Virgil Thomson)

Ernest Bloch (Roger Sessions, Quincy Porter, Leon Kirchner, Douglas Moore)

II. FUNCTION OF MUSIC

Since the middle of the century there has been a particular emphasis on the employment of composers and performers as teachers in colleges and universities. This tradition has grown exponentially in the last half of this century. In addition, "Composers in Residence," whose responsibilities are exclusively to compose music, occupy positions in schools parallel to those who served in Renaissance and Baroque courts. The function of the composer in these situations is twofold: to provide instruction through precept and example to those who wish to compose, and to provide opportunities whereby the general university community can experience the music of contemporary composers.

Because many colleges and universities have resources in teaching and performance, they have become fertile ground for experimental and avant-garde composers. In fact, some of the most elaborate resources for electronic music are to be found in educational institutions. Moreover, educational institutions can also supply audiences that are eager to experience new sounds and techniques of composing and performance. In Europe, broadcasting studios have also been in the vanguard of this movement.

Special festivals and concert series organized for the purpose of presenting works of contemporary composers, especially the avant-garde, have multiplied since the middle of the century. Such festivals occur in many countries. In addition, there are festivals devoted to non-Western music, old and new. Some receive the sponsorship of universities and schools of music, governments, foundations, or individuals who give support to the composition and performance of music of the twentieth century. Important festivals are held in

Edinburgh, Scotland; Spoleto, Italy; Salzburg, Austria; and Aspen, Colorado. Central to the festival season in some cities is the production of opera. These include Bayreuth and Munich, Germany, and Santa Fe, New Mexico.

In this century, the number of cities in the United States that have developed opera companies has increased dramatically. Many of these opera companies produce far more operas from the traditional repertory than contemporary or experimental works. On the other hand, many European opera houses commit a portion of their effort to contemporary works. University workshops and opera studios provide some opportunity for contemporary opera in America.

During the second half of the twentieth century, the musical play has experienced some decline, despite the significant contributions of such composers as Stephen Sondheim and Andrew Lloyd Webber. In the same period, ballet has achieved a position of high importance in Europe and North America, where in addition to traditional classical movements, such a variety of expressive gestures and positions has developed that it is often called Modern Dance. The techniques developed by Martha Graham, Merce Cunningham, George Balanchine, Glen Tetley, John Cranko, and Jerome Robbins, all outstanding choreographers, have led to the composition of ballet music by contemporary composers.

In television there has not yet been an artistically satisfying union of music and media. European television and public television in the United States, however, broadcast numerous concerts and operatic performances that include contemporary works. These telecasts are for the most part adaptations of stage or concert presentations. Television offers a different avenue of communication that continues to challenge imaginative composers and directors.

III. STYLE AND PERFORMANCE PRACTICE

Following midcentury, experiments with twelve-tone technique and other forms of atonality continued, but by the 1980s there was a slackening interest in serial technique. Experimentalism flourished in the postwar atmosphere as imaginations ran rampant, employing unusual sound effects, unorthodox instruments, and new principles of construction. Advances in electronic tone production led to the development of sophisticated synthesizers used to create sounds of infinitely small pitch differential and tone color. As a reaction to these experiments, there has also been an increased interest in a kind of new Romanticism (neoromanticism) among some composers.

Formal Organization

Complete serial composition is the term that describes works that treat all the elements of music in serial fashion. These compositions are not formally organized around a tone row, but rather around the serial arrangement of all musical elements. Messiaen was a proponent of this genre.

A unique development in the second half of the twentieth century has been chance music, often referred to as *aleatory* or *indeterminate* music. In its written appearance it takes various forms, which necessarily affect the sound outcome in performance. In some instances a prose description of what is intended is all that is presented. In other instances, graphic or representational symbols suggest matters of pitch, timbre, or time. Sometimes actual musical passages are written in traditional notation, with the order of their presentation left to the performers. Some composers choose to control the temporal element and allow the performers to control the pitches. Other composers may choose a different pattern of freedom and control. Karlheinz Stockhausen's *Klavierstück XI* uses a type of indeterminacy by presenting nineteen musical fragments on a large piece of cardboard. The pianist is to play whatever fragment the eyes fall on, while following a few rules that suggest appropriate tempos and articulations. The piece is concluded when a fragment is played more than twice.

Minimalism is a musical development of the 1960s that has achieved broader acceptance in more recent decades. The origins of musical minimalism are found both in the music of Satie and Cage and in the visual art of such painters as Ad Reinhardt and the sculptor David Smith. Minimalist music employs such techniques as drones, static harmonies, and ostinatos, all repetitious devices. The composers most readily associated in America with minimalism are Terry Riley, Steve Reich, John Adams, and Philip Glass. Instrumental ensembles lend themselves well to the stylistic conventions of minimalism, and in the 1980s such composers as the Canadian, R. Murray Schafer, and the Estonian, Arvo Pärt, have written minimalist music for choir. Minimalist music from the world of opera includes Philip Glass's trilogy *Satyagraha* (based on the life of Gandhi), *Akhnaten* (based on the life of an Egyptian Pharaoh), and *Einstein on the Beach*. More recently, John Adams's *Nixon in China* and Bernd Alois Zimmerman's *Die Soldaten* have met with success.

Melody

Strictly speaking, in the more radical compositions since World War II, melody, as previously expressed, has nearly disappeared. Many contemporary compositions are devoted to displays of tone color and rhythmic complexity. This is true not only for electronic music but for many works written for traditional instruments as well. One development has been in the exploration of *multiphonics*, the simultaneous production of more than one tone by wind instruments or voices. This technique, based on pitch clusters, introduces significantly different tone colors as well. There has been a gradual movement away from the serial techniques that were so important earlier in the century.

Rhythm

The rhythmic complexities cultivated in the music of non-Western cultures have been influential in recent music. The rhythmic freedom of popular music has also had a significant influence on the art music of the twentieth century. Electronic composition makes it possible to create intricate rhythmic patterns and complexities that defy human performance. Such music exists primarily in recorded form.

Rhythm is sometimes emphasized to the extent that a total composition, or parts of a work, are made up of rhythmically enhanced sonorities that are lacking melodic significance and harmonic purpose. Free rhythms, such as were found in medieval and Renaissance music, are once more used. Bar lines are often omitted. Nontraditional meter signatures often indicate only the unit of measure—quarter note, eighth note, half note without designating the number of notes comprising a unit. In some more recent music, traditional metric units are no longer viable. Time is often measured by a stopwatch, or even left to the discretion of performers. In minimalism, the rhythms are highly repetitive, creating a hypnotic effect. Departures from these rhythmic ostinati can be so subtle as to become almost imperceptible.

Harmony

Traditional harmony is completely denied in some works, particularly those of electronic origin. The combination of different pitches is no longer based on their function within a tonal system but rather on independent patterns of tonal movement and the effect of massed harmonic colors. Hence, tones of different pitches are combined in clusters or constellations and not by any principle of tension set up by consonance and dissonance.

Texture

Sound blocks, clusters, or constellations replace voice leading. Such clusters can be transparent or thick and opaque, depending on the pitches selected and the number of tones in the cluster. In contrast to imitative counterpoint of earlier periods, a new kind of counterpoint persists in which each of several independent groups engage in a simultaneous presentation of individual material.

Instrumentation and Tone Color

Contemporary experiments with timbre have led to a revival of instruments that have long been neglected or infrequently used in art music. Such instruments as the harpsichord, guitar, mandolin, and a list of percussion instruments, such as the xylophone and tuned drums, are often used. In fact, percussion instruments receive greater attention, and their number and variety are greatly increased. Exotic instruments, especially those of India and Indonesia, have intrigued contemporary composers because they provide new sources of tone color.

Electronic sound synthesizers provide perhaps the greatest addition to the timbral resources of contemporary composers. These instruments can be used independently or can be used with more traditional instruments, sometimes even substituting for existing instruments.

Electronic instruments are capable of producing sounds of definite pitch that are rich in overtones, pure tones that are completely devoid of overtones, and white sounds. White sounds contain the entire spectrum of audible frequencies, just as white light contains all colors of the spectrum. By filtering out selected overtones, a variety of sound coloring is possible. Through such electronic manipulation, normal tone qualities of traditional instruments are distorted to create totally fresh sound experiences. This has been commonly employed in jazz and popular music. Variation in speed of recording is another means of achieving new tone colors. A tuba, for example, can be pitched at the level of a piccolo by accelerating the recording speed. Such new tone colors are achievable only through electrical or electronic means.

Performance Practice

Notation of modern music may be expressed in terms of graphs, charts, and symbols that are specifically defined for particular compositions. This practice of developing new notational symbols for specific compositions has become widespread. It has even led to the publication of books devoted to the topic of *devised notation.* To date there is little standardization of these symbols.

The rise of jazz as a vehicle for creative expression is an important phenomenon that had a strong influence on composers in the twentieth century. Its influence has been felt rhythmically, harmonically, timbrally, and through its improvisatory nature.

There has been a marked revival of interest in early instruments such as harpsichord, recorder, krummhorn, viol, lute, and guitar. This interest has been stimulated through amateur performance and music instruction in schools and colleges. *Early Music,* a scholarly journal published in England, is a response to the serious interest of amateur and professional musicians in preclassic music and its "correct" performance.

Many of the outstanding performers and conductors who were active during the time of the Second World War continue to flourish. The following list includes some of these people as well as the younger generation, who are widely known through concerts, recordings, television, and radio appearances.

Among the pianists are Glenn Gould (d. 1982), Emil Gilels (d. 1985), Sviatoslav Richter, André Watts, Vladimir Ashkenazy, Radu Lupu, Marta Argerich, Alfred Brendel, Murray Perahia, Andras Schiff, Maurizo Pollini, Mitsuko Uchida, and Alicia DeLarrocha. Sergei Prokofiev (d. 1953) and Leonard Bernstein (d. 1990) both gained fame as pianists and composers. Prominent violinists include David Oistrakh (d. 1974), Yehudi Menuhin, Isaac Stern, Itzhak Perlmann, Pinchas Zukerman, Gidon Kramer, and Anne-Sophie Mutter. Several cellists have international reputations as well: Gregor Piatigorsky (d. 1976), Lynn Harrell, Yo-Yo Ma, Janos Starker, and Mstislav Rostroprovitch, who for years directed the National Symphony Orchestra. Jean-Pierre Rampal and James Galway are flutists who are universally known. Among the outstanding singers of our generation are Joan Sutherland, Jessye Norman, and Elly Ameling, sopranos; Janet Baker, Marilyn Horn, Cecilia

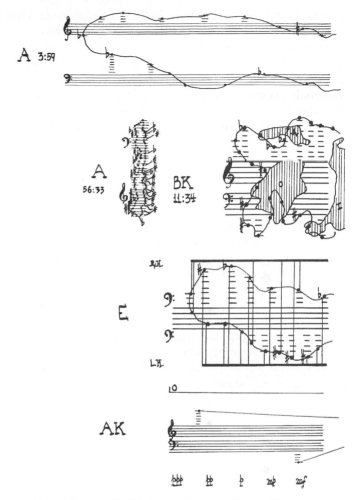

Nontraditional notation by John Cage. (© 1958 by Henmar Press Inc. Reprinted by permission of C. F. Peters Corporation.)

Bartoli, and Ann Sofie von Otter, mezzo-sopranos; Luciano Pavarotti, Placido Domingo, José Carreras, Ben Hepner, and Peter Schreier, tenors; and Dietrich Fischer-Dieskau, Sherill Milnes, Bryn Terfyl, and Dmitri Hvorostovsky, baritones; and Samuel Ramey, bass. The list of conductors includes several people who have also had careers as solo performers. Leonard Bernstein and André Previn head this list. Other conductors include Fritz Reiner (d. 1963), George Szell (d. 1970), Otto Klemperer (d. 1973), Eugene Ormandy (d. 1985), Herbert von Karajan, (d. 1989), Zubin Mehta, Seiji Ozawa, Bernard Haitink, and Sir George Solti. The list of the fine younger generation of conductors should include Christoph von Dohnányi, James Conlon, Michael Tilson

Thomas, Simon Rattle, Riccardo Muti, Claudio Abbado, Daniel Bärenboim, James Levine, John Eliot Gardiner, Nikolaus Harnoncourt, Phillipe Herreweghe, and Leonard Slatkin.

IV. MUSIC FOR VOICES

The vocal music of the Baroque is sometimes mildly criticized for its instrumental character. In the twentieth century, certain writing for voices is similarly criticized, but for somewhat different reasons. Successions of intervals that could be easily negotiated by instruments, often outside any tonal scheme, are demanded of singers. Compositions based on twelve-tone and aleatoric principles deprive singers of the orientation to a tonal center, which for many singers is almost essential. During this time, in solo and choral works, the voice is often freed from verbal considerations. Shouts, screams, and grunts are used. An entirely new and separate school of vocal production has evolved around "extended vocal techniques," and music is being written to utilize the new possibilities of sound derived from these. Pauline Oliveros, Morton Feldman, Meredith Monk, and other composers have experimented with these new sounds.

There continues to be vocal music written using the pitch conventions of twelve-tone and aleatoric techniques, but a noticeable return to the more comfortable tonality of neoromanticism has also occurred. This return to the harmonic vocabulary of late Romanticism is broadly based and reveals itself in a surprising variety of compositional styles.

Single-Movement Forms

Art Song

The art song, in individual and cyclic settings, continues to be a medium of choice for many composers. These composers wed the voice to a varied array of traditional and electronic instruments and often to poetry and prose of high quality.

The second half of this century has been fortunate to have a number of the finest song performers of all time. However, the song recital regrettably has declined in popular favor. Despite this, a substantial amount of recent song repertoire has become available to the public through recordings. (Ex. 9.1–9.9)

Choral Works

Choral writing during the second half of the century has been cast in virtually all of the experimental and traditional forms the period inherited. Writing for the church and schools has occupied some composers' time, and concert music has been in some demand. (Ex. 9.10–9.18)

The spirit of experimentation remains active even in sacred music, which has traditionally lagged behind the developments in other areas of musical composition. Few of the large religious works are appropriate for liturgical services. Often the liturgical music uses a style that might be called neo-baroque, an adaptation of contrapuntal style to the dissonant idioms of the twentieth century. (Ex. 9.19–9.28)

Composite Forms

Opera and Musical Theater

Opera continues to examine historic (*The Rake's Progress,* Stravinsky) and current (*La cubana,* Henze) themes. In the United States there has been a growing need for chamber operas capable of being produced with small forces and modest expenditures. The harmonic and timbral resources available to all composers in this century find their way into opera. There are also many works that have multimedia characteristics; works of an experimental nature that involve action, words, and other elements commonly associated with the theater. Musical theater flourished in the 1950s and 1960s in the United States, and has shown a resurgence of vitality in England in the 1970s and 1980s. The musical play is characterized by substantial spoken dialogue in the vernacular, music in the popular style of the day, and plots that vary from the historical to the contemporary and from the serious to the farcical. As the century has progressed, the rather artificial distinction between opera and musical play has become eroded further. European opera houses have for years offered musical plays in the same season with operas. With each successive year there appear to be fewer and fewer successful musicals. (Ex. 9.29–9.46)

V. MUSIC FOR INSTRUMENTS

Thus far, this book has followed the evolution of numerous set forms that continued from one period to another. In some degree this is possible with contemporary music, but not nearly to the extent possible in earlier chapters. For this reason the authors are abandoning some aspects of the previous outline in favor of a more general discussion of contemporary musical structures. Still, some composers use the traditional titles of the past, even when their music stretches the terminology in unexpected ways.

Traditional Genre

Among the forms and genre that continue to interest composers are the concerto, symphony, theme and variation, and ballet. The concerto principle has always been the exploration and contrast of unequal sound sources. That principle applies particularly well to the sound aspirations of contemporary composers and has resulted in numerous concertos in recent years. The terms *symphony* and *sonata* have always carried a certain ambiguity that has allowed composers great latitude in adapting them to their needs. At no time is this

A computer and sound synthesizer laboratory. (The Bettmann Archive)

more evident than today, when the term *symphony* has come to designate little more than a composition for a large number of instrumentalists on stage. Theme and variation continues to give composers opportunities to state something musically, and then explore the various mutations and transformations possible with that musical idea. Ballet and modern dance have prospered in this century, and ballet music has as well. As dance movements have changed, composers for the dance have explored a wide-ranging variety of appropriate musical sounds. (Ex. 9.47–9.61)

Nontraditional Musical Compositions Using Traditional Instruments

During the last three hundred years, the art of instrument making has given composers instruments of great versatility. These instruments are being used in new and unconventional ways, producing sounds that were never heard before. Such performance techniques as "prepared piano" in John Cage's *Sonatas and Interludes,* and multiphonics in Berio's *Sequenzas,* are the result of such experimentation. Concomitant with the experimental treatment of instruments is the experimental treatment of musical forms in which their sounds are presented free of historical antecedents. (Ex. 9.62–9.67)

Electronic Music

The first electronic compositions were created through the manipulation of sounds of common objects or musical instruments. The invention of the electronic synthesizer made it possible to create unique sounds, entirely independent of preexisting sources such as musical instruments, machines, and voices. In many works, traditional instruments and voices are combined with taped recordings of electronically produced sounds or with live sounds generated by synthesizers. Musical compositions have also been created by programming computers to produce unique sounds. One of the stranger effects of the use of computers for composition is that humans can be programmed out of the compositional process. This is done by giving the computer the capacity to produce numerous musical events, and then giving it the added capacity to determine the sequence of events without intervention.

Television frequently employs electronically generated sound as background for dramatic performances, the presentation of station signatures, and advertising. More often than not, this use of electronic music seeks anonymity by using these techniques in an almost conventional way. (Ex. 9.68–9.72)

VI. COMPOSERS

As acknowledged several times previously, the roots of virtually every movement since World War II are plainly discernible in the first half of the century. For example, many of the characteristics of electronic music (new tone colors, terse themes, extreme pitch ranges, microtonal pitches, and total serial construction) on which much emphasis has been placed since 1950, were already present in the works of Varèse, Webern, Habá, Stravinsky, Cage, Partch, and many others.

(Any of the following composers whose names are identified by an asterisk have already been discussed to some degree in the previous chapter.)

Ralph Vaughan Williams * continued writing in his typically English style, adding three symphonies and an opera, *The Pilgrim's Progress.*

Igor Stravinsky * adopted the serial technique only after 1950. One such work is his music for the ballet, *Agon.* Another is *In Memoriam—Dylan Thomas,* for tenor, string quartet, and trombone quartet, based on a five-note tone row. His opera of 1951, *The Rake's Progress,* is based on a libretto by Auden and Kallman, whose inspiration was Hogarth's engravings of the same name. (Ex. 9.20, 9.31, 9.53)

Edgar Varèse * moved strongly into electronic music with his *Deserts,* which is for fourteen winds, pianoforte, five percussion instruments, and two-track tape. Its dates are 1950–1954, and it was revised at least three times. Another composition, *Poème electronique* (1957–1958), is for three-track tape.

*Sergei Prokofiev** continued to write prolifically after the war, although he was severely censured by the Soviet government. As a result he remained sufficiently conservative in his compositions to accommodate the tastes of the Soviet government. One such orchestral composition is *The Meeting of the Volga with the Don River,* written in 1952.

*Darius Milhaud** is remembered not only as a composer, but as a teacher of composition in Europe and the United States. Like Stravinsky and others, he wrote a composition commemorating the assassination of John F. Kennedy, *Murder of a Great Chief of State* (1963).

*Paul Hindemith** became an American citizen in 1946, and thereafter conducted and taught in the United States and abroad. His *Symphony in B flat for Concert Band* premiered in 1951. The *Concerto for Organ and Orchestra* is one of his last compositions.

*Roger Sessions** made a strong contribution through his compositions, essays, and teaching. His cantata, *When Lilacs Last in the Dooryard Bloom'd,* was written between 1967 and 1970. He wrote eight symphonies, seven of which premiered after 1947.

*Ernst Krenek** continued to write experimentally in his later years. Representative works are *Aulokithara,* for oboe, harp, and tape, Op. 213a (1971); *Spätlese,* Op. 218, a song cycle written in 1973; and *They Knew What They Wanted,* for narrator, oboe, piano, and percussion, Op. 227 (1976–1977).

*Aaron Copland** was for years recognized as the Dean of American composers. One of his early postwar works is the song collection *Twelve Poems of Emily Dickinson* (1948–1950). More recent compositions are *Connotations* (1962) using the twelve-tone technique and an orchestral work, *Inscape,* in 1967.

Luigi Dallapiccola (1904–1975) was the foremost of the modern Italian composers. He combined dodecaphonic technique with Italian tradition of vocal line in a very expressive fashion. His masterful adaptation of the twelve-tone system to lyrical expression is well illustrated in *Canti di liberazione* (Songs of Liberty, 1951–1955), a set of choral songs, and in his opera *Il Prigioniero* (The Prisoner). A number of chamber works employing voice and instruments of various kinds are also noteworthy. (Ex. 9.2, 9.23, 9.56)

Michael Tippett (1905–) is an English composer whose texted music shows a deep interest in social issues. His compositional style is characterized by a continuing emphasis on vigorous rhythms and luminous textures, with harmonies that go beyond the late nineteenth and early twentieth centuries without embracing serialism. The oratorio, *A Child of Our Time* (1944), based on American Negro spirituals, is his most popular work in this country. His opera, *The Midsummer Marriage* (1952), continues to be performed thirty years after its premiere at Covent Garden. (Ex. 9.26, 9.35)

*Dmitri Shostakovitch** excelled in instrumental music but very often included vocal solos and choruses in his large symphonic works, including several of his last symphonies. (Ex. 9.1)

Louise Talma (1906–), French by birth and American by adoption, was educated in both countries. Her early compositions are based on neoclassical

Aaron Copland conducting. (The Bettmann Archive)

principles, but after 1950, twelve-tone techniques began to appear in her compositions, albeit primarily in a loosely defined tonal context. The *Piano Sonata No. 2* (1944–1955) shows her stylistic movement in this direction. *Let's Touch the Sky* (1952), a work for choir and woodwind trio, expresses the freshness and energy of the poem by e. e. cummings. In 1974 she was selected to become a member of the National Institute of Arts and Letters, the first female composer to be so honored.

Olivier Messiaen (1908–1992) was a French composer, theoretician, and organist who pioneered in the area of *total serialism,* a serial organization of sounds, durations, dynamics, and articulations. In his efforts to find new effects he made use of exotic percussion instruments, generators, and bird calls, of which he was particularly fond. His importance as a theoretician can be noted through the works of his students such as Boulez, Stockhausen, and Nono. Among his important compositions are *Réveil des oiseaux* (1953), *Oiseaux exotique* (1955–1956), and *Catalogue d'oiseaux* (1956–1958). (Ex. 9.21, 9.66)

Elliott Carter (1908–) is an American composer whose music is concerned with contrapuntal texture and with rhythm and meter as form-building elements. His works are infused with modal counterpoint, though he has made use of a personal type of twelve-tone technique. In some works he employed a system of *metric modulation,* whereby he has been able to modulate from one speed to another by changing the rhythmic values of the basic units. Carter is not a prolific composer, but his works are refined. His *Variations for Orchestra* (1955); *String Quartet, No. 2* (1959); the *Double Concerto for Harpsichord, Piano and Two Chamber Orchestras* (1961) are typical of his output. More recent works include *In Sleep, In Thunder,* six poems by Robert Lowell (1981), and *Changes, for Solo Guitar* (1983). (Ex. 9.47, 9.61)

John Cage (1912–1992) was an American composer whose ruminations concerning sound and whose radical tendencies in composition have expressed themselves in the derivation of new tone colors. One such experiment involved preparing the piano by placing on the strings of the instrument such objects as paper, erasers, and screws. For such a "prepared piano" Cage wrote *Sixteen Sonatas* and *Four Interludes.* He has also experimented in the area of aleatoric or random composition in, for example, *Imaginary Landscape, No. 4* (1951). In this work, twelve radios, dialed according to predetermined wavelengths, give forth whatever is presently being programmed. (Ex. 9.57, 9.64, 9.65)

Benjamin Britten (1913–1976), perhaps the most eminent of the twentieth-century British composers, wrote for many musical genres, but achieved worldwide recognition through his operas and choral works. Britten's style was essentially vocal. He was clearly a classicist in his approach to composition and consequently was not interested in the Wagnerian idea of endless melody, but rather espoused the principle of closed forms. He was not an adherent of any set method or technique of composition, but was influenced by a number of composers in whose individual styles he found elements of interest. His operas include *The Rape of Lucretia* (1946), *Peter Grimes* (1945), *Albert Herring* (1947), *Billy Budd* (1951), and *A Midsummer Night's Dream* (1960). Two of his well-known choral works were written aboard ship during World War II—*A Ceremony of Carols* (1942) and *Hymn to St. Cecilia* (1942). A more dramatic work involving far larger performance forces is the *War Requiem* (1962), which combines texts from the Latin requiem with poems by Wilfred Owen, who was killed during World War I. Britten's song cycles are among the most important contributions to twentieth-century vocal music. These include the *Canticles* (various dates) and *Phaedra* (1970), one of his last vocal works. Not least of his compositions, and illustrative of his love for the variation form is the very popular *The Young Person's Guide to the Orchestra.* (Ex. 9.3, 9.10, 9.18, 9.24, 9.29)

Witold Lutoslawski (1913–1994) was a composer whose early concern with twelve-tone technique gave way to more recent practices, including electronic composition. He has been widely recognized as one of the most significant of the modern Polish composers. He composed principally for orchestra and chamber music ensembles. Among his best-known works are his First and Second Symphonies (1941–1947, 1966–1967), and *Paroles tissées* (1965) for tenor and chamber orchestra. The daring of his music can be seen in *Trois poèmes d'Henri Michaux* for choir, wind instruments, percussion, two pianos, and harp (1963), which requires two separate conductors using different scores.

Milton Babbitt (1916–) is an American composer whose mathematical genius contributed to his exploration of the relationships between music and mathematics, even to the point of adapting mathematical vocabulary to music. His music is characterized by a strict adherence to serial technique, and he has a long-term interest in sound synthesizers and computer music. *Philomel* (1964) combines tape with live performance. Much of his music is cerebral and nearly inaccessible to the average listener. (Ex. 9.5)

Ulysses Kay (1917–), an important African American composer and teacher, may be best known for the film score of *The Quiet One* (1948). Kay wrote for instrumental ensembles of all sizes, and for various vocal combinations. His latest opera is about the American abolitionist *Frederick Douglass* (1980–1985).

George Rochberg (1918–), an American composer, combines twelve-tone influences with a logical harmonic style into a singularly personal idiom. For a decade he wrote extensively using the serial technique, concluding that period with the *Piano Trio* (1963). His compositions cover a wide range of instrumental and vocal forms. He has also published a number of articles dealing with the problems of twelve-tone composition. Rochberg taught at the University of Pennsylvania. A number of his works employ quotations from other composers from the sixteenth to the twentieth century, such as Schütz, Bach, Mahler, Ives, Boulez, and Varèse. Among his works are five symphonies, a violin concerto, seven string quartets, and a recent opera, *The Confidence Man* (1982).

Leon Kirchner (1919–), an American composer, teacher, and brilliant pianist, came under the influence of Schoenberg in his early musical studies. Later he studied with Ernest Bloch. These men influenced him greatly, but he never adopted a system from either of them. His music fluctuates between highly chromatic and atonal idioms. Whether the medium is the orchestra, the piano, or the string quartet, his music is known for its motoric drive. It is imbued with an intensity of expression that is almost exhausting in its demands on the listener. Kirchner's importance in the midcentury musical scene of America is demonstrated by the large number of awards and commissions he received, including the New York Music Critics' Circle Award, the Naumburg Award, and a Pulitzer Prize for his third string quartet, written in 1967. His *Concerto for Piano and Orchestra* (1953), *Sinfonia* (1951), and *String Quartet No. 1* (1949) are representative of his finest writing. His vocal music has included a song cycle and an opera. (Ex. 9.60)

Lukas Foss (1922–), an American, began his compositional career as a neoclassicist. After approximately 1960, his interest in improvisation led him to explore various aspects of indeterminacy. *Time Cycle* (1960), for soprano and orchestra, has been recorded and enjoys considerable success. His

Baroque Variations (1967) plays on compositions by Handel, Scarlatti, and Bach. (Ex. 9.55)

Iannis Xenakis (1922–) was born in Greece but has lived in the United States and Paris. He was a student of Messiaen and was also associated with the architect Le Corbusier. His music is structured on the principles of mathematical probability (stochastic principles) in terms of traditional instruments and traditional notation. His interest in the aesthetics of music and mathematics led him to establish Centers for Musical Mathematics and Automation, first in Paris and then in Bloomington, Indiana, where he taught for a time. His important works include *Pithoprakta,* for fifty instruments (1955–1956); *Achoripsis* (1956–1957); *Stratégie,* for two small orchestras (1959–1962); *Metastasis* (1953–1954) for orchestra; and *Eonta* (1963–1964) for piano and brass. A sizable list of works for tape, and still others, for which a computer is helpful in performance, is also included among his compositions. (Ex. 9.63)

György Ligeti (1923–) was born in Hungary but later became a naturalized citizen of Austria. His activities have taken him into almost all European countries as well as the United States. He has been associated with the Studio for Electronic Music in Cologne and is one of the leaders of the International Courses for New Music in Darmstadt. His early works, published in eastern Europe prior to his departure from Hungary in 1956, are mostly simple, folk-derived works. His later works are characterized by an emphasis on color and masses of sound. To achieve this he employs all varieties of noisemakers, as well as electronically generated sounds. His compositions, however, have exploited all musical media, from the organ and string quartet to the symphony orchestra, as well as small and large vocal ensembles. Among his works are *Volumina,* for organ (1961–1962); *Requiem,* for solo voices, chorus, and orchestra (1963–1965); and *Lux aeterna,* for sixteen solo voices (1966). In several compositions Ligeti has made critical comments about contemporary compositions. One such composition is his *Poème symphonique* (1962) for one hundred metronomes all operating at different speeds. (Ex. 9.14)

Luciano Berio (1925–), Italian composer of the avant-garde, developed an interest in electronic music after his first visit to the United States. He has frequently combined performances with electronic tapes. His most significant works show a deep concern for music combined with gesture and dramatic action. *Circles* (1960), a setting of poems by e. e. cummings for voice, harp, and percussion instruments, is designed for visual and spatial realization. Berio's further involvement with music and dramatic action, as well as the relation between words and music, is illustrated in his opera *Passaggio* (1961–1962), and the composition *Visages* (1961), a taped composition using both electronic and vocal sounds. Many of these compositions were written for his wife, Cathy Berberian. *Recital I (for Cathy, 1962)* includes a tour de force catalogue of vocal and dramatic styles. (Ex. 9.7)

Pierre Boulez (1925–), a twentieth-century French composer, developed a complex style of serial composition in which, like Messiaen, his teacher, he employs serialization of pitches and durations (totally controlled music). He has also explored electronic music. The best-known work of Boulez is *Le Marteau sans maître* (The Hammer Without a Master), written between 1952 and 1954 and revised in 1957. The unusual instrumentation of contralto, flute in G, viola, guitar, vibraphone, and percussion is indicative of his concern with tone color, particularly with that created by percussion instruments. As a conductor, Boulez has been an active participant in festivals of contemporary music. During his tenure as conductor of the New York Philharmonic he championed serial music, and continues to do so.

Hans Werner Henze (1926–) is a German composer active in all fields of composition. His early works showed a mastery of the twelve-tone technique, which he later utilized in a manner that appealed more readily to the larger audience. He has been particularly successful in operatic composition. Many of his operas are intended to convey strong social and sometimes Marxist messages. Such works as *Der junge Lord* (1965) and *Der Prinz von Homburg* (1960) have had great success. A year spent teaching and writing in Cuba influenced the social focus of his writing. (Ex. 9.39, 9.59)

Thea Musgrave (1928–), a native of Scotland, matriculated at Edinburgh University and later studied composition with Nadia Boulanger. Her compositional style mixes serial writing with more conservative practices. Attention was first drawn to her in the United States through her operatic works, most notably *Mary, Queen of Scots* (1976). She has written concerti for a number of instruments, and her film scores are numerous. (Ex. 9.41, 9.72)

Karlheinz Stockhausen (1928–) is a German composer who has given most of his attention to electronic music, although he started his career as a disciple of Webern, using conventional instruments. *Kontra-Punkte* (1953), for ten solo instruments, is a representative work of this period. Another phase is represented by *Klavierstücke XI* (1956), a work constructed on the basis of random selection and improvisatory treatment of nineteen notated fragments. In 1988 he wrote the fourteenth of his *Klavierstücke*. The best known of his electronic compositions is *Gesang der Jünglinge* (Song of the Youths, 1955–1956, revised for four-track tape in 1956), which is written for voice and electronic sound generator. The notation of such music in graphs and geometric figures precludes any performances by other than those persons tutored in reading such notation. Much of his work embraces "open" form, leaving many decisions to the performers, as in *Mixtur* (1964). The electronic equipment employed by Stockhausen, and those associated with him at the Northwest German Radio Studio in Cologne, did not attempt to imitate the sounds of conventional instruments. The sounds produced by signal generators and electronic synthesizers were exploited for their intrinsic value as new sounds. Much of Stockhausen's music includes a theatrical element, utilizing space and movement, as in *Momente,* written in 1961 and revised several times.

George Crumb (1929–), an American composer, combined study at American universities with study in Berlin. His compositions reflect a tendency

Thea Musgrave (© Martha Swope/Time, Inc.)

to relate traditional formalities with very extreme demands on technical resources. Exceptional combinations of electronic instruments and conventional instruments, as well as electrically amplified instruments, result in extraordinary tonal effects. This interest in unusual sound qualities demands that his vocal forces sing microtonal intervals, shriek, hiss, whisper, and produce other non-traditional vocal sounds. Works such as *Night of the Four Moons,* for alto flute, banjo, electric cello, and percussion (1969); *Songs, Drones and Refrains of Death,* for baritone, electric guitar, electric double bass, electric piano, and percussion (1968); and *Lux aeterna for Five Masked Players,* for soprano, bass flute, sitar, and two percussion players (1971) are representative of Crumb's interest in such sound effects. In addition to writing for groups of instruments with vocalists, he has written extensively for piano. *Zeitgeist* (1988) is for two amplified pianos. An *Idyl for the Misbegotten* (for amplified flute and three percussionists, 1986) combines electronically altered and traditional sounds. Crumb is on the faculty of the University of Pennsylvania.

Sofia Gubaïdulina (1931–) is a prolific Russian composer whose popularity has grown enormously, especially in the post-Soviet years. Her works
draw on her Jewish and Russian heritage and demonstrate a great independence of imagination and solidity of technique. Her recorded works include
Hommage à T. S. Eliot for Octet and Soprano (1987) and *Offertorium*
(Concerto for Violin and Orchestra, 1980).

Henryk Górecki (1933–) is a Polish composer whose star seems to be in
the ascendency. Eclectic in his techniques, his works that include voices have
received special recognition. *Symphony No. 3* (Symphony of Sorrowful Songs,
1976) for soprano and orchestra has been performed and recorded widely.

Krzysztof Penderecki (1933–), whose compositions are represented by
various instrumental and vocal combinations, is perhaps the most widely
known of today's Polish composers. He has developed a style that is quite
original and independent of any of the fixed systems of the twentieth century.
His works allow a certain amount of freedom to improvise for the performer,
which is only governed by specific time limits. He has achieved novel tonal
effects in the use of traditional orchestral instruments in his well known
Threnody for the Victims of Hiroshima (1960). The *Passion According to St.
Luke* (1962–1965) is one of the most impressive choral works of the twentieth
century. Likewise, the opera *The Devils of Loudon* (1969) is a powerfully dramatic work. His best-known recent work is *A Polish Requiem,* which premiered in 1984. (Ex. 9.16, 9.25, 9.28, 9.49, 9.50, 9.62)

R. Murray Schafer (1933–) is a Canadian composer and pedagogue
occupied with the exploration of the nature and potential of physical sounds.
His compositions range from chamber music of unusual instrumentation to
operatic and symphonic pieces employing electronic music as well as
aleatoric devices. Among his many compositions are a *String Quartet*
(1970); *North/White,* for orchestra (1973); and *Apocolypsis,* for five hundred
performers (1976). A composer with a sense of humor, his *Son of
Heldenleben* (1968) quotes and manipulates the music of Richard Strauss.
His more serious side is revealed in *Threnody* (1966), which uses the words
of Japanese children who survived the bombing of Hiroshima. With a grant
from the Donner Foundation, he studied the relationship of people worldwide and the sounds that surround them. Schafer has a compelling interest
in language, and its use and misuse in communication is a source of his
musical inspiration.

Peter Maxwell Davies (1934–) is an English composer whose works are
characterized by controlled improvisation and by an abundance of styles and
idioms, from Renaissance polyphony to complete serialism. Some of his
important works are the *Saint Michael Sonata* (1957), *Eight Songs for a Mad
King* (1969), and the *Second Fantasia on Taverner's "In Nomine,"* (1964).
Since 1970, Davies has lived in the Orkney Islands, where he has written many
works based on Scottish and English themes. Like Schafer, he has written
music for children. (Ex. 9.11)

Alfred Schnittke (1934–), a Russian composer, has written prodigiously for traditional orchestral instruments and ensembles. Many of his works bear standard names such as concerto, concerto grosso, sonata, and symphony. His style contrasts moments of clarity and order with moments of disintegration and chaos. It also shows the influence of such symphonists as Bruckner, and of Russian folk song. He enjoys international popularity among great performers, and is represented on recordings with an extended catalogue. The *Concerto for Viola and Orchestra* (1985) has been particularly well received. Despite recent ill health, he has continued to compose a remarkable quantity of music, including his *Symphony No. 8,* completed in 1994.

Arvo Pärt (1935–), was born in Estonia, and has lived in Germany in recent years. Prior to 1986 his works were predominantly serial. Since then his writing, especially the vocal works, reflects his deep religious feelings in compositions that exhibit the influence of medieval music in a usually succinct and personal contemporary style. His works include *Passio Domini nostri Jesu Christi secundum Joannem* (1982), *Sarah Was Ninety Years Old, Cello Concerto* (1983), *Stabat Mater* (1985), and *Litany* (1995). (Ex. 9.19)

Philip Glass (1937–), American minimalist, has studied with many of the important teachers in the United States and France. His travels in India, as well as his work with Ravi Shankar, have certainly influenced his movement in the direction of minimalism. He is probably best known in this country for his film score for *Koyaanisqatsi* (1981). This work is illustrative of his collaborative artistic efforts with filmmakers and visual artists of all kinds, as is *Einstein on the Beach* (1976). (Ex. 9.42)

Ellen Zwillich (1939–) is an active American composer whose talent has been recognized with many grants and commissions, including grants from the National Endowment for the Arts and a Guggenheim Fellowship. Two of her recent works are a flute concerto (1990) and an oboe concerto (1991). She received a Pulitzer Prize in 1983 for her *Symphony No. 1: three movements for orchestra.*

Judith Zaimont (1945–) enjoys increasing importance, especially for her solo vocal and choral music. Recognition of her abilities in the setting of texts has been acknowledged through the commissions of such professional choral ensembles as the Gregg Smith Singers and the Western Wind. Additionally, she has written successfully for various chamber ensembles and for the piano. (Ex. 9.9)

Schulamit Ran (1949–), an Israeli composer, studied piano and composition at the Mannes College of Music in New York. She has taught at the University of Chicago. Her music is basically atonal, and sometimes includes electronic sources. The *Symphony No. 1* (1990) was premiered by the Philadelphia Orchestra. (Ex. 9.51)

ADDITIONAL COMPOSERS

A. Argentina
    Alberto Ginastera (1916–1983)
    Mauricio Kagel (1931–)
    Mario Davidovsky (1934–)
B. Austria
    Johann N. David (1895–1977)
    Hans Jelinek (1901–1969)
    Hans F. Apostel (1901–1972)
    Gottfried von Einem (1918–1996)
C. Belgium
    Henri Pousseur (1929–)
D. Canada
    Harry Somers (1925–)
    John Beckwith (1927–)
E. Czech Republic
    Václav Dobiáš (1909–1978)
    Karel Husa (1921–)
    Jindřich Feld (1925–)
    Oldřich Flossman (1925–)
F. Denmark
    Vagn Holmboe (1909–)
    Niels Viggo Bentzon (1919–)
G. England
    Arthur Bliss (1891–1975)
    Elisabeth Maconchy (1907–1994)
    Elizabeth Lutyens (1909–1983)
    Peter Racine Fricker (1920–1990)
    Robert Simpson (1921–)
    Harrison Birtwistle (1934–)
    Oliver Knussen (1952–)
    Dominic Muldowney (1952–)
    Robert Saxton (1953–)
H. Finland
    Joonas Kokkonen (1921–)
    Einojuhani Rautavaara (1928–)
I. France
    Jean Françaix (1912–)
    Jean Martinon (1920–1976)
J. Germany
    Werner Egk (1901–1983)
    Boris Blacher (1903–1975)

Wolfgang Fortner (1907–1979)
Bernd Alois Zimmerman
    (1918–1970)
K. Greece
    Yannis Papaioannau (1910–1989)
    Dimitri Terzakis (1930–)
L. Hungary
    Matyas Seiber (1905–1960)
M. Italy
    Bruno Maderna (1920–1973)
    Luigi Nono (1924–1990)
    Sylvano Bussotti (1931–)
N. Japan
    Yasushi Akutagawa (1925–1989)
    Toshiro Mayuzumi (1929–)
    Toru Takemitsu (1930–1996)
    Yori Aki Matsudaira (1931–)
O. Mexico
    Rodolfo Halffter (1900–1987)
    Blas Galindo (1910–)
P. Netherlands
    Henk Badings (1907–1987)
    Ton de Leeuw (1926–)
    Peter Schat (1935–)
Q. Norway
    Klaus Egge (1906–1979)
    Finn Mortensen (1922–1983)
    Arne Nordheim (1931–)
R. Poland
    Kazimierz Serocki (1922–1981)
    Tadeusz Baird (1928–1981)
    Boguslaw Schaeffer (1929–)
S. Russia
    Tikhon Khrennikov (1913–)
    Georgi Sviridov (1915–)
    Edison Denisov (1929–1996)
    Giya Kancheli (1935–)
T. Slovak Republic
    Jan Cikker (1911–1989)
U. Spain
    Carlos Surinach (1915–)
    Cristóbal Halffter (1930–)

V. Sweden
    Lars-Erik Larsson (1908–1986)
    Karl-Birger Blomdahl (1916–1968)
    Bo Nilsson (1937–)
    Jan W. Morthenson (1940–)
    Sven-David Sandstrom (1942–)
W. Switzerland
    Rolf Liebermann (1910–)
X. Ukraine
    Leonid Grabovsky (1935–)
    Valentin Silvestrov (1937–)
Y. United States of America
    Roy Harris (1898–1979)
    Randall Thompson (1899–1984)
    Otto Luening (1900–)
    Harry Partch (1901–1974)
    Richard Rodgers (1902–1979)
    Marc Blitzstein (1905–1964)
    Norman Lockwood (1906–)
    Halsey Stevens (1908–1989)
    Samuel Barber (1910–1981)
    William Schuman (1910–1992)
    Alan Hovhaness (1911–)
    Vladimir Ussachevsky (1911–1990)
    Gian Carlo Menotti (1911–)
    Ingolf Dahl (1912–1971)
    Hugo Weisgall (1912–)
    Norman Dello Joio (1913–)
    Vivian Fine (1913–)
    Vincent Persichetti (1915–1987)
    David Diamond (1915–)
    Lou Harrison (1917–)
    William Bergsma (1921–)

    Peter Mennin (1923–1983)
    Daniel Pinkham (1923–)
    Ned Rorem (1923–)
    William Kraft (1923–)
    Gunther Schuller (1925–)
    Earle Brown (1926–)
    Barney Childs (1926–)
    Emma Lou Diemer (1927–)
    Donald Erb (1927–)
    Dominick Argento (1927–)
    Donald Martino (1931–)
    Pauline Oliveros (1932–)
    Morton Subotnik (1933–)
    Roger Reynolds (1934–)
    Terry Riley (1935–)
    Steve Reich (1936–)
    David Del Tredici (1937–)
    William Bolcom (1938–)
    John Corigliano (1938–)
    Joan Tower (1938–)
    Charles Wuorinen (1938–)
    Barbara Kolb (1939–)
    Doris Hays (1941–)
    Meredith Monk (1942–)
    Victoria Bond (1945–)
    Beth Anderson (1950–)
    Libby Larsen (1950–)
Z. Yugoslavia
    Milko Keleman (1924–)

VII. HISTORIANS AND THEORISTS

Arnold Schoenberg (1874–1951) was known as a teacher and theorist as well as a composer. His most important literary work, *Harmonielehre* (1911), appeared in English as *Theory of Harmony* (New York, 1948). In this work, as well as in subsequent English volumes, Schoenberg discussed his theory and aesthetics of music. *Style and Idea* (New York, 1950) and *Structural Functions of Harmony* (New York, 1954) are two volumes among a large number of articles and monographs by Schoenberg.

Igor Stravinsky (1882–1971) delivered a series of lectures at Harvard which were subsequently published under the title *Poetics of Music* (Cambridge, 1947). In them he discussed his own musical aesthetics as well as the musical aesthetics of a number of other composers, past and present. A later series of six volumes under the title, *Conversations with Igor Stravinsky,* were written in collaboration with Robert Craft and discuss all manner of musical questions, particularly those concerning modern music.

Rudolf Reti (1885–1957), a Serbian by birth, lived most of his life in the United States and wrote several books, the most important is *Tonality-Atonality-Pantonality* (New York, 1958), which was published after his death.

Howard Hanson (1896–1981) was a composer, conductor, and teacher. His influence on the musical life of the United States has been very great, especially because of his position at Eastman School of Music. His book, *The Harmonic Materials of Modern Music* (New York, 1960), gives a midcentury view of music theory.

Roger Sessions (1896–1985) was actively engaged in university teaching for most of his life. His keen, analytical mind and his long years of experience as composer and teacher prompted him to write several books. *The Musical Experience of Composer, Performer, Listener* (Princeton, 1950) and *Reflections on the Music Life in the United States* (1956) are two important works dealing with then-current problems in music.

Theodor Wiesengrund Adorno (1903–1969) was a German philosopher, musicologist, and composer. Adorno championed the new composers of the twentieth century, particularly those of the Schoenberg school, and wrote profusely concerning the relation of music and society. Among his many works are *Einleitung in der Musiksoziologie* (Frankfurt, 1949) and the *Philosophie der neuen Musik* (Tübingen, 1949). The latter, his most important contribution, an excursion into dialectic, shows how the antagonism of the social condition, along with ruling consciousness, hinders composers from achieving self-expression.

Felix Salzer (1904–1986), an Austrian-born musical theorist, had been in America since 1940. His two-volume work, *Structural Hearing, Tonal Coherence in Music* (New York, 1952; an unabridged and corrected edition by Dover Publications, New York, appeared in 1962) is based on Heinrich Schenker's conception of tonality and musical coherence.

John Cage (1912–1992), in his writings and lectures, was a major influence in twentieth century music. *Silence* (1961), one of his publications of essays and lectures, urges that people break down the distinctions between life and art, and enjoy life as it is.

Milton Babbitt (1916–) was attracted throughout his career to the second Viennese school and its descendents. His writings combine his interests in mathematics and twelve-tone technique, based on vocabulary borrowed from other disciplines. Among them are *The Function of Set Structure in the Twelve-tone System* (1946), *Twelve-tone Invariants as Compositional Determinants* (1960), and *Twelve-tone Rhythmic Structure and the Electronic Medium* (1962).

Leonard B. Meyer (1918–) is an American musicologist and aesthetician. A student of the humanities and musical composition, he has written many articles and several books on aesthetic issues. Among his books are *Emotion and Meaning in Music* (Chicago, 1956) and *Music, the Arts and Ideas* (Chicago, 1967). He also collaborated with Grosvenor Cooper on a volume *The Rhythmic Structure of Music* (Chicago, 1960).

George Rochberg (1918–), a teacher and composer, has written extensively about music in the twentieth century, especially about twelve-tone or serial music. Many of his essays first appeared in the *Journal of Music Theory* and *Perspectives of New Music*. In 1955 *The Hexachord and Its Relation to the Twelve-tone Row* appeared in print. *The Aesthetics of Survival: A Composer's View of Twentieth-century Music* (1984) is a collection of his essays, edited by the composer William Bolcom.

Iannis Xenakis (1922–) has always been interested in the connection between mathematics and music, as reflected in his writings—*Wahrscheinlichkeitstheorie und Musik* (1956) and *Elements of Stochastic Music* (1960–1961).

Pierre Boulez (1925–) has written on a wide variety of musical topics, with an emphasis on twentieth-century music. Most of these essays have appeared in such journals as *The Listener* (England), *Darmstädter Beiträge zur neuen Musik* (Germany), and *Nouvel observateur* (France). In 1978 Boulez became the director of IRCAM, an institute in Paris that specializes in the study of electronic and computer music and in electronic instrument building.

Andrew Porter (1928–) was for many years the music critic for the *New Yorker* magazine. As such, his critical reviews are of major consequence, both to contemporary performers and composers. Many of his critical essays have been published in book form. In 1991 Porter returned to England, where he is the music critic for *The Observer.*

Other historians of note from this period include Carolyn Abbate, Meg Bent, Howard Mayer Brown, Margot Fassler, Phillip Gossett, Richard H. Hoppin, Joseph Kerman, Roger Parker, Harold Powers, Paul Henry Lang, Charles Rosen, Stanley Sadie, Maynard Solomon, and Richard Taruskin.

The Beatles (AP Wide World Photos, Inc.)

10

Jazz and Popular Music of the Twentieth Century

1958	*Michael Jackson* (1958–)	1979	*Frank Zappa,* Joe's Garage, vol. 1–3
1961	*Wynton Marsalis* (1961–)	1980	*Rap movement emerges*
1963	*Early Beatles tours*	1982	Michael Jackson's album, *Thriller;* best-selling album of all time
1967	*Beatles,* Sgt. Pepper's Lonely Heart's Club Band	1984	*Bruce Springsteen,* Born in the USA
1969	*Woodstock Festival*	1996	*Jerry Garcia,* founder of the Grateful Dead, died
1975	*Elton John,* Captain Fantastic		
1976	*Punk Rock emerges*		
1978	*Disco becomes popular*		

I. SOCIOCULTURAL INFLUENCES ON POPULAR MUSIC

The first nine chapters of the *Outline History of Music* dealt with an historical account of the development of the art music of the Western world. This chapter is concerned almost exclusively with popular music in the United States. Besides the countless musical examples that constitute the evidence of such a history, there has always been a comparably large amount of information about performers, composers, styles, and locations.

Any attempt to define popular music in a strict sense will fail because the border between popular and art music is often indistinguishable. The term *popular* is used here to denote music that is more immediate in its perception and appreciation, whereas art music normally demands more study and reflection. It also denotes music that is more readily accessible to the general public. Popular music and art music can evoke responses from the simple and immediate to the complex and analytical. Under no circumstance is the difference between art and popular music to be construed as a difference in quality. At best, popular and art designations are only attempts at describing differences of compositional style, performance practice, and function.

Popular music was almost entirely unnotated until the nineteenth century. Its record is fragmentary, depending on two sources: the oral tradition and its incorporation in notated art music. Illustrations and accounts of folk song and dance give evidence of the existence of popular music from earliest times, but it was not until the nineteenth century that any real attempt was made to collect and notate such music.

During the second half of the nineteenth century, popular folk music was being collected and published, and began to be a commercial success. Songs and dances were being written and published for the general public by such composers as Stephen Foster. The market was flooded with popular tunes as unnamed composers created folk music. Copyright laws were established to protect composers, and production of sheet music increased. The twentieth century saw the widespread dissemination of popular music through mass printing and the electronic media. "Tin Pan Alley" refers to the places in New York City where popular sheet music was being published until the 1940s.

The social and political upheavals resulting from the two world wars, and concomitant technological developments, spread popular culture, including music, throughout the world. An increase in the pervasiveness of popular music in the twentieth century can be attributed to the following: (1) the development of electronic media of all kinds: radio, sound recordings, motion pictures, and television; (2) the dissemination of popular music by means of these media; (3) the possibility of commercial profit from the sale and distribution of popular music; and (4) the discovery, by entrepreneurs, of a substantial disposable income controlled by the youth of the world. All of these have resulted in the production of popular music in quantities never before seen.

Without attempting to reconstruct the many details of its development, an account of the popular music of the twentieth century seems justifiable because of its widespread acceptance, sociological significance, and musical implications. It appears that the spread of twentieth-century popular music is of a magnitude never before experienced.

II. FUNCTION OF MUSIC

Many of the functions of popular music are the same as they have been throughout history: to entertain, to dance to, and to express love. Some functions, however, are now either greatly intensified or are peculiar to the present. Ragtime was a style of popular music at the turn of the century which was primarily associated with the piano but was also performed on other instruments and was employed for singing and dancing. In the decades that followed, larger ensembles evolved that were almost exclusively intended to accompany dancing. This period, between 1930 and 1945, may be referred to as the "big-band era." The waltz and polka craze of the nineteenth century yielded to the foxtrot, two-step, Lindy Hop, Charleston, and more recently the twist, the monkey, and disco.

After World War II, the interest in popular music turned from dance to entertainment in concert settings. One expression of popular music—rock— employed loud volumes, throbbing rhythms, and stroboscopic lighting.

The acclaim of performers, as in so many periods of history, became an important element in the success of individual musicians and groups. The adulation of such stars and groups as Frank Sinatra, Elvis Presley, The Beatles, The Grateful Dead, Elton John, Madonna, Michael Jackson, and Bruce Springsteen has exceeded that accorded military and political heroes of the past.

The ubiquitousness of movies, recordings, and television, and the more recent development of satellite communication, has made it possible for music to reach a worldwide audience. Miniature radios and "boom boxes" have made music, and especially popular music, an easily portable and nearly constant part of daily life, especially among youth.

Singing Saints, 1940, Sargent Johnson. Lithograph, 18.25 × 15.5 in. (framed). (Collection of the Oakland Museum of California. Gift of Arthur C. Painter)

III. STYLE AND PERFORMANCE PRACTICE

Popular music by its very nature is not given to large forms. The many forms employed by composers of popular music are marked by their variety. The song is the basic single-movement form, and the composite form is a series of varied presentations of the single unit or a mingling of two or more different units. In the last two decades, and even before that in the works of certain composers such as Kenton, Ellington, and Brubeck, forms of longer duration have become much more prevalent.

In many cases there is no real division between vocal and instrumental compositions in popular music. In many instances, vocal and instrumental performances are combined. Song tunes are readily and frequently adapted to become instrumental works, and sometimes they acquire an independent life in the new form. Popular music of the twentieth century encompasses a great variety of music, including folk, gospel, jazz, country and western, rock music, and all their permutations.

It is generally accepted that jazz originated in the late nineteenth and early twentieth century in New Orleans. This occurred because of the mixture of African, French, and Spanish influences stemming from the Creole and French portions of what had been the Louisiana Purchase. These peoples treasured their music and wanted to keep alive the sounds of their cultures. This amalgamation of cultural differences, which also included the influence of African American church music and the use of instruments common to Civil War military bands, resulted in an exotically romantic popular music.

Other features of this music that derived from non-European traditions were its improvisatory style, its unnotated, or oral tradition, and its relation to the practice of call-and-response. The forms and length of popular music were influenced by such diverse factors as the form of Civil War marches and the technology surrounding sound production. For example, the ten-inch, 78 RPM recording disc could accommodate no more than approximately three minutes of music per side. Thus, many early popular songs were limited to that duration.

Blues

The term is difficult to define with precision. In the broadest sense it represents music that originated among African American people of the South as an outgrowth of their sorrow songs. The blues have both the ingredients of pain and humor; pain at the many indignities of life one must suffer, and sufficient humor to make that pain bearable. W. C. Handy played a significant role in codifying the blues, which have a common poetic form (AAB), a distinctive yet fluid scale, and a harmonic progression that was widely but not consistently used. There are times when the only thing that identifies these songs as "blues" is the title. The blues normally are based on a regular twelve-bar pattern with a free interpolation of both words and music. Performers suggested their feelings by manipulating various pitches of the scale, most often the third and seventh degrees, and by altering the timbre of the singing voice.

Country or folk blues were the expression of rural southern African American people, usually accompanied on a folk instrument by the male singer. In contrast, urban blues ultimately moved into popular entertainment, including recordings and stage performances. Blues singers were both male and female, accompanied by ensembles of mixed instruments.

Blues have existed for so long that they are frequently cited as one of the forerunners of jazz. Although modified frequently, they remain a vital part of popular music today, currently known as blues, rhythm and blues, or soul.

Scott Joplin (1868–1917) (The Bettmann Archive)

Ragtime

Ragtime, one of the earliest forms of African American popular music, was performed almost exclusively on the piano. Later it took on orchestral form. The first published "rag" appeared in 1897, from which time it developed concurrently with New Orleans jazz. Unlike many forms of popular music, it was soon more precisely notated, although not necessarily performed exactly, thereby reducing an essential characteristic of jazz, namely, improvisation. Its earliest development was associated with African American song. Later it was related to dance. The dissemination of rags was promoted through piano rolls and solo performers. Rags were virtually always in moderate tempo in duple meter, and were characterized by strong syncopations over a regular rhythmic beat in the bass. Its form was rather predictable. The greatest composer of ragtime was Scott Joplin.

New Orleans Jazz

The city of New Orleans is frequently identified as the birthplace of jazz, although it was emerging in other localities as well. Early New Orleans jazz was characterized by a type of free counterpoint most often played by three instruments: clarinet, trombone, and trumpet, with the trumpet as the dominant or "lead" instrument. These instruments were supported by a rhythm section of drums, tuba (later string bass), and piano or banjo (later guitar). The music was more or less improvisatory, with the trumpet stating the melody and being accompanied by the other instruments in their own variations of the melody. In jazz, the saxophone was originally a novelty instrument, but it came into its own in the jazz of the 1920s. The earliest recordings of jazz were made in 1917.

Dixieland

Earlier jazz was largely the province of African Americans and creoles, but white bands came on the scene with what is generally known as Dixieland jazz. It was through this movement that jazz went north to Chicago and New York. Dixieland became popular about the time of World War I. It was in 1917 that the first recordings were made of Dixieland jazz. Stimulated by the

Louis Armstrong (1900–1971) (The Bettmann Archive)

Dixieland style, young white high-school and college students developed what was known as the Chicago style of jazz, usually called two-beat jazz.

Swing

Swing came into its own in the early thirties, and soon became the dominant style of jazz. Between 1935 and 1945, jazz and swing were almost synonymous. It introduced substantially larger bands and a four-beat style with a more even emphasis on all four beats of the measure. Most of the music was heavily arranged. Benny Goodman, Count Basie, Duke Ellington, and Jimmie Lunceford were among the most important big-band leaders. These big bands provided important opportunities for many outstanding soloists. The orchestra and soloists, many of them trained instrumentalists, combined to produce the big sounds that typify the style. It is a style that pits the solo against the larger ensemble in much the same manner as the concerto grosso of the seventeenth century.

Bop (Bebop)

By the end of the thirties, swing had become a big business in popular music. As so often happens, there was soon a movement to turn away from the established style, which had with time become cliché-ridden. The new style, an essentially black movement called "bebop," originated in New York City. As a reaction to swing, it rejected the set format of the large band and sought an outlet for personal creativity in small combos. Among the distinguishing musical characteristics of bop are extreme tempos, changing rhythms, unequal phrase lengths, and unpredictable starting and stopping places for the phrases. The impression given by the music of bebop was that of an excited, improvisatory style with melodic fragments—not a sustained melodic line—and active rhythms.

Cool Jazz

During the fifties, jazz entered a period of greater restraint in reaction to the intricacies of bebop, which immediately preceded it. The new style was referred to as "cool jazz." Although there was still improvisation, it emphasized long,

"Duke" Ellington (1899–1974) (© Bob Coyle)

linear melodies and eschewed the extreme registers of the instruments. It was a jazz influenced by European style, with advanced harmony and rhythmic writing. Dotted and disconnected rhythms were replaced by predominantly even, legato notes. The melodic rhythm lagged behind the beat rather than pushing ahead as in bebop styles. Among the leaders of this style were Stan Getz and Miles Davis. In the late 1950s a related style, modal jazz, created the effect of exoticism through the use of modal scales and harmonies.

Free Jazz

The atonal innovations of art music encountered the freedom of jazz in the 1960s in a movement called "free jazz." Atonality appeared in concert music almost fifty years earlier. Free jazz led to the disintegration of beat, meter, and symmetry as it explored the realm of the aleatoric. It also incorporated some aspects of non-Western music from such regions as India, Africa, and the Far

East. There was an intensity of sound that bordered on the ecstatic and frenetic, especially in the performances of Ornette Coleman and John Coltrane.

Rock

If there was any single revolution in twentieth-century popular music, it began in the 1950s with Rock and Roll, with its origins in rhythm and blues. It was more commonly referred to in the 1960s and thereafter as rock. It is generally characterized by an amplified, hard rhythmic beat, and simple, throbbing harmonic patterns. Rock lyrics include references to sex, drugs, and social and political rebellion. The loud volume of the music, central to the aesthetics of rock, left no place for acoustic instruments in rock bands. Consequently they were replaced by electric guitars, electric pianos, synthesizers, and countless other electronically controlled instruments.

This movement has enjoyed an extended period of success. Its adherents have explored an unusually wide variety of sounds, resulting in numerous movements and names such as Heavy Metal, Acid Rock, Grunge, Punk, and Pop Rock. Some of these sounds are so extreme that the music seems to achieve its purpose through some degree of ugliness and vulgarity. If classicism is viewed as order and restraint, romanticism may be viewed as a move from order toward freedom and even chaos. On that continuum, it could be argued that rock music is the epitome of the romantic.

Rock music continues to be controversial. It has, however, in many ways moved into mainstream American music. In 1985, then Senator Al Gore's wife, Tipper, encouraged the government to regulate rock albums with a rating system. Rap became a strong part of popular American culture, accepted by white and black, urban and suburban youth in 1988. In 1990 the Heavy Metal group, Judas Priest, was sued in civil court, when the parents of two young men claimed that the album *Stained Class* was responsible for the suicide deaths of the men. The case was thrown out of court. In 1991, the alternative album *Nevermind* by Nirvana opened mainstream radio to Grunge Rock. In 1992, at President Clinton's Inaugural Ball, Fleetwood Mac's *Don't Stop* was played.

Country and Western

Country and western music is a uniquely American expression originally based on a romantic vision of rural and western life. Some of those themes continue to be used, while more modern examples deal with the vicissitudes of country life. In performance it consists, even today, of a relatively unsophisticated vocal style and simple accompaniments. The vocal line is commonly supported by violin, string bass, and guitar. In recent years, country and western music has been influenced by other popular music while preserving its traditional topics and instrumentation. Nashville, Tennessee, the home of Grand Ole Opry, has become the mecca of the country and western style. Its performers are subject to adulation in the same way as other popular musicians. It is possible that the

Cats. A musical play by Andrew Lloyd Webber. (© Carol Rosegg/Martha Swope/Time, Inc.)

dramatic increase in popularity of country and western music in the last two decades is in part a reaction to the excesses of rock.

Bluegrass

This style of country music springs from the rural areas of the south, especially Kentucky and its neighboring states. Bluegrass depends on such acoustic instruments as the banjo, guitar, and the violin, played in the fashion of old-time fiddlers. Melodies are derived from Appalachia and adjacent regions of the south, with influence from the folk music of the British Isles. An immediately apparent feature is its rapid tempos.

Musical Theater

One of the most successful musical forms of this century in England and America is the so-called musical play or Broadway musical. These developed from the European operetta, vaudeville, and even burlesque, and typically include solo songs, ensembles, and dances. Plots could be tightly constructed or practically nonexistent. In the 1920s and 1930s these musicals achieved great success and were the sources of much popular music. In recent decades musicals have become extravagant technical productions featuring technologically advanced visual and aural effects. Early preeminent composers of this genre include Jerome Kern, George Gershwin, and Richard Rogers. Andrew

Lloyd Webber's *The Phantom of the Opera,* and Claude-Michel Schonberg's two works, *Miss Saigon* and *Les Misérables* are more recent hits. One of the most successful composers is Stephen Sondheim, who had five musicals playing simultaneously on the West End in London during the summer of 1996. His *Sweeney Todd* (1979) is almost operatic in style.

IV. MUSICAL COMPOSITIONS

Comprehensive lists of popular music are beyond the scope of this book. However, the following list of popular songs represents a much longer list of music that has enriched the lives of many people.

1900–1910
Bill Bailey, Won't You Please Come Home? Hughie Cannon (1902)
Some of These Days, Shelton Brooks (1910)
Give My Regards to Broadway, George M. Cohan (1904)

1911–1920
Alexander's Ragtime Band, Irving Berlin (1911)
St. Louis Blues, W. C. Handy (1914)
Rock-a-bye Your Baby With a Dixie Melody, Jean Schwartz, Sam Lewis,
  Joe Young (1918)

1921–1930
April Showers, Louis Silvers, Muddy DeSylva (1921)
Stardust, Hoagy Carmichael, Mitchell Parish (1929)
Ain't Misbehavin', Thomas "Fats" Waller, Harry Brooks, Andy Razaf
  (1929)

1931–1940
As Time Goes By, Herman Hupfield (1931)
Sophisticated Lady, Edward "Duke" Ellington, Mitchell Parish, Irving
  Mills (1933)
Over the Rainbow, Harold Arlen, E. Y. Harburg (1939)
How High the Moon, Nancy Hamilton, Morgan Lewis (1940)

1941–1950
Don't Sit Under the Apple Tree, Les Brown, Charlie Tobias, Sam H.
  Stept (1942)
Sentimental Journey, Bud Green, Les Brown, Ben Homer (1944)
On the Atchison, Topeka and the Santa Fe, Johnny Mercer, Harry
  Warren (1945)

1951–1960
I Could Have Danced All Night, Alan Jay Lerner, Frederick Loewe
  (1956)
Seventy-Six Trombones, Meredith Willson (1957)
Satin Doll, Johnny Mercer, Billy Strayhorn, "Duke" Ellington (1958)

1961–1970
Yesterday, John Lennon, Paul McCartney (1965)
Hello, Dolly! Jerry Herman (1963)
Raindrops Keep Fallin' on My Head, Hal David, Burt Bacharach (1969)
Bridge Over Troubled Waters, Paul Simon, Art Garfunkel (1970)

1971–1980
Send in the Clowns, Stephen Sondheim (1973)
Evergreen, Barbra Streisand, Paul Williams (1976)
One, Marvin Hamlisch, Edward Kleban (1975)
Shadows in the Moonlight, Rory Bourke, Charlie Black (1979)

1981–1990
Memory, Andrew Lloyd Webber, Trevor Nunn, T. S. Eliot (1981)
Hello Again, Neil Diamond, Alan Lindgren (1980)
We Are the World, Michael Jackson, Lionel Ritchie (1984)

Similarly, many albums represent the music of certain performers, composers, or styles. Some examples follow.

Swing: *Carnegie Hall Concert,* Benny Goodman (1938); *Carnegie Hall Concert,* "Duke" Ellington (1943)

Bop: *Greatest Jazz Concert Ever,* Charlie Parker, "Dizzy" Gillespie, Charles Mingus, Bud Powell, Max Roach (1953)

Cool Jazz: *Kind of Blue,* Miles Davis (1959); *Take Five,* Dave Brubeck (1955)

Modern Jazz: *Giant Steps,* John Coltrane (1959)

Free Jazz: *The Shape of Jazz to Come,* Ornette Coleman (1959)

Jazz-Rock: *Bitch's Brew,* Miles Davis (1969)

Rock: *Sgt. Pepper's Lonely Hearts Club Band,* Beatles; *The Magic of ABBA* (1980)

V. COMPOSERS, ARRANGERS, AND PERFORMERS

Scott Joplin (1868–1917) is America's most famous composer of Ragtime. Although best known for his "rags," he was the first American to write a significant opera, *Treemonisha.* His best-known composition is *Maple Leaf Rag.* The 1974 film, *The Sting,* with its hit tune *The Entertainer,* brought a renewed interest in Ragtime as a musical style.

Edward Kennedy "Duke" Ellington (1899–1974) began his musical career as a Ragtime musician. He is probably the most important composer in jazz history. *Mood Indigo* and *Caravan* are among his many early works of enduring importance. In addition to his extensive compositions for jazz band, Ellington wrote for the stage and films. His creation of "sacred concerts" and works in symphonic style brought the jazz idiom to the symphony orchestra.

The Three Black Kings was written in that style, and was completed by his son after his death. In the 1940s he became a proponent of the Swing movement, continuing to conduct a big band. He performed on virtually every continent, and in 1969 received the Presidential Medal of Freedom.

Louis "Satchmo" Armstrong (1900–1971) was the single most important performer in jazz history. His combo, the "Hot Five," was one of the most successful bands of the late 1920s. He took solo performing to a new level of virtuosity, using special effects and a personal expressive style. In his later years he became known as America's Musical Ambassador. One of his great vocal hits was "Hello Dolly."

Billie Holiday (1915–1959) is likely the most important female singer in jazz history. Her style was warm and intense and is documented in a series of recordings made between 1936 and 1944. Two of her best numbers were *He's Funny That Way* and *All of Me.*

Ella Fitzgerald (1918–1996), probably the most important female jazz singer since World War II, began her singing career in New York when she was sixteen. As a soul singer she performed with most of the important bands of her time. She had an unusual gift for improvisation which led to her reputation as the best of the "scat" singers. Early in her career she recorded *A-tisket, A-tasket,* one of her signature tunes.

Elvis Presley (1935–1977), the American baritone, used his natural rich voice to express intense emotional themes. He became one of the central figures of Rock and Roll, and enjoyed a successful though short career in popular music. Among his many hits are *Heartbreak Hotel, Blue Suede Shoes,* and *Love Me Tender.*

Many of the artists of popular music were simultaneously composers, arrangers, and performers. It seems practical to list them in terms of the styles of music with which they were involved. Because of their large number, the authors make no attempt to be inclusive. Only those who seem to be most influential have been listed. A number of these people were involved in more than one style, but they appear where they have had their greatest importance.

Blues:
Huddy (Leadbelly) Ledbetter, Blind Lemon Jefferson, B. B. King, W. C. Handy, Mamie Smith, Ma Rainey, and Bessie Smith.

Ragtime:
Scott Joplin, Joseph Lamb, Ferdinand "Jelly Roll" Morton, Eubie Blake, and Thomas "Fats" Waller

New Orleans Jazz:
W. C. Handy, "Jelly Roll" Morton, Sidney Bechet, Bunk Johnson, Jack Teagarden, and King Oliver

Dixieland:
Louis Armstrong, Bix Beiderbecke, Fletcher Henderson, Duke Ellington, and Earl "Fatha" Hines

Swing:
Louis Armstrong, Duke Ellington, Woody Herman, Harry James,
  Tommy Dorsey, Benny Goodman, Gene Krupa, Charlie Barnet, Count
  Basie, Artie Shaw, and Glenn Miller

Bop (Bebop):
Dizzy Gillespie, Thelonious Monk, Lennie Tristano, Charlie Parker, and
  Charlie Mingus

Cool Jazz:
Gerry Mulligan, Stan Getz, Lester Young, Lennie Tristano, Miles Davis,
  Dave Brubeck, and the Modern Jazz Quartet

Free Jazz:
John Coltrane, Ornette Coleman, Miles Davis, and John Lewis

Rock:
Bill Haley, Elvis Presley, Beatles, Jefferson Airplane, The Who, Rolling
  Stones, Blood, Sweat & Tears, Grateful Dead, Stevie Wonder, Little
  Richard, Elton John, and Michael Jackson

Country and Western:
Jimmy Rodgers, Hank Williams, Chet Atkins, Patsy Cline, Glenn
  Campbell, Johnny Cash, Charley Pride, Loretta Lynn, Roger Miller,
  Bobbie Gentry, Anne Murray, Dolly Parton, Kenny Rogers, Garth
  Brooks, and Crystal Gayle

Bluegrass:
Earl Scruggs, Lester Flatt, William "Bill" Monroe, and the Osborne
  Brothers

Musical Theater:
Victor Herbert, Cole Porter, Jerome Kern, George Gershwin, Richard
  Rodgers, Frederick Loewe, Jerry Herman, Andrew Lloyd Webber, and
  Stephen Sondheim

In addition to the aforementioned jazz and popular artists, following are a
number of gifted popular songwriters: Vincent Youmans, Irving Berlin, Hoagy
Carmichael, Frederick Loewe, Alan Lerner, Cole Porter, Jerome Kern, George
Gershwin, Sammy Cahn, John Lennon, and Burt Bacharach.

The best-known singers of popular music in the twentieth century include
the following: Al Jolson, Bessie Smith, Bing Crosby, Billie Holiday, Ethel
Merman, Ella Fitzgerald, Frank Sinatra, Nat "King" Cole, Aretha Franklin,
Elvis Presley, Barbra Streisand, Michael Jackson, Bruce Springsteen, and
Madonna.

Appendix 1

Musical Instruments

I. STRINGS

A. Bowed Strings

Rebec: A stringed instrument introduced into Europe from Arabia around the tenth century. It has a long neck with a small round or pear-shaped body, usually with three strings. It is played with a loosely haired bow and has a nasal timbre. The rebec was an ancestor of modern bowed string instruments.

Viols: A large group of bowed string instruments in use from the Gothic through the Renaissance and Baroque periods. The viols differ from the violin family in that (a) they had deeper ribs, (b) the shoulders sloped from the neck, (c) the number of strings was generally six but might be more or less, (d) frets were placed on the fingerboard, (e) the bridge was quite flat, enabling the playing of chords, (f) the viol bow stick was convex and held palm up, and (g) the instruments were held on or between the legs of the performer. The viol tone quality was light and somewhat nasal. Viols were made in various sizes: bass, tenor, alto, and discant (soprano). The revival of viol playing in the twentieth century has been generally concerned with the tenor instrument that was the model used for solo performance in the works of Baroque composers.

Violins: The modern bowed string instruments date from the early Baroque. The most important members of the family are the violin (soprano), the viola (alto), the violoncello (tenor), and the contrabass or bass viol, the latter taken over from the viol family and often built in that form. The most famous makers were Italians, dating from the seventeenth and eighteenth centuries. Among them were Gaspar da Salo, Amati, Stradivari, and Guarneri, who made Cremona famous as the center for violin construction.

The violin, viola, and cello are all four-stringed instruments tuned in fifths. The bass viol retains the tuning in fourths of the viol family. The bow used in playing instruments of the violin family differs from the earlier bow in its curvature in relation to its hair. It is held with the palm down, except for the bass viol, for which both bowing styles are still in use. The violin and viola are held on the shoulder, the cello and string bass in a modified vertical position, resting on the floor. The tone of the violin family is of a rich, sweet quality rivaling that of the human voice.

B. Plucked String Instruments

Harp: One of the oldest known instruments. It was used by civilizations c. 3000 years B.C. It appears in various forms among all folk peoples. The modern instrument (double harp) was invented by Erard in 1810 and by use of pedals is capable of a complete chromatic scale of six octaves. While already called for by composers of the sixteenth century, the harp as a solo and orchestral instrument made its appearance in the nineteenth century.

Psaltery: An ancient instrument, found throughout the world in one form or another. It has a flat soundboard over which a number of strings are stretched. The strings are plucked by both hands of the performer.

Lute and Guitar: Plucked string instruments that are held in the lap. They have fretted fingerboards of varying lengths and numbers of strings. Strings are fingered with the left hand and plucked by the right. Lutes are characterized by pear-shaped bodies. The guitar is a flat instrument, the body of which in other respects has somewhat the shape of the violin.

The lute was the most important instrument of the Renaissance. Players of virtuoso capacity encouraged a large literature to be written. The introduction of keyboard instruments resulted in the decline and eventual disappearance of the lute. The guitar, because it was more easily played, became very popular in the seventeenth century and has remained so to the present day. The lute has been revived in the twentieth century due to renewed interest in Renaissance and Baroque music.

Harpsichord: Includes a large variety of instruments in which the strings are plucked by a set of plectra attached to key levers. The key levers are arranged like the keys of the modern piano, and when depressed, the plectra pluck the strings, resulting in a sound very much like that of the lute or harp. Harpsichords were built in various shapes and sizes and given various names such as clavicembalo, cembalo, clavecin, virginal, and spinet. It is well to remember that the harpsichord mechanism was not the forerunner of the piano action. It could be regarded more reasonably as a mechanized lute or harp.

C. Struck Strings

Dulcimer: Includes a variety of psaltery whose strings are struck by small hammers held in the hand rather than plucked. In this manner it becomes the forerunner of the piano.

Clavichord: A small keyboard string instrument, usually in the form of a rectangular box in which metal wedges attached to keys strike the individual strings. The placement of the wedges determines the length of the vibrating strings and, therefore, their individual pitches. The tone is very soft, and the instrument was often used in the household for teaching and practice purposes. The clavichord might be thought of as a mechanized dulcimer.

Pianoforte: A popular instrument invented by Cristofori in 1709. It is a string instrument in which the strings are sounded by the striking of a set of felted hammers attached to keys. Improvements in the mechanical construction of the piano have been concerned with the various intricacies of the key and hammer action, the construction of the sounding board, and the frame of the instrument upon which the strings are stretched. The full name of the pianoforte was an indication that this instrument could play both loudly and softly, and indeed could sustain a tone without having to keep the keys depressed. Unlike earlier keyboard instruments, this could be accomplished because of its action and the use of sostenuto and damper pedals.

II. WIND INSTRUMENTS

A. Woodwinds
Non-Reed Woodwinds

Flute: One of the oldest and most widespread of all instruments. The flute appears in a variety of shapes and sizes. Both the whistle or recorder type as well as the transverse type were known in earliest times and used simultaneously throughout music history. The transverse type consists of a tube of wood or metal closed at one end, with a side hole across which the player blows. A number of finger holes enable the performer to play the entire chromatic scale. Modern flutes are made of metal and are fitted with a refined mechanism that enables rapid technical performance and accuracy of pitch. In addition to the more common soprano flute, there is the very high-pitched piccolo and the alto and bass flutes.

Recorder: Recorders are of the flute family and are fitted with mouthpieces into which the performer blows. They were made of wood and at one time were preferred to the transverse flute, which largely replaced them about 1750. In the twentieth century the recorder was revived with great enthusiasm by the interest in Renaissance and Baroque music. Because of limited range, recorders are made in various sizes and designated as sopranino, soprano, alto, tenor, bass, and contrabass.

Obsolete and Folk Flutes: The ocarina is a globular flute, usually made of clay, with an embouchure hole and finger holes. The syrinx or pan pipes is a set of individual closed pipes, bound together, that can be sounded by blowing over the open ends.

Single Reeds

Clarinet: A cylindrical pipe of wood with a bell-shaped opening at the lower end and a beaklike mouthpiece at the upper end, to which is attached a single reed of cane. The breath of the player activates this reed and, with the aid of holes and keys, can produce a wide range of pitches as well as distinctly varied tone colors in the several registers of the instrument. The modern clarinet dates from the early eighteenth century. The fingering mechanism was greatly improved in the nineteenth century. The clarinet is made in several sizes: E flat (very high), B flat (most common), A, E flat alto, B flat bass, and B flat contrabass.

Saxophone: A family of single reed instruments that consist of conical metal pipes. Soprano (B flat), alto (E flat), tenor (B flat), baritone (E flat), and bass (B flat) constitute the usual members of the family. They were invented by Adolphe Sax in the middle of the nineteenth century. The alto and tenor saxophones are especially used in jazz and symphonic bands. A wide variety of tone qualities is possible with all types of saxophones.

Double Reeds

Oboe: A conical pipe made of wood and fitted with a double reed at the upper end. Its timbre is reedy and nasal. The modern instrument, which made its appearance in the middle of the seventeenth century, is highly mechanized. The reed is held directly by the lips of the performer, who therefore has considerable control over the tone quality.

English Horn: An alto oboe, longer than the oboe, fitted with a pear-shaped bell at its lower end, and with the reed attached to a bent tube. It produces a rich, muffled, soft sound.

Oboe da caccia and Oboe d'amore: Baroque alto oboes that have been largely replaced by the English horn. These oboes are occasionally used in the performance of Baroque music.

Shawm: A family of double reed instruments, forerunners of the oboe. Shawms were commonly used until the seventeenth century. The tone was very strident, and the instruments were particularly used for outdoor music. Its mechanization was minimal.

Bassoon: The bass instrument of the modern double reeds. It has not changed materially from its earlier predecessors in shape or fingering. Its long wooden pipe is doubled upon itself, enabling the player to finger the instrument with comparative ease despite its great length. It has a large range and serves as a very agile bass instrument. The *contrabassoon* can reach the lowest-pitched notes of all orchestral instruments.

Dulzian: The forerunner of the bassoon. It was made in a number of sizes, and differed from the bassoon in that it was made of a single block of wood.

Crumhorn, Rauschpfeif, and Kortholt: Instruments of various sizes and shapes with encapsulated double reeds. The double reed was covered by a wooden cap into which the performer blew. The resulting wind pressure activated the reed. The range of these instruments was very limited, since they could not produce harmonics by overblowing.

B. Wind Instruments with Cupped Mouthpieces (Brass Instruments)

These instruments, originally made of wood or animal horns, were later made of various metals. The instruments were fitted with cupped mouthpieces; the performer set the column of air into vibration with the lips pressed against the cupped shape of the mouthpiece. The single column of air could only sound the natural overtones of the fundamental pitch of the pipe. Early instruments solved this problem in two ways. One was by boring holes in the pipe that could be covered or opened as in a flute, and the other was by the use of a slide mechanism in metal trumpets and trombones. The introduction of valves in the nineteenth century enabled all brass instruments to play the entire chromatic scale.

Trumpet: The high-pitched metal tube with a cupped mouthpiece comes pitched variously: B flat, A, E flat, and C. By the addition of three valves, either piston or rotary, the modern trumpet, with its brilliant tone, has become a versatile instrument. The *cornet* is a variant of the trumpet. Its shorter length and longer conical section give it a less brilliant tone than that of the trumpet.

Horn (French Horn):   A conical metal tube wound into a spiral and played with a funnel-shaped mouthpiece. Because of its narrow bore, its playable natural tones enabled it to be one of the most versatile brass instruments even before the invention of valves. Its tone is rich and suited to solo work. It blends with other brasses and with the woodwinds.

Zink or Cornetto: Wooden tube with a cup-shaped mouthpiece and fitted with finger holes. These Renaissance and Baroque instruments were made in various sizes: soprano, alto, tenor, and bass. The latter was shaped like a letter and called a serpent. It continued to be used into the nineteenth century, when it was replaced by the modern valved tuba.

Trombone: A lower-pitched brass instrument most generally fitted with a slide mechanism, which enables the performer to shorten or lengthen the tubing and thereby play the entire chromatic scale. It has maintained its form since the fifteenth century. The predecessors of trombones were known as sackbuts and had a smaller and less brilliant tone quality due to the smaller bore of the tube and mouthpiece. Two sizes of modern trombones are generally in use today, the tenor and bass. Some use is also made of a valve trombone in brass bands.

Tuba: The largest and deepest sounding instrument of the brass family. Conically bored, it is played with a cup-shaped mouthpiece. Tubas come in various sizes, allowing them to play in different ranges. The most common are the tenor, bass, and double bass.

C. Organ

The organ is a wind instrument consisting of many individual pipes that are activated by wind from a wind chamber. By the use of keys connected to the wind chest either mechanically or electronically, the performer can cause different pipes to speak. Through the various shapes, the addition of metal reeds, and the combination of pipes, tone qualities characteristic of the organ itself and of various orchestral instruments are available. Organs vary in size from the small portative (movable) organ of the Renaissance, consisting of a single set of pipes, to the large nineteenth-century instruments with several thousand pipes and several manuals. Other instruments using the principle of the wind organ are the *regal, bagpipe, accordion,* and *harmonium.*

III. PERCUSSION

A. Instruments with Indefinite Pitch

Drums, Tabor, and Tambourine: These instruments are found among all peoples in all shapes, sizes, and in all periods of history. Those of indefinite pitch vary from very high (*snare drum*) to very low (*bass drum*). All consist of wooden or metal frames over which

membranes are stretched. They are played with the hand or by striking with wooden or metal sticks.

Cymbals, Gong, Castanets, Triangle, Tam-tam, and others: Along with numerous other sound generators, these are all instruments of a single fixed pitch or sound quality made of metal or wood. Some are struck with hammers or rods, as in the case of the *gong* and *triangle*. Others are self-sounding, like the *castanets* or *cymbals.*

B. Instruments with Definite Pitch

Timpani (Kettledrums): The name given to the drum whose membrane is stretched over a large metal, kettlelike form. They can be tuned within a limited range. They are the most important orchestral percussion instruments.

Glockenspiel, Bells, Xylophone, Marimba, Celesta, and others: These tuned bars of metal or wood form several chromatic octaves and can be played with various types of hammers: wood, metal, or rubber. The celesta is played by means of a keyboard.

IV. ENSEMBLES

In the course of music history the constituency of some musical ensembles has become standardized. There are many exceptions to the instrumentation of these common ensembles, but the following groups are frequently encountered.

> String trio: violin, viola, violoncello or two violins, violoncello
> Piano trio: piano, violin, violoncello
> String quartet: two violins, viola, violoncello
> Piano quartet: piano, violin, viola, violoncello
> Woodwind quintet: flute, clarinet, bassoon, oboe, horn

Brass quintet: two trumpets, horn, trombone, tuba

Piano quintet: piano, two violins, viola, violoncello

String quintet: two violins, two violas, violoncello; or two violins, viola, violoncello, string bass; or two violins, viola, two violoncellos

String sextet: two violins, two violas, two violoncellos

Septet: various combinations of wind and stringed instruments

Woodwind octet: two clarinets, two oboes, two bassoons, two horns or other combinations.

There are several seating arrangements for symphony orchestras. One of the most common arrangements follows:

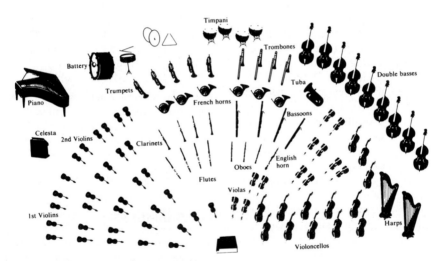

An orchestral seating plan. (From Leon Dallin, *Listener's Guide to Musical Understanding.* 8th ed. Copyright © 1994 The McGraw-Hill Companies, Inc. All Rights Reserved. Reprinted by permission.)

Appendix 2

Musical Examples for Examination and Listening

Each of the musical examples in this appendix was chosen for its availability in printed and recorded form. The sources for the examples in the first five chapters are identified by the following acronyms:

DWMA, vol. 1: Stolba, K Marie (ed.) *The Development of Western Music: An Anthology, vols. 1 and 2,* (2nd ed.). Dubuque, Iowa: Brown and Benchmark, 1994.

EMH: Fuller, Sarah (ed.) *The European Musical Heritage: 800–1750.* New York: McGraw-Hill, Inc., 1987.

HAM: Apel, Willi (ed.) *Historical Anthology of Music,* Cambridge, Mass.: Harvard University Press, 1949.

HMS: *History of Music in Sound,* London: Oxford University Press, 1953.

MM: Parrish, Carl & John F. Ohl, *Masterpieces of Music Before 1750,* New York: W. W. Norton and Co. Inc., 1951.

NAWM: Palisca, Claude V. (ed.) *Norton Anthology of Western Music, vol. 1,* New York: W. W. Norton and Co. Inc., 1980.

TEM: Parrish, Carl, *A Treasury of Early Music,* New York: W. W. Norton and Co. Inc., 1958.

CHAPTER 1: ANCIENT PRECURSORS OF WESTERN MUSIC

Ex. 1.1: For fifty-two additional musical compositions of non-Western cultures see HMS, vol. 1, pp. 13–38.

Further examples of recorded non-Western music may be found under the labels of Bärenreiter-Musicaphon, Phillips, and Folkways. Many libraries continue to hold these LP records.

CHAPTER 2: EARLY MIDDLE AGES (300–1100)

Ex. 2.1: Byzantine Music
HMS, vol. 2, p. 2

Ex. 2.2: *Ambrosian psalmellus for Quadragesima:* Redde mihi
TEM, p. 3

Ex. 2.3: Ambrosian chant: Verse, *Eructavit*
HAM, p. 11

Ex. 2.4: Gallican Improperia for Good Friday: *Popule meus*
TEM, p. 8

Ex. 2.5: Mozarabic Antiphon for Easter: *Gaudete populi*
TEM, p. 12

Ex. 2.6: Gregorian hymn for Whitsunday: *Veni Creator Spiritus*
TEM, p. 16

Ex. 2.7: Gregorian chant: *Ut queant laxis*
HAM, p. 12 or DWMA, vol. 1, p. 20

Monophonic Mass

Ex. 2.8: First Mass for Christmas
Liber Usualis
Ex. 2.9: *Easter Mass: Proper* and *Ordinary* EMH, pp. 2–20

Antiphon

Ex. 2.10: *Laus Deo Patri* and *Psalm 113,*
Laudate pueri
MM, p. 3

Ex. 2.11: *Psalm 146* with Antiphon
HAM, p. 11

Ex. 2.12: *Alma Redemptoris Mater*
DWMA, vol. 1, p. 3

Ex. 2.13: *Salve, Regina*
DWMA, vol. 1, p. 3

Ex. 2.14: *Ave regina caelorum* EMH, p. 38

Alleluia

Ex. 2.15: *Vidimus stellam*
MM, p. 6

Ex. 2.16: *Alleluia: Angelus Domini*
HAM, p. 12

Trope

Ex. 2.17: *Agnus Dei*
MM, p. 18

Ex. 2.18: *Kyrie Jhesu dulcissime,*
Fronciaco
TEM, p. 66

Ex. 2.19: Kyrie-Trope: *Omnipotens*
HAM, p. 13

Ex. 2.20: *Gloria with Trope*
NAWM, p. 31

Sequence

Ex. 2.21: *Victimae Paschali*
MM, p. 8

Ex. 2.22: *Rex caeli, Domine*
MM, p. 16 or DWMA, vol. 1, p. 21

Ex. 2.23: *Alleluia: Dominus in Sina,*
with Sequence *Christus hunc diem,*
Balbulus
HAM, p. 13

Ex. 2.24: *Dies Irae, Sequence,* Thomas
of Celano
DWMA, vol. 1, p. 17

Conductus

Ex. 2.25: *Song of the Ass*
Christo psallat
Beata viscera
Sol oritur
HAM, p. 14

Secular Monophony

Ex. 2.26: *O Admirabile Veneris*
HMS, vol. 2, p. 25

Ex. 2.27: Sequence: *Sancti Spiritu avidit*
nobis gratia
HMS, vol. 2, p. 21

CHAPTER 3: LATE MIDDLE AGES: ARS ANTIQUA–ARS NOVA (1100–1400)

Musical Forms
Virelai

Ex. 3.1: *C'est la fin*
HAM, p. 17

Ex. 3.2: *Or la truix* (trouvère song)
MM, p. 11, or DWMA, vol. 1, p. 57

Ex. 3.3: *Dame a vous sans retollir*
EMH, p. 113

EX. 3.4: *Ma trédol rossignol joly,* Borlet
EMH, p. 125

Rondeau

Ex. 3.5: *Ma fin est mon commencement,*
Machaut
DWMA, vol. 1, p. 55

Ex. 3.6: *Prendes i garde,* Gui llaume
d'Amiens
EMH, p. 51

Ex. 3.7: *Quant j'ay l'espar,* Machaut
EMH, p. 112

Ballade

Ex. 3.8: *Je puis trop bien,* Machaut
(ballade)
HAM, p. 48

Ex. 3.9: *Quant Theseus—Ne quier veoir,*
Machaut (double ballade)
NAWM, p. 78

Ex. 3.10: *Nes que on porroit,* Machaut
EMH, p. 109

Canzo

Ex. 3.11: *Be m'an perdut,* Bernart de
Ventadorn
TEM, p. 27

Ex. 3.12: *Can vei la lauzeta mover,*
Ventadorn
EMH, p. 42

Ex. 3.13: *Reis glorios,* Guiraut de Bornelh
HAM, p. 15, or DWMA, vol. 1, p. 43

Bar Form

Ex. 3.14: *Nu al'rest,* Walther von der
Vogelweide
HAM, p. 18

Ex. 3.15: *Palästinalied,* Crusade Song,
Walther von der Vogelweide
DWMA, vol. 1, p. 48

Routrouenge

Ex. 3.16: *Pour mon coeur*
HAM, p. 17

Cantiga

Ex. 3.17: *Gran dereit',* Alfonso El Sabio
TEM, p. 33

Lauda

Ex. 3.18: *Ogne homo*
TEM, p. 37

Lai (Leich)

Ex. 3.19: *Ey ich sach in dem trone*
HMS, vol. 2, p. 32

Ex. 3.20: *Espris d'ire,* Guillaume le Vinier
HAM, p. 17

Organum

Ex. 3.21: *Rex caeli Domine,* from
Musica Enchiriadis
EMH, p. 32

Ex. 3.22: *Sit gloria Domini,* from
Musica Enchiriadis
EMH, p. 33

Ex. 3.23: *Hec dies,* attributed to Leonin
HAM, p. 27

Ex. 3.24: *Alleluya (Nativitas),* Perotin
(organum)
MM, p. 22, or DWMA, vol. 1, p. 27

Ex. 3.25: *Viderunt omes,* Leonin
(organum duplum)
TEM, p. 41

Ex. 3.26: *Mors,* Perotin (organum
quadruplum)
DWMA, vol. 1, p. 30

Ex. 3.27: *Ipsi soli,* Guido d'Arezzo
EMH, p. 33

Ex. 3.28: *Alleluia Pascha nostrum,*
Leonin (organum duplum)
EMH, p. 58

Ex. 3.29: *Alleluia Pascha nostrum,*
Perotin? (organum triplum)
EMH, p. 67

Clausulae

Ex. 3.30: *Regnat*
EMH, p. 78

Ex. 3.31: *Domino,* School of Notre Dame
HAM, p. 25

Ex. 3.32: *Hec Dies*
HAM, p. 30

Conductus

Ex. 3.33: *De castitatis thalamo*
MM, p. 31

Ex. 3.34: *Ave virgo virginum*
NAWM, p. 64

Ex. 3.35: *Hac in anni janua* (three-voice
conductus)
HAM, p. 41, or DWMA, vol. 1, p. 31

Motet

Ex. 3.36: *En non Diu! Quant voi; Eius in
Oriente* (Motet of the Notre Dame
School)
MM, p. 27, or DWMA, vol. 1, p. 32

Ex. 3.37: *Ave gloriosa mater-Ave Virgo-Domino* (thirteenth-century motet)
TEM, p. 46

Ex. 3.38: *Ad solitum vomitum/Regnat* (two-voice motet)
EMH, p. 78

Ex. 3.39: *Pucelete-Je languis-Domino* (motet)
DWMA, vol. 1, p. 34

Ex. 3.40: *Aucun-Lonc tans—Annuntiantes,* Petrus de Cruce (motet)
HAM, p. 36

Ex. 3.41: *Aucuns vont souvent-Amor qui cor-Kyrie,* Petrus de Cruce (motet)
DWMA, vol. 1, p. 35

Ex. 3.42: *Garrit Gallus—In nova fert—* N[euma], Philippe de Vitry (motet)
DWMA, vol. 1, p. 49

Isorhythmic Motet

Ex. 3.43: *O Maria-Virgo-Davidica* (isorhythmic motet)
HMS, vol. 2, p. 53

Ex. 3.44: *Tribum que/Quouiam secta/Merito hec patimur,* Philippe de Vitry
EMH, p. 99

Ex. 3.45: *Bone pastor Guillerme/Bone pastorqui pästores/Bone pastor,* Machaut
EMH, p. 104

Ex. 3.46: *S'il estoit nulz,* Machaut (isorhythmic motet)
HAM, p. 46

Rota

Ex. 3.47: *Sumer is icumen in*
HAM, p. 44, or DWMA, vol. 1, p. 36

Ballata

Ex. 3.48: *Questa fanciullámor,* Landini
EMH, p. 122

Ex. 3.49: *Chi più le vuol sapere,* Landini
MM, p. 40

Ex. 3.50: *Non avrà ma' pietà,* Landini
DWMA, vol. 1, p. 63

Ex. 3.51: *Dieus soit,* Adam de la Halle
DWMA, vol. 1, p. 56

Ex. 3.52: *Io son un pellegrin,* Giovanni da Florentia
HAM, p. 54

Chace and Caccia

Ex. 3.53: *Si je chante main* (chace)
HMS, vol. 3, p. 13

Ex. 3.54: *Con brachi assai,* Giovanni da Firenze (caccia)
TEM, p. 76

Ex. 3.55: *Tosto che l'alba,* Ghirardello da Firenze (caccia)
HAM, p. 55, DWMA, vol. 1, p. 75, or EMH, p. 118

Madrigal

Ex: 3.56: *Sì dolce non sonò,* Landini
DWMA, vol. 1, p. 77

Ex: 3.57: *Non al suo amante,* Jacopo da Bologna
HAM, p. 52, DWMA, vol. 1, p. 57, or EMH, p. 116

Mass

Ex: 3.58: *Agnus Dei,* Machaut (mass movement)
DWMA, vol. 1, p. 68, or NAWM, p. 52

Ex: 3.59: *Agnus Dei* from the *Mass of Tournai*
TEM, p. 62

Ex. 3.60: *Credo* (mass movement), Power
EMH, p. 132

Ex. 3.61: *Et in terra pax,* Johannes Ciconia (mass movement)
HAM, p. 59

Liturgical Drama

Ex. 3.62: *Ordo Virtutum* (excerpt), Hildegard von Bingen
DWMA, vol. 1, p. 38

Instrumental Motet

Ex: 3.63: *In seculum longum*
TEM, p. 54

Ex: 3.64: Organ paraphrase of a Kyrie
TEM, p. 72

Estampie

Ex. 3.65: *Kalenda Maya,* Raimbaut de
Vaqueiras
DWMA, vol. 1, p. 43

Ex: 3.66: *Lamento di Tristan,* with *Rotta,
Saltarello*
HAM, p. 63

Ex: 3.67: *Estampie*
MM, p. 33

Ex: 3.68: *English Dance*
HAM, p. 43

Composers

Leonin

See Ex. 3.23, 3.25, 3.28

Perotin

Ex: 3.69: *Sederunt principes* (organum)
NAWM, p. 56
See also Ex. 3.24, 3.26, 3.29

Adam de la Halle

Ex: 3.70: *Le jeu de Robin et de Marion*
TEM, p. 16, or DWMA, vol. 1, p. 59, or
NAWM, p. 46
See also Ex. 3.51

Landini

Ex: 3.71: *Amar si le alti tue gentil
costumi* (madrigal)
HMS, vol. 3, p. 21

Ex: 3.72: *Sì dolce non sonò* (madrigal)
HAM, p. 57 or DWMA, vol. 1, p. 61
See also Ex. 3.48–3.50, 3.56

Machaut

See Ex. 3.5, 3.7–3.10, 3.45, 3.46

CHAPTER 4: RENAISSANCE (1400–1600)

**Musical Forms
Isorhythmic Motet**

Ex. 4.1: *Veni Sancte Spiritus,* Dunstable
TEM, p. 87

Motet

Ex. 4.2: *Beata Mater,* Dunstable
EMH, p. 141

Ex. 4.3: *Parce, Domine,* Obrecht
MM, p. 55

Ex. 4.4: *Ave Maria,* Josquin
DWMA, vol. 1, p. 77

Ex. 4.5: *Tu pauperum refugium,* Josquin
HAM, p. 92

Ex. 4.6: *Tu solus, qui facis mirabilia,*
Josquin
NAWM, p. 111

Ex. 4.7: *Ave regina caelorum,* Gombert
EMH, p. 218

Ex. 4.8: *Tristis est anima mea,* di Lasso
MM, p. 78, or DWMA, vol. 1, p. 124

Ex. 4.9: *Tristis est anima mea,* di Lasso
EMH, p. 233

Ex. 4.10: *Magnificat octavi toni,* Morales
TEM, p. 108

Ex. 4.11: *Sicut cervus,* Palestrina
HAM, p. 153

Ex. 4.12: *Veni sponsa Christi,* Palestrina
EMH, p. 224

Ex. 4.13: *Miserere mihi Domini,* Byrd
EMH, p. 239

Polychoral Motet

Ex. 4.14: *Laudate Dominum,* Hassler
TEM, p. 138

Hymn

Ex. 4.15: *Conditor alme siderum,* Dufay
NAWM, p. 99

Ex. 4.16: *Beata de Genetrix,* Damett
HAM, p. 69

Chorale

Ex. 4.17: *Komm, Gott Schöpfer, heiliger
Geist,* Johann Walter
TEM, p. 120

Ex. 4.18: *Aus tiefer Not,* Luther
EMH, p. 213

Ex. 4.19: *Aus tiefer Not,* Johann Walter
HAM, p. 115, or EMH, p. 214

Psalms

Ex. 4.20: *Mon Dieu me paist,* Goudimel
TEM, p. 126

Ex. 4.21: Two Settings of *Psalm 35,*
Goudimel and Claude le Jeune
HAM, p. 135

Anthem

Ex. 4.22: Verse Anthem: *This is the
Record of John,* Gibbons
HAM, p. 195

Ex. 4.23: Anthem: *Heare the voyce and
prayer of thy servants,* Tallis
TEM, p. 13

Ex. 4.24: Verse Anthem: *Christ rising
again,* Byrd
HAM, p. 165

Ex. 4.25: Anthem: *When David heard,*
Tomkins
HAM, p. 191

Frottola

Ex. 4.26: *Io non compro più speranza,* Cara
EMH, p. 210

Ex. 4.27: *O mia cieca e dura sorte,* Cara
TEM, pp. 97 and 99

Ex. 4.28: *Non vol aqua,* Tromboncino
HAM, p. 97

Madrigal

Ex. 4.29: *Il bianco e dolce cigno,*
Arcadelt
EMH, p. 263

Ex. 4.30: *Voi ve n'andat' al cielo,*
Arcadelt
HAM, p. 141

Ex. 4.31: *S'io parto, i'moro,* Marenzio
MM, p. 100

Ex. 4.32: *Scaldava il sol,* Marenzio
EMH, p. 272

Ex. 4.33: *Thyrsis? Sleepest thou?* Bennet
MM, p. 109, or DWMA, vol. 1, p. 148

Ex. 4.34: *Io pur respiro,* Gesualdo
HAM, p. 182

Ex. 4.35: *Moro, lasso, al mio duolo,*
Gesuáldo
EMH, p. 282

Ex. 4.36: *Aspro core e selvaggio e cruda
voglia,* Willaert
NAWM, p. 242

Ex. 4.37: *Hark, all ye lovely saints,*
Weelkes
HAM, p. 193

Ex. 4.38: *Datemi pace, o duri miei
pensieri,* Rore
NAWM, p. 250

Ex. 4.39: *Da le belle contrade d'oriente,*
Rore
EMH, p. 266

Ex. 4.40: *Cruda Amarilli,* Monteverdi
EMH, p. 278

Chanson

Ex. 4.41: *Adieu m'amour,* Binchois
MM, p. 48

Ex. 4.42: *Ce moys de may,* Dufay
EMH, p. 168

Ex. 4.43: *Adieu m'amour,* Dufay
EMH, p. 169

Ex. 4.44: *Faulte d'argent,* Josquin
EMH, p. 195

Ex. 4.45: *Pour ung plaisir,* Créquillon
MM, p. 64

Ex. 4.46: *L'Alouette,* Janequin
HAM, p. 109

Ex. 4.47: *Ou mettra l'on ung baiser,*
Janequin
EMH, p. 254

Polyphonic Lied

Ex. 4.48: *Oho, so geb' der Mann ein'n Pfenning,* Senfl
TEM, p. 177

Ex. 4.49: *Zwischen Berg und tiefem Tal,* Isaac
HAM, p. 91, or DWMA, vol. 1, p. 82

Quodlibet

Ex. 4.50: *Fricassée,* Anon.
TEM, p. 170

Ex. 4.51: *Veni sancte spiritus, Veni creator spiritus,* Finck
HAM, p. 84

Ayre

Ex. 4.52: *My thoughts are winged with hope,* Dowland
TEM, p. 189

Ex. 4.53: *Stay, cruel, stay,* Danyel
HAM, p. 184

Miscellaneous Secular Forms

Ex. 4.54: Villancico: *Soy contento y vos servido,* Juan del Encina
TEM, p. 94

Ex. 4.55: *Señora de hermosura,* Encina
EMH, p. 205

Ex. 4.56: Meistersinger Melody: *Gesangweise,* Hans Sachs
TEM, p. 105

Ex. 4.57: Virelai: *Ma bouche rit,* Ockeghem
HAM, p. 79

Ex. 4.58: Rondeau: *De plus en plus,* Binchois
HAM, p. 74, or DWMA, vol. 1, p. 72

Composite Forms
Mass

Ex. 4.59: *Missa Mi-mi, Agnus Dei,* Ockeghem
EMH, p. 161

Ex. 4.60: Cantus firmus Mass on a secular tune: *Missa, L'Homme armé, Kyrie I and II,* la Rue
HAM, p. 95

Ex. 4.61: Cantus firmus Mass on a secular tune: *Missa, Se la face ay pale, Kyrie I,* Dufay
MM, p. 43.
Agnus Dei, Dufay
EMH, p. 146
(Ballade *Se la face ay pale,* Dufay, DWMA, vol. 1, p. 65)

Ex. 4.62: *Missa L'homme armé, Agnus Dei II,* Josquin
EMH, p. 182

Ex. 4.63: *Missa Pange Ringua, Kyrie,* Josquin
EMH, p. 185

Ex. 4.64: Parody Mass: *Missa Veni sponsa Christe,* Palestrina
Kyrie, EMH, p. 228
Agnus Dei, MM, p. 86

Ex. 4.65: Credo from *Missa Papae Marcelli,* Palestrina
NAWM, p. 200

Ricercar

Ex. 4.66: *Ricercar No. 7,* Willaert
HMS, vol. 4, p. 51

Ex. 4.67: *Ricercar arioso,* A. Gabrieli
HMS, vol. 4, p. 61

Ex. 4.68: *Ricercar,* Cavazzoni
HAM, p. 121, or DWMA, vol. 1, p. 130

Canzona

Ex. 4.69: *Canzona francese deta Pour ung plaisir,* A. Gabrieli
MM, p. 64

Ex. 4.70: *Canzona Septimi Toni a 8,* G. Gabrieli
EMH, p. 246

Ex. 4.71: *Canzona,* Maschera
HAM, p. 201

In Nomine

Ex. 4.72: *In nomine,* Bull
DWMA, vol. 1, p. 133

Toccata

Ex. 4.73: *Toccata Quinta, Secondo Tuono,* Merulo
TEM, p. 152

Ex. 4.74: *Toccata,* Merulo
HAM, p. 168

Fantasia

Ex. 4.75: *Three part Fantasia, No. 3,* Gibbons
HMS, vol. 4, p. 53

Ex. 4.76: *Fantasia in Echo,* Sweelinck
HAM, p. 209

Prelude

Ex. 4.77: *Praeludium,* Bull
HAM, p. 205

Variation

Ex. 4.78: *Loth to depart,* Farnaby
MM, p. 115

Ex. 4.79: *Goe from my window,* Munday
HAM, p. 204

Ex. 4.80: *Diferencias sobra O Gloriosa Domina,* Luis de Narvaez
HAM, p. 130

Dance Forms

Ex. 4.81: *Danseries a 4 Parties, Second Livre,* Attaignant
NAWM, p. 280

Ex. 4.82: *Pavana for the virginal,* John Bull
TEM, p. 161

Ex. 4.83: *Passamezzo d'Italie,* Anon
TEM, p. 194

Ex. 4.84: *Der Prinzen-Tanz; Proportz,* Anon
MM, p. 74

Ex. 4.85: *Paduan and Intrada,* Puerl
HMS, vol. 4, p. 51

Ex. 4.86: *Galliard* for Cittern and Bass, Holborne
NAWM, p. 293

Composite Forms

Ex. 4.87: *Three Dances,* Gervaise
HAM, p. 148

Composers
John Dunstable

Ex. 4.88: *O rosa bella*
HAM, p. 65

Ex. 4.89: Motet: *Sancta Maria*
HAM, p. 66
See also Ex. 4.1–4.2

Guillaume Dufay

Ex. 4.90: *Ave Regina Coelorum*
HMS, vol. 3, p. 42

Ex. 4.91: *Missa L'Homme Armé*
DWMA, vol. 1, p. 69
See also Ex. 4.15, 4.42, 4.43, 4.61

Gilles Binchois

Ex. 4.92: *Filles a marier*
HMS, vol. 3, p. 45

Ex. 4.93: *De plus en plus*
DWMA, vol. 1, p. 72
See also Ex. 4.41

Johannes Ockeghem

Ex. 4.94: Chanson: *Prenez sur moi*
Collected Works, Breitkopf and Härtel

Ex. 4.95: Mass: *Fors seulement*
Collected Works, Breitkopf and Härtel

Ex. 4.96: *Missa Prolationum*
Kyrie, DWMA, vol. 1, p. 73
Sanctus, MM, p. 51

Ex. 4.97: Virelai: *Ma maîtresse*
HAM, p. 78
See also Ex. 4.57, 4.59

Josquin des Prez

Ex. 4.98: Frottola: *El Grillo*
HMS, vol. 3, p. 55

Ex. 4.99: Chanson: *Mille regretz*
NAWM, p. 219

Ex. 4.100: Motet: *Tribulatio et angustia*
HMS, vol. 3, p. 58

Ex. 4.101: Motet: *Ave Maria*
DWMA, vol. 1, p. 77
See also Ex. 4.4–4.6, 4.44, 4.62–4.63

Heinrich Isaac

Ex. 4.102: Polyphonic Lied: *Innsbruck, ich muss dich lassen*
HMS, vol. 3, p. 75, or NAWM, p. 231
See also Ex. 4.49

Jacob Obrecht

Ex. 4.103: Motet: *Si oblitus fuero*
HMS, vol. 3, p. 51

Ex. 4.104: Motet: *Pater Noster*
HAM, p. 80
See also Ex. 4.3

Clement Janequin

Ex. 4.105: Chanson: *À ce joly moys de may*
DWMA, vol. 1, p. 108
See also Ex. 4.46–4.47

Adrian Willaert

Ex. 4.106: Motet: *Victimae paschali laudes*
HAM, p. 116, or DWMA, vol. 1, p. 85
See also Ex. 4.66

Nicholas Gombert

See Ex. 4.7

Ludwig Senfl

Ex. 4.107: Polyphonic Lied: *Da Jakob nu das Kleid ansah*
HAM, p. 114
See also Ex. 4.48

Thomas Tallis

Ex. 4.108: Motet: *Adeste nunc propitius*
HMS, vol. 4, p. 34

Ex. 4.109: Responsorium: *Audivi vocem*
HAM, p. 137
See also Ex. 4.23

Jacobus Clemens

Ex. 4.110: Motet: *Vox in Rama*
HAM, p. 134

Antonio de Cabézon

Ex. 4.111: Variations: *Diferencias sobre el canto llano del Caballero*
DWMA, vol. 1, p. 136

Andrea Gabrieli

Ex. 4.112: *Sonata pian' e forte*
NAWM, p. 168, or HAM, p. 198

Ex. 4.113: Prelude: *Intonazione settimo tono*
HAM, p. 146
See also Ex. 4.67, 4.69

Philippe de Monte

Ex. 4.114: Mass: *Benedicta es*
HMS, vol. 4, p. 24

Ex. 4.115: Parody Mass: *Missa super Cara la vita*
HAM, p. 160

Giovanni Pierluigi Palestrina

Ex. 4.116: Madrigal: *Alla riva del Tebro*
HAM, p. 155

Ex. 4.117: Mass (excerpts): *Missa Papae Marcelli*
NAWM, p. 200, and HAM, p. 152

Ex. 4.118: Motet: *Sicut cervus*
HAM, p. 153
See also Ex. 4.11–4.12, 4.64–4.65

Orlando di Lasso

Ex. 4.119: Chanson: *Bon jour mon coeur*
HAM, p. 159

Ex. 4.120: *Penitential Psalm III*
HAM, p. 157
See also Ex. 4.8–4.9

William Byrd

Ex. 4.121: Motet: *Ego sum panis vivus*
MM, p. 91, or DWMA, vol. 1, p. 162

Ex. 4.122: Motet: *Non vos relinquam*
HAM, p. 164
See also Ex. 4.13, 4.24

Tomás Luis de Victoria

Ex. 4.123: Motet: *O vos omnes*
HAM, p. 163, or DWMA, vol. 1, p. 123

Ex. 4.124: Motet: *O Domine Jesu*
HMS, vol. 4, p. 23

Luca Marenzio

Ex. 4.125: Madrigal: *Scendi dal
Paradiso*
HMS, vol. 4, p. 14

Ex. 4.126: Madrigal: *Solo e pensoso*
DWMA, vol. 1, p. 95

Ex. 4.127: Madrigal: *Madonna mia
gentil*
HAM, p. 173
See also Ex. 4.31–4.32

Giovanni Gabrieli

Ex. 4.128: from the Sacrae Symphoniae:
In ecclesiis
HAM, p. 175, or DWMA, vol. 1, p. 140

Ex. 4.129: *Sonata pian' e forte*
HAM, p. 198, or DWMA, vol. 1, p. 126
See also Ex. 4.70

Thomas Morley

Ex. 4.130: Madrigal: *Thyrsis and Milla*
HMS, vol. 4, p. 48

Ex. 4.131: Madrigal: *April is in my
mistress' face*
DWMA, vol. 1, p. 111

Ex. 4.132: Ballett: *My bonny lass*
HAM, p. 180

Ex. 4.133: Ballett: *Sing we and chant it*
DWMA, vol. 1, p. 105

Don Carlo Gesualdo

Ex. 4.134: Madrigal: *Moro lasso*
TEM, p. 181, or DWMA, vol. 1, p. 103

Ex. 4.135: Madrigal: *Io pur respiro*
HAM, p. 182
See also Ex. 4.35

John Dowland

Ex. 4.136: Ayre: *In darkness let me dwell*
DWMA, vol. 1, p. 112

Hans Leo Hassler

Ex. 4.137: Polyphonic Lied: *Ach Schatz*
HAM, p. 187

Ex. 4.138: Motet: *Quia vidisti me*
HAM, p. 186

Claudio Monteverdi

Ex. 4.139: Madrigal: *Cruda amarilli*
DWMA, vol. 1, p. 199, or NAWM, p. 154
See also Ex. 4.40

Thomas Weelkes

Ex. 4.140: Madrigal: *O care thou wilt
dispatch me*
HMS, vol. 4, p. 17, or NAWM, p. 265

CHAPTER 5: BAROQUE (1600–1750)

Music for Voices
Recitativo Accompagnato

Ex. 5.1: *Comfort Ye* from *Messiah,*
Handel
DWMA, vol. 1, p. 261

Recitativo Secco

Ex. 5.2: *Al valor del mio brando* from
Rinaldo, Handel
MM, p. 189

Aria

Ex. 5.3: *Cara sposa* from *Rinaldo,*
Handel
MM, p. 189

Ex. 5.4: *Every Valley* from *Messiah,*
Handel
DWMA, vol. 1, p. 263

Arioso

Ex. 5.5: *O Jour affreux* from *Dardanus,*
Rameau
HMS, vol. 5, p. 23

Ex. 5.6: *Ach Golgotha,* from the *St.
Matthew Passion,* J. S. Bach
MM, p. 226, or DWMA, vol. 1, p. 250

Chorus

Ex. 5.7: *With Drooping Wings* from *Dido
and Aeneas,* Purcell
Oxford University Press

Motet

Ex. 5.8: *Hodie completi sunt dies
pentecostes,* G. Gabrieli
NAWM, p. 416

Ex. 5.9: *In ecclesiis,* G. Gabrieli
EMH, p. 313

Ex. 5.10: *Jesu, meine Freude,* J. S. Bach
DWMA, vol. 1, p. 245

Spiritual Concerto

Ex. 5.11: Sacred Cantata: *O Herr, hilf,*
Schütz
MM, p. 135

Ex. 5.12: *O quam tu pulchra es,* Schütz
EMH, p. 326

Ex. 5.13: *Saul, Saul was verfolgst du
mich?,* Schütz
EMH, p. 336

Ex. 5.14: Chorale concerto: *Erschienen
ist der herrliche Tag,* Schein
TEM, p. 217

Anthem

Ex. 5.15: Verse Anthem: *Hear, O
heav'ns,* Humfrey
HMS, vol. 5, p. 38, or NAWM, p. 457

Solo Song

Ex. 5.16: Solo madrigal: *Perfidissimo
volto,* Caccini
NAWM, p. 294, and EMH, p. 287

Ex. 5.17: *Cruda Amarilli,* d'India
EMH, p. 282

Ex. 5.18: Duet: *Ohimè dov' è il mio ben,*
Monteverdi
NAWM, p. 303

Ex. 5.19: *Zefiro torna,* Monteverdi
EMH, p. 300

Ex. 5.20: Lute song: *Flow my tears,*
Dowland
NAWM, p. 312, and EMH, p. 295

Ex. 5.21: *Meine Seufzer, meine Klagen,*
Erlebach
HMS, vol. 5, p. 18

Composite Forms
Italian Opera

Ex. 5.22: Excerpt from *Euridice,* Peri
EMH, p. 348

Ex. 5.23: Excerpts from *Orfeo,* Monteverdi
DWMA, vol. 1, p. 157, NAWM, p. 333,
and EMH, p. 355

Ex 5.24: Excerpt from *Scipione
Africano,* Cavalli
EHM, p. 385

Ex. 5.25: Opera buffa: Excerpt from *La
Serva Padrona,* Pergolesi
DWMA, vol. 1, p. 297, and EMH, p. 507

Ex. 5.26: Opera seria: Excerpts from
Giulio Cesare, Handel
HMS, vol. 5, p. 17, and NAWM, p. 395

Ex. 5.27: Excerpt from *Admeto,* Handel
EMH, p. 481

French Opera

Ex. 5.28: Excerpts from *Alceste,* Lully
HMS, vol. 5, p. 20, and EMH, p. 393

Ex. 5.29: *Séjour de l'éternelle paix* from
Castor et Pollux, Rameau
MM, p. 172, or DWMA, vol. 1, p. 238

Ex. 5.30: Excerpt from *Hippolyte et
Aricie,* Rameau
EMH, p. 499

Ex. 5.31: *Chaconne* from the opera-
ballet, *Les Fêtes Vénitiennes,* Campra
TEM, p. 270

English Opera

Ex. 5.32: Excerpts from *Dido and
Aeneas,* Purcell
DWMA, vol. 1, p. 176, and EMH, p. 400

Ex. 5.33: Excerpt from *The Beggar's
Opera,* John Gay
NAWM, p. 403

German Opera

Ex. 5.34: *Ach! Nero ist nicht Nero mehr,*
from *Octavia,* Keiser
HMS, vol. 5, p. 26

Ex. 5.35: *Hoffe noch* from *Croesus,*
Keiser
TEM, p. 277

Oratorio

Ex. 5.36: Excerpts from *Jepthe,* Carissimi
NAWM, p. 436, DWMA, vol. 1,
p. 178, and EMH, p. 373

Ex. 5.37: *Draw the tear from hopeless
love,* from *Solomon,* Handel
MM, p. 200

Ex. 5.38: *Via, via, false Sirene* from
Rappresentazione di Anima e di Corpo,
Cavalieri
TEM, p. 208

Passion Music

Ex. 5.39: Excerpts from *St. Matthew
Passion,* J. S. Bach
DWMA, vol. 1, pp. 250, 255

Cantata

Ex. 4.40: Excerpt from *Alpi nervose e
dure,* Cesti
EMH, p. 388

Ex. 5.41: *Laudate Dominum,* Buxtehude
Bärenreiter, ed.

Ex. 5.42: Excerpts from *Su le sponde del
Tebro,* A. Scarlatti
EMH, p. 472

Ex. 5.43: *Ein feste Burg,* Cantata No. 80,
J. S. Bach
Bach Gesellschaft edition

Ex. 5.44: Chorale and Chorus from
Christ lag in Todesbanden, Cantata
No. 4, J. S. Bach
MM, pp. 208, 215

Ex. 5.45: *Jesu, der du meine Seele,*
Cantata No.78, J. S. Bach
EMH, p. 514

Ex. 5.46: Recitative and aria, *Amor tu
sei,* from *Stravaganze d' Amore,*
Marcello
TEM, p. 304

Mass

Ex. 5.47: *Messe de Minuit,* Charpentier
Concordia Publishing House

Ex. 5.48: Excerpts from *B Minor Mass,*
J. S. Bach
NAWM, p. 499

Music for Instruments
Toccata

Ex. 5.49: *Toccata No. 8 . . .,* Frescobaldi
EMH, p. 421

Ex. 5.50: *Toccata in E minor for Organ,*
Pachelbel
MM, p. 156

Prelude

Ex. 5.51: *Prélude a l'imitation de Mr.
Froberger,* L. Couperin
EMH, p. 434

Ex. 5.52: *Prelude and Fugue in A minor,*
BWV 543, J. S. Bach
NAWM, p. 574

Ex. 5.53: *Prelude and Fugue in D minor,*
WTCI, J. S. Bach
EMH, p. 555

Ex. 5.54: Chorale preludes: *Wenn wir in
höchsten Nöten sein,* BWV 641 and
668a, J. S. Bach
NAWM, p. 576

Ricercar

Ex. 5.55: *Ricercar dopo il Credo,*
Frescobaldi
MM, p. 144

Fugue

Ex. 5.56: *Das Wohltemperierte Klavier,*
J. S. Bach
See also Ex. 5.51

Ex. 5.57: *Contrapunctus III,* from *Kunst
der Fuge,* J. S. Bach
MM, p. 230

Ex. 5.58: *Capriccio über dass
Hennengeschrey,* Poglietti
TEM, p. 232

Fantasia

Ex. 5.59: *Fantasie a 4,* Sweelinck
NAWM, p. 602

Ex. 5.60: *Fantasie for violin solo,*
Telemann
TEM, p. 297

Overture

Ex. 5.61: *Overture to Armide,* Lully
MM, p. 152, or NAWM, p. 367

Theme and Variation

Ex. 5.62: *John come kiss me now,* from
The Fitzwilliam Virginal Book, Byrd
EMH, p. 407

Ex. 5.63: *Jesus Christus unser Heiland,
der du uns,* Scheidt
EMH, p. 413

Ex. 5.64: *La Folia,* Corelli
Schott, ed.

Ex. 5.65: *Goldberg Variations,* J. S. Bach
Eulenburg, ed.

Passacaglia and Chaconne

Ex. 5.66: *Passacaglia and Fugue in C
minor,* J. S. Bach

Ex. 5.67: *Chaconne for Violin,* Vitali
Schirmer, ed.

Chorale Prelude

Ex. 5.68: *In dulci jubilo,* Buxtehude and
J. S. Bach
HMS, vol. 6, p. 26

Ex. 5.69: *Christ lag in Todesbanden,*
J. S. Bach
MM, p. 212

Ex. 5.70: *Nun komm, der Heiden
Heiland,* Buxtehude
TEM, p. 237
See also Ex. 5.53.

Composite Forms
Suite

Ex. 5.71: *Suite VI in C,* Froberger
EMH, p. 428

Ex. 5.72: *Suite in E minor,* Froberger
MM, p. 147, or DWMA, vol. 1, p. 201

Ex. 5.73: Lute piece: *Tombeau de
Mademoiselle Gaultier,* Gaultier
TEM, p. 227

Orchestral Suite

Ex. 5.74: *Suite no. 3 in D major for
Orchestra,* J. S. Bach
Eulenburg, ed.

Sonata da Chiesa

Ex. 5.75: *Sonata da chiesa in E minor,*
Op. 3, No. 7, Corelli
MM, p. 162

Ex. 5.76: *Sonata da chiesa in D major,*
Op. 5, No. 1, Corelli
DWMA, vol. 1, p. 221, and EMH, p. 459

Ex. 5.77: *Rosary Sonata X,* Biber
EMH, p. 454

Sonata da Camera

Ex. 5.78: *Trio Sonata, La Raspona,*
Legrenzi
NAWM, p. 525

Ex. 5.79: *Sonata da camera a tre,* Opus 4,
no. 5, Corelli
EMH, p. 450

Ex. 5.80: Trio Sonata: *Concert Royal,*
F. Couperin
Editions de l'Oiseau Lyre, Complete
Works of Couperin, vol. 7

Ex. 5.81: *Violin Sonata in E major,* J. S.
Bach
Schirmer, ed.

Keyboard Sonata

Ex. 5.82: *Sonata in C minor,* D. Scarlatti
MM, p. 179

Ex. 5.83: *Sonata in D minor,* D. Scarlatti
EMH, p. 560

Ex. 5.84: *Sonata in D major,* D. Scarlatti
EMH, p. 564

Solo Concerto and Concerto Grosso

Ex. 5.85: *Violin Concertos, Nos. 1* and *2,*
J. S. Bach
Schirmer, ed.

Ex. 5.86: *Concerto in A major for Violin
and Orchestra,* Op. 9, No. 2, Vivaldi
DWMA, vol. 1, p. 228

Ex. 5.87: *Concerto Grosso in C major*
(first movement), Handel
MM, p. 182

Ex. 5.88: *Brandenburg Concerti Nos.
1–6,* J. S. Bach

Ex. 5.89: *La Primavera,* Op. 8, No. 1
(first movement), Vivaldi
TEM, p. 286
Ex. 90: *Violin Concerto in G minor,*
Op. 8, No. 8, Viraldi
EMH, p. 571

Composers
Giulio Caccini

Ex. 5.91: Madrigal: *Dovrò dunque
morire*
MM, p. 120

Ex. 5.92: Solo madrigal: *Amarilli mia bella*
DWMA, vol. 1, p. 152
See also Ex. 5.16

Jacopo Peri

Ex. 5.93: Excerpts from the opera
Euridice
NAWM, p. 324
See also Ex. 5.22

Jan Pieterzoon Sweelinck

Ex. 5.94: Chorale Variation: *Ach Gott,
von Himmel sieh' darein*
HMS, vol. 4, p. 62

Ex. 5.95: *Fantasia chromatica*
DWMA, vol. 1, p. 197
See also Ex. 5.58

Claudio Monteverdi

See Ex. 5.18–5.19, 5.23

Michael Praetorius

Ex. 5.96: *Wie schön leuchtet der
Morgenstern*
HMS, vol. 4, p. 39

Ex. 5.97: *Vater unser im Himmelreich*
HAM, p. 189

Girolamo Frescobaldi

Ex. 5.98: *Il secondo libro di toccate:
Toccata nona*
DWMA, vol. 1, p. 202

Ex. 5.99: *Partite 12 sopra l'Aria di
Ruggiero*
NAWM, p. 611
See also Ex. 5.48

Heinrich Schütz

Ex. 5.100: Introit from *Die Sieben Wortte*
DWMA, vol. 1, p. 195

Ex. 5.101: *Symphoniae Sacrae: O quam tu pulchra es*
DWMA, vol. 1, p. 190, or NAWM, p. 448
See also Ex. 5.11–5.13

Hermann Schein
See Ex. 5.14

Samuel Scheidt
Ex. 5.102: Chorale prelude: *Vater unser im Himmelreich*
DWMA, vol. 1, p. 205
See also Ex. 5.62

Pier Francesco Cavalli
Ex. 5.103: Duet from *Egisto, Musici della selva*
HMS, vol. 5, p. 11
See also Ex. 5.24

Jacques Champion Chambonnières
Ex. 5.104: Keyboard Music
HMS, vol. 6, p. 20

Giacomo Carissimi
Ex. 5.105: *Afferte gladium; Judicium Salomonis*
MM, p. 129
See also Ex. 5.35

Johann Jakob Froberger
See Ex. 5.70–5.71

Marc' Antonio Cesti
Ex. 5.106: *E dove t' aggiri* from *Il Pomo d'oro*
HMS, vol. 5, p. 12

Jean-Henri d'Angelbert
Ex. 5.107: *Prelude, Allemande, Sarabande* from a suite for harpsichord
HAM, vol. 2, p. 96

Jean-Baptiste Lully
See Ex. 5.27, 5.60

Marc-Antoine Charpentier
Ex. 5.108: Oratorio scene from *Le Reniement de St Pierre*
TEM, p. 242
See also Ex. 5.46

Dietrich Buxtehude
See Ex. 5.40, 5.67

Johan Pachelbel
See Ex. 5.49

Arcangelo Corelli
See Ex. 5.74–5.75, 5.78

Henry Purcell
Ex. 5.109: *A New Ground*
MM, p. 159
See also Ex. 5.31

Johann Kuhnau
Ex. 5.110: *Biblical Sonata No. 2*
Broude, ed.

Alessandro Scarlatti
Ex. 5.111: Quartet: *Idolo mio ti chiamo Tito* from *Tito Sempronio Gracco*
HMS, vol. 5, p. 16

Ex. 5.112: Aria, *Mi rivedi, o selva ombrosa,* from *Griselda*
NAWM, p. 391
See also Ex. 5.41

François Couperin
Ex. 5.113: *Vingt-cinquième ordre, Pièces de Clavecin,* 4ième Livre
NAWM, p. 617

Ex. 5.114: *La Galante*
MM, p. 169

Ex. 5.115: *Pièces de clavecin,* Premier
livre, F. Couperin
EMH, 548
See also Ex. 5.79

Antonio Vivaldi

Ex. 5.116: *Concerto in A Major for
Violin and Orchestra,* Op. 9, No. 2
DWMA, vol. 1, p. 228
See also Ex. 5.88–5.89

Georg Telemann

See Ex. 5.59

Jean-Philippe Rameau

See Ex. 5.5, 5.28–5.29

Johann Sebastian Bach

See Ex. 5.6, 5.10, 5.38, 5.42–5.44, 5.47,
5.51–5.53, 5.55–5.56, 5.65, 5.67–5.68,
5.73, 5.80, 5.84, 5.87

Domenico Scarlatti

See Ex. 5.81

George Frideric Handel

Ex. 5.117: Chorus, *All we like sheep,*
from *Messiah*
DWMA, vol. 1, p. 269
See also Ex. 5.1–5.4, 5.26, 5.36, 5.86

Giovanni Battista Pergolesi

Ex. 5.118: Recitative and Aria from the
opera buffa, *Livietta e Tracollo*
TEM, p. 314
See also Ex. 5.25

CHAPTER 6: CLASSIC (1750–1820)

(Because of the large number of
recordings available for many works
from the Classic period to the present,
beginning with chapter 6 the authors

have chosen to recommend
compositions, but not specific
recordings for these more readily
available examples.)

Music for Voices
Recitative

Ex. 6.1: *Hai già vinta la cause* (the
Count), from *Le Nozze di Figaro,* Mozart

Aria

Ex. 6.2: *Che farò senza Euridice*
(Orfeo), from *Orfeo ed Euridice,* Gluck
DWMA, vol. 1, p. 351

Choruses and Ensembles

Ex. 6.3: *Le Nozze di Figaro* (Marriage of
Figaro), Mozart

Vocal Polyphony

Ex. 6.4: *Der Greis,* Haydn

Ex. 6.5: *Più non si trovano,* K. 549,
Mozart

Lied

Ex. 6.6: *An Chloe,* K. 524, Mozart

Ex. 6.7: *My mother bids me bind my
hair,* Haydn

Composite Vocal Forms
Opera

Ex. 6.8: *Alceste,* Gluck

Ex. 6.9: *Orfeo ed Euridice,* Gluck
DWMA, vol. 1, p. 342

Ex. 6.10: *Don Giovanni,* Mozart
See 6.1

Ex. 6.11: *Die Entführung aus dem Serail*
(The Abduction from the Seraglio),
Mozart

Ex. 6.12: *Il matrimonio segreto,*
Cimarosa

Ex. 6.13: *Médée,* Cherubini

Oratorio

Ex. 6.14: *Die Schöpfung,* Haydn

Ex. 6.15: *Die Jahreszeiten,* Haydn

Mass

Ex. 6.16: *Missa Solemnis in D minor* (Nelson Mass), Haydn

Ex. 6.17: *Mass in C major* (Coronation), K. 317, Mozart

Ex. 6.18: *Requiem in C minor,* Cherubini

Music for Instruments
Sonata-Allegro Form

Ex. 6.19: *Symphony No. 104, D major* (London), first movement, Haydn
DWMA, vol. 1, p. 358

Ex. 6.20: *Piano Sonata in C minor,* K. 457, first movement, Mozart
DWMA, vol. 1, p. 373

Ex. 6.21: *String Quartet No. 1, F major,* Op. 18, No. 1, first movement, Beethoven

Rondo

Ex. 6.22: *String Quintet in G minor,* K. 516, last movement, Mozart

Ex. 6.23: *Piano Sonata No. 2, A major,* Op. 2, last movement, Beethoven

Variation Form

Ex. 6.24: *Clarinet Quintet, A major,* K. 581, last movement, Mozart

Ex. 6.25: *String Quartet in C major,* Op. 76, second movement, Haydn

Ex. 6.26: *Variation for piano in F minor,* Haydn

Three-Part Song Form

Ex. 6.27: *Piano Sonata No. 1 in F minor,* second movement, C. P. E. Bach

Ex. 6.28: *Symphony No. 101, D major* (Clock), second movement, Haydn

Minuet and Trio, and Other Dance Forms

Ex. 6.29: *Eine kleine Nachtmusik,* K. 525, Menuetto, Mozart

Ex. 6.30: *Symphony No. 101, D major* (Clock), third movement, Haydn

Overture

Ex. 6.31: *Overture* to *Orfeo ed Euridice,* Gluck

Ex. 6.32: *Overture* to *Le Nozze di Figaro,* Mozart

Polyphonic Instrumental Music

Ex. 6.33: *String Quartet, B major,* K. 387, last movement, Mozart

Ex. 6.34: *Symphony No. 41, C major,* K. 550, last movement, Mozart

Composite Forms
Sonata

Ex. 6.35: *Sonatas for Harpsichord,* H. 24–29, C. P. E. Bach

Ex. 6.36: *Sonata in C minor for Piano,* K. 457, Mozart
DWMA, vol. 1, p. 373

Ex. 6.37: *Sonata in G major for Violin and Piano,* K. 301, Mozart

Ex. 6.38: *Sonata No. 44 in E flat major for Piano,* Haydn

Symphony

Ex. 6.39: *Symphony No. 3 in F major,* C. P. E. Bach

Ex. 6.40: *Symphony No. 1 in C major,* Op. 21, Beethoven

Ex. 6.41: *Symphony No. 92 in G major* (Oxford), Haydn

Ex. 6.42: *Symphony in D major,* Op. 5, No. 2, Johann Stamitz

Concerto

Ex. 6.43: *Cello Concerto in B flat major,* Boccherini

Ex. 6.44: *Piano Concerto No. 27 in B flat major,* K. 595, Mozart
DWMA, vol. 1, p. 323

Ex. 6.45: *Concerto No. 10 in E flat major for Two Pianos,* K. 365, Mozart

Ex. 6.46: *Concerto in E flat major for Trumpet and Orchestra,* Hummel

Chamber Music

Ex. 6.47: *Quintet in G major for Strings,* G. B. Sammartini

Ex. 6.48: *Quintet for flute, oboe, violin, viola and continuo,* Op. 11, J. C. Bach

Ex. 6.49: *Piano Trio No. 1 in G major,* Haydn

Ex. 6.50: *Piano Quartet No. 2 in E flat major,* K. 493, Mozart

Ex. 6.51: *String Quartet No. 19 in C major,* K. 465, Mozart

Serenades, Divertimenti, Cassations, Notturni

Ex. 6.52: *Divertimenti,* Haydn

Ex. 6.53: *Serenata Notturna in D major,* K. 239, Mozart

CHAPTER 7: ROMANTIC (1820–1900)

Music for Voices
Art Song

Ex. 7.1: *Dichterliebe,* Op. 48, Schumann

Ex. 7.2: *Die Winterreise,* D. 911, Schubert

Ex. 7.3: *Songs and Dances of Death,* Mussorgsky

Choral Music

Ex. 7.4: *Te Deum,* Verdi

Ex. 7.5: *Ein Deutsches Requiem,* Op. 45, Brahms

Ex. 7.6: *Mass in F major,* Bruckner

Ex. 7.7: *Symphony No. 9 in D minor,* Op. 125 (choral), Beethoven

Ex. 7.8: *Warum ist das Licht gegeben?* (motet), Op. 74, No. 1, Brahms

Opera
Italian Opera

Ex. 7.9: *Il barbieri di Siviglia,* Rossini
DWMA, vol. 2, p. 58

Ex. 7.10: *Lucia di Lammermoor,* Donizetti

Ex. 7.11: *La traviata,* Verdi

Ex. 7.12: *Tosca,* Puccini

Ex. 7.13: *Pagliacci,* Leoncavallo

French Opera

Ex. 7.14: *Les Hugenots,* Meyerbeer

Ex. 7.15: *Carmen,* Bizet

German Opera

Ex. 7.16: *Der Freischütz,* Weber
DWMA, vol. 2, p. 29

Ex. 7.17: *Tristan und Isolde,* Wagner
DWMA, vol. 2, p. 168

Ex. 7.18: *Parsifal,* Wagner

Nationalistic Opera

Ex. 7.19: *Boris Godunov,* Mussorgsky
DWMA, vol. 2, p. 207

Ex. 7.20: *Bartered Bride,* Smetana

Oratorio

Ex. 7.21: *Elijah,* Op. 70, Mendelssohn
DWMA, vol. 2, pp. 69–81

Ex. 7.22: *L'enfance du Christ,* Op. 25, Berlioz

Music for Instruments
Sonata Form

Ex. 7.23: *Piano Sonata No. 23,* Op. 57
(Appassionata), Beethoven
DWMA, vol. 2, p. 5

Ex. 7.24: *Symphony No. 3 in E flat
major,* Op. 55 (Eroica), first movement,
Beethoven
DWMA, vol. 3, p. 13

Ex. 7.25: *Symphony No. 3 in F major,*
Op. 90, first movement, Brahms
DWMA, vol. 2, p. 188

Two-Part and Three-Part Song Forms

Ex. 7.26: *Nocturnes,* Chopin
DWMA, vol. 2, p. 66

Ex. 7.27: *Caprices for Violin,* Op. 1,
Paganini

Ex. 7.28: *Ballade No. 4,* Op. 52, Chopin

Ex. 7.29: *Ballade,* Op. 10, No. 1,
Brahms

Variations

Ex. 7.30: *Variations on a Theme by
Handel,* Op. 24, Brahms

Ex. 7.31: *Variations in D major,* Op. 76,
Beethoven

Dance Movements

Ex. 7.32: *Polanaise Fantasie,* Op. 61,
Chopin

Ex. 7.33: *Mephisto Waltz,* Liszt

Ex. 7.34: *Danse Macabre,* Op. 40, Saint-
Saëns

Rhapsody

Ex. 7.35: *Hungarian Rhapsody No. 2,*
Liszt

Ex. 7.36: *Rhapsody in E flat major,* Op.
119 No. 4, Brahms

Ex. 7.37: *Spanish Rhapsody,* Op. 70,
Albeniz

Études

Ex. 7.38: *Etudes,* Op. 25, Chopin
DWMA, vol. 2, p. 62

Ex. 7.39: *Transcendental Etudes for
Piano,* Liszt

Concert Overture

Ex. 7.40: *Hebrides Overture,* Op. 26,
Mendelssohn

Ex. 7.41: *Academic Festival Overture,*
Op. 80, Brahms

Symphonic Poem

Ex. 7.42: *Les Préludes,* Liszt

Ex. 7.43: *Vltava* (Moldau), Smetana

Ex. 7.44: *Till Eulenspiegels lustige
Streiche,* Richard Strauss

Sonata and Symphony

Ex. 7.45: *Sonata for Violin and Piano in
C minor,* Op. 30, Beethoven

Ex. 7.46: *Sonata for Cello and Piano in
F major,* Op. 90, Brahms

Ex. 7.47: *Sonata No. 2,* Op. 35, Chopin

Ex. 7.48: *Symphony No. 3 in E flat
major,* Op. 55 (Eroica), Beethoven

Ex. 7.49: *Symphony No. 2 in C minor*
(Resurrection), Mahler

Ex. 7.50: *Symphony No. 5 in E minor,*
Op. 64, Tchaikovsky

Ex. 7.51: *Symphonie Fantastique,* Op.
14, Berlioz
DWMA, vol. 2, p. 129

Ex. 7.52: *Symphony No. 9 in E minor,*
Op. 95, Dvořák

Ex. 7.53: *Symphony No. 2 in D major,*
Sibelius

Concerto

Ex. 7.54: *Piano Concerto in A minor,*
Op. 54, Schumann

Ex. 7.55: *Violin Concerto in D major,*
Op. 77, Brahms

Ex. 7.56: *Piano Concerto in B flat
minor,* Tchaikovsky

Ex. 7.57: *Violoncello Concerto in B
minor,* Op. 104, Dvorák

Chamber Music

Ex. 7.58: *String Quartet No. 16 in F
major,* Op. 135, Beethoven

Ex. 7.59: *Piano Quintet in E flat major,*
Op. 44, Schumann

Ex. 7.60: *Clarinet Quintet in B minor,*
Op. 115, Brahms

Ex. 7.61: *String Quartet No. 2 in D
major,* Borodin

Ballet

Ex. 7.62: *Creatures of Prometheus,*
Beethoven

Ex. 7.63: *Swan Lake,* Tchaikovsky

Symphonic Suite

Ex. 7.64: *Nutcracker Suite,* Op. 71A,
Tchaikovsky

Ex. 7.65: *Peer Gynt Suite No. 1,* Op. 46,
Grieg

CHAPTER 8: EARLY TWENTIETH CENTURY (1900–1945)

Music for Voices
Art Song

Ex. 8.1: *Five Poems of Charles
Baudelaire* (1890), Debussy

Ex. 8.2: *Songs,* Ives

Ex. 8.3: *Chansons madécasses* (1926),
Ravel

Ex. 8.4: *Das Marienleben,* Op. 27 (1923,
rev. 1948), Hindemith

Ex. 8.5: *Pierrot Lunaire* (1912),
Schoenberg
DWMA, vol. 2, pp. 291, 293

Choral Works

Ex. 8.6: *The Peaceable Kingdom* (1936),
Randall Thompson

Ex. 8.7: *Mörike Lieder,* Op. 19
(1938–39), Distler

Ex. 8.8: *Twelve Welsh Folk Songs* (1931),
Holst

Opera and Musical Theater

Ex. 8.9: *Pelléas et Mélisande*
(1901–1902), Debussy

Ex. 8.10: *Wozzeck* (1931), Berg
DWMA, vol. 2, p. 311

Ex. 8.11: *Mathis der Mahler* (1938),
Hindemith

Ex. 8.12: *Moses und Aron* (begun 1932,
incompl.), Schoenberg

Ex. 8.13: *Die Dreigroschenoper* (1928),
Weill

Ex. 8.14: *Porgy and Bess* (1935),
Gershwin

Ex. 8.15: *Die lustige Witwe* (1905),
Lehar

Ex. 8.16: *Desert Song* (1926), Romberg

Ex. 8.17: *Showboat* (1927), Kern

Ex. 8.18: *Anything Goes* (1934), Porter

Oratorio/Choral Works with Orchestra

Ex. 8.19: *La Damoiselle élue*
(1887–88,1902), Debussy

Ex. 8.20: *The Hymn of Jesus,* Op. 37
(1917), Holst
DWMA, vol. 2, p. 269

Ex. 8.21: *Symphony of Psalms* (1930),
Stravinsky
DWMA, vol. 2, p. 336

Ex. 8.22: *Psalmus Hungaricus* (1923), Kodály

Ex. 8.23: *Belshazzar's Feast* (1931), Walton

Ex. 8.24: *Carmina Burana* (1937), Orff

Liturgical Music

Ex. 8.25: *Sacred Service, "Avodath Hakodesh"* (1934), Bloch

Ex. 8.26: *Choral-Passion* (1933), Distler

Music for Instruments
Overture and Symphonic Poems

Ex. 8.27: *Outdoor Overture* (1938), Copland

Ex. 8.28: *Big Ben Overture* (1934), Toch

Variation

Ex. 8.29: *Enigma Variations*, Op. 36 (1898–99), Elgar

Ex. 8.30: *Variations for Orchestra*, Op. 31 (1938), Schoenberg
DWMA, vol. 2, pp. 296, 299

Ex. 8.31: *Variations for Piano*, Op. 27 (1936), Webern

Short Forms: Dances,
Poetic Pieces

Ex. 8.32: *Three Pieces in the Shape of a Pear* (1890–1903), Satie (piano)

Ex. 8.33: *Mikrokosmos* (1926–37), Bartók (piano)

Ex. 8.34: *Sarcasms* (1912–14), Prokofiev (piano)

Sonata, Chamber Music,
and Symphony

Ex. 8.35: *Sonata for Violin and Piano* (1921–22), Bartók

Ex. 8.36: *Piano Sonata* (1941), Copland

Ex. 8.37: *Sonata for Trombone and Piano* (1941), Hindemith

Ex. 8.38: *Sonata for Cello Unaccompanied* (1909–10), Kodály

Ex. 8.39: *String Quartet No. 6* (1939), Bartók

Ex. 8.40: *Sonata for Violin and Cello* (1920–22), Ravel

Ex. 8.41: *Ode to Napoleon* (1942), Schoenberg

Ex. 8.42: *London Symphony* (1914, rev. 1920), Vaughan Williams

Ex. 8.43: *Symphony for Chamber Orchestra*, Op. 21 (1928), Webern

Concerto:

Ex. 8.44: *Piano Concerto* (1942), Schoenberg

Ex. 8.45: *Violin Concerto* (1936), Berg

Ex. 8.46: *Violin Concerto No. 2* (1935), Prokofiev

Ex. 8.47: *Concerto Grosso No. 1* (1924–25), Bloch

Ex. 8.48: *Concerto for Orchestra* (1944), Bartók

Suite

Ex. 8.49: *Lyric Suite* (1927), Berg (string quartet)

Ex. 8.50: *Appalachian Spring Suite* (1945), Copland (orchestra)
DWMA, vol. 2, p. 342

Ex. 8.51: *Lieutenant Kije Suite* (1934), Prokofiev (for orchestra)

Ex. 8.52: *Suite No. 2 for Orchestra* (1902, rev. 1943), Bartók

Ex. 8.53: *Suite*, Op. 25 (1924), Schoenberg (piano)

Ballet–Modern Dance

Ex. 8.54: *El sombrero de tres picos* (1919), de Falla

Ex. 8.55: *Le Sacre du printemps* (1913), Stravinsky
DWMA, vol. 2, p. 322

Ex. 8.56: *Le Création du monde* (1923), Milhaud

Ex. 8.57: *The Golden Age* (1930), Shostakovitch

Ex. 8.58: *Romeo and Juliet* (1938), Prokofiev

Incidental Music for Film and Drama

Ex. 8.59: *Of Mice and Men* (1939), Copland (film)

Ex. 8.60: *Quiet City* (1939), Copland (film)

Ex. 8.61: *Major Barbara* (1941), Walton (film)

Ex. 8.62: *Divertissement* (1930), Ibert (drama)

CHAPTER 9: MUSIC SINCE WORLD WAR II

Music for Voices
Art Song

Ex. 9.1: *Six Songs,* Op. 62, Dmitri Shostakovich (1942, orchestrated, 1971)

Ex. 9.2: *Goethe-Lieder,* for voice and three clarinets, Luigi Dallapiccola (1953)

Ex. 9.3: *Still Falls the Rain—The Raids (1940), Night and Dawn,* for tenor, horn, and piano, Benjamin Britten (1954)

Ex. 9.4: *Poems of Love and the Rain,* Ned Rorem (1962–63)

Ex. 9.5: *Philomel,* for voice and magnetic tape, Milton Babbitt (1964)

Ex. 9.6: *Eight Songs for a Mad King,* for baritone and instruments, Peter Maxwell Davies (1969)

Ex. 9.7: *Recital I (for Cathy),* sop. solo with seventeen instruments, Luciano Berio (1972)

Ex. 9.8: *Final Alice,* for soprano, folk group, and orchestra, David del Tredici (1976)

Ex. 9.9: *In the Theater of Night: Dream Songs on Poems of Karl Shapiro,* Judith Lang Zaimont (1983)

Choral Works

Ex. 9.10: *Five Flower Songs,* Benjamin Britten (1950)

Ex. 9.11: *Ave Maria,* Peter Maxwell Davies (1961)

Ex. 9.12: *Sound Patterns,* Pauline Oliveros (1961)

Ex. 9.13: *Motetti per la Passione,* Goffredo Petrassi (1965)

Ex. 9.14: *Lux aeterna,* György Ligeti (1966)

Ex. 9.15: *Campian Suite,* Halsey Stevens (1967)

Ex. 9.16: *Ecloga VIII,* Krzysztof Penderecki (1972)

Ex. 9.17: *Three Evangelienmotetten,* Johann Nepomuk David (1971)

Ex. 9.18: *Sacred and Profane—Medieval Lyrics,* Op. 91, Benjamin Britten (1974–75)

Ex. 9.19: *Litany,* Arvo Pärt (1995)

Ex. 9.20: *Mass,* Igor Stravinsky (1948)

Ex. 9.21: *Messe de la Pentacôte,* Olivier Messiaen (1950)

Ex. 9.22: *Christmas Cantata,* Arthur Honneger (1953)

Ex. 9.23: *Canti di liberazione,* Luigi Dallapiccola (1955)

Ex. 9.24: *War Requiem,* Benjamin Britten (1962)

Ex. 9.25: *Passion According to St. Luke,* Krzysztof Penderecki (1962–65)

Ex. 9.26: *The Vision of St. Augustine,* Michael Tippett (1963–65)

Ex. 9.27: *Mass,* Leonard Bernstein (1971)

Ex. 9.28: *A Polish Requiem,* Krzysztof Penderecki (1980–84)

Opera and Musical Theater

Ex. 9.29: *Peter Grimes,* Benjamin Britten (1945)

Ex. 9.30: *The Consul,* Gian-Carlo Menotti (1950)

Ex. 9.31: *The Rake's Progress,* Igor Stravinsky (1951)

Ex. 9.32: *My Fair Lady,* Frederick Loewe (1956)

Ex. 9.33: *Sound of Music,* Richard Rodgers (1959)

Ex. 9.34: *Fiddler on the Roof,* Jerry Bock (1964)

Ex. 9.35: *The Midsummer Marriage,* Michael Tippett (1965)

Ex. 9.36: *West Side Story,* Leonard Bernstein (1965)

Ex. 9.37: *A Water Bird Talk,* Domenick Argento (1974)

Ex. 9.38: *The Mask of Orpheus,* Harrison Birtwistle (1974–77)

Ex. 9.39: *We Come to the River,* Hans Werner Henze (1974–76)

Ex. 9.40: *Chorus Line,* Marvin Hamlisch (1975)

Ex. 9.41: *Mary, Queen of Scots,* Thea Musgrave (1977)

Ex. 9.42: *Satyagraha,* Phillip Glass (1980)

Ex. 9.43: *Cats,* Andrew Lloyd Webber (1981)

Ex. 9.44: *Nixon in China,* John Adams (1987)

Ex. 9.45: *Phantom of the Opera,* Andrew Lloyd Webber (1987)

Ex. 9.46: *Into the Woods,* Stephen Sondheim (1987)

Music for Instruments
Traditional Genres

Ex. 9.47: *Double Concerto for Harpsichord and Piano,* Elliott Carter (1961)

Ex. 9.48: *Concerto for Piano and Woodwinds,* Wallingford Riegger (1954)

Ex. 9.49: *Concerto for Viola and Orchestra,* Krzysztof Penderecki (1983)

Ex. 9.50: *Violin Concerto,* Krzysztof Penderecki (1976–77)

Ex. 9.51: *Concerto da Camera II,* Shulamit Ran (1987)

Ex. 9.52: *Symphony No. 2* (Mysterious Mountain), Alan Hovhannes (1955)

Ex. 9.53: *Symphony in Three Movements,* Igor Stravinsky (1946)

Ex. 9.54: *Symphony No. 1,* John Corigliano (1990)

Ex. 9.55: *Baroque Variations,* Lukas Foss (1967)

Ex. 9.56: *Variazione per Orchestra,* Luigi Dallapiccola (1954)

Ex. 9.57: *Landrover,* John Cage (1972) (ballet)

Ex. 9.58: *Winterbranch,* La Monte Young (1964) (ballet)

Ex. 9.59: *The Labyrinth,* Hans Werner Henze (1952) (ballet)

Ex. 9.60: *Piano Trio,* Leon Kirchner (1954)

Ex. 9.61: *Quintet for Brass,* Elliott Carter (1974) (woodwind quartet)

Nontraditional Musical Compositions Using Traditional Instruments

Ex. 9.62: *Threnody for the Victims of Hiroshima,* Krzysztof Penderecki (1959–60)

Ex. 9.63: *Pithoprakta,* Iannis Xenakis (1957)

Ex. 9.64: *A Collection of Rocks, Orchestra Without Conductor,* John Cage (1984)

Ex. 9.65: *Fontana Mix,* John Cage (1958)

Ex. 9.66: *Chronochromie,* Olivier Messiaen (1960)

Ex. 9.67: *Distant Runes and Incantations, for Piano and Orchestra,* Joseph Schwantner (1983)

Electronic Music

Ex. 9.68: *Silver Apples of the Moon,* Morton Subotnik (1967)

Ex. 9.69: *Computer Piece,* Vladimir Ussachevsky (1965)

Ex. 9.70: *And God Created Great Whales,* Op. 229/1, for taped whale sounds and orchestra, Alan Hovhannes (1970)

Ex. 9.71: *Synchronisms No. 7,* Mario Davidovsky (1974)

Ex. 9.72: *Orfeo,* for dancer, flute, and tape, Thea Musgrave (1975)

Appendix 3
Additional Resources

The following resources are included in this appendix:

1. General readings
2. Music references
3. Music periodicals
4. Scores and recordings
5. Musical anthologies
6. Readings by chapter

1. General Readings

Abraham, Gerald. *The Concise Oxford History of Music.* New York: Oxford University Press, 1985.

Borroff, Edith. *Music in Europe and the United States.* 2d ed. Engelwood Cliffs, N.J.: Prentice-Hall Inc., 1990.

Crocker, Richard L. *A History of Musical Style.* New York: Dover, 1986.

Grout, Donald Jay, and Claude Palisca. *A History of Western Music.* 4th ed. New York: W. W. Norton, 1988.

Lang, Paul Henry. *Music in Western Civilization.* New York: W. W. Norton, 1941.

Le Huray, Peter. *Authenticity in Performance.* New York: Cambridge University Press, 1990.

Rosenstiel, Leonie, ed. *Schirmer History of Music.* New York: Schirmer Books, 1982.

Stevens, Denis, ed. *History of Song.* Rev. ed. New York: W. W. Norton, 1970.

Stolba, K Marie. *The Development of Western Music: A History.* 3d ed. Dubuque, Iowa: Brown and Benchmark, 1997.

Strunk, Oliver. *Source Readings in Music History.* Rev. ed. New York: W. W. Norton, 1996.

Wold, Milo, et al. *An Introduction to Music and Art in the Western World.* 10th ed. Dubuque, Iowa: Wm. C. Brown Co., 1996.

2. Music References

Blume, Friedrich, ed. *Die Musik in Geschichte und Gegenwart.* 16 vols. Kassel, West Germany: Bärenreiter, 1949–1986 (New edition begun c. 1994).

Hitchcock, H. Wiley, and Stanley Sadie, ed. *The New Grove Dictionary of American Music.* 4 vol. London: Macmillan Press, 1986.

Kernfeld, Barry, ed. *The New Grove Dictionary of Jazz.* 2 vols. London: Macmillan, 1988.

New Oxford History of Music. 10 vols. London: Oxford, 1954–1975. The volumes are: I. Ancient and Oriental Music (1957); II. Early Middle Ages to 1300 (2nd ed. 1990); III Ars Nova and the Renaissance, 1300–1540 (1960); IV. The Age of Humanism, 1540–1630 (1968); V. Opera and Church Music, 1630–1750 (1975); VI. Concert Music, 1630–1750 (1986); VII. The Age of Enlightenment, 1745–1790 (1973); VIII. The Age of Beethoven, 1790–1830 (1982); IX. Romanticism, 1830–1890 (1990); and X. The Modern Age, 1890–1960 (1974).

Randel, Don, ed. *The Harvard Biographical Dictionary of Music.* Cambridge: Harvard University Press, 1996.

Randel, Don, ed. *The New Harvard Dictionary of Music.* Cambridge: Harvard University Press, 1990.

Sadie, Julie Anne, and Rhian Samuel, ed. *The Norton-Grove Dictionary of Women Composers.* New York: W. W. Norton, 1995.

Sadie, Stanley, ed. *New Grove Dictionary of Music and Musicians.* 20 vols. London: Macmillan, 1980. This edition is by far the most comprehensive in the English language. It contains extended articles on every facet of music as well as extensive biographical entries.

Sadie, Stanley, ed. *The New Grove Dictionary of Opera.* 4 vols. London: Macmillan, 1992.

Shestack, Melvin, and Tad Richards. *The New Country Music Encyclopedia.* New York: Simon and Schuster, 1993.

Slonimsky, Nicholas. *Baker's Biographical Dictionary of Musicians.* 8th ed. New York: Shirmer Books, 1992.

Thompson, Oscar. *International Cyclopedia of Music and Musicians.* 10th ed. Edited by Oscar Thompson and Bruce Bohle. New York: W. W. Dodd, 1975.

3. Music Periodicals

Black Music Research Journal
The Cambridge Opera Journal
Die Reihe
Early Music
Gramophone
Journal of the American Musicological Society
Journal of the Royal Musical Association
Modern Music Quarterly (1923–1946)
Music and Letters
The Musical Quarterly
The Musical Times
Nineteenth Century Music
Notes: Quarterly Journal of the Music Library Association
The Opera Quarterly
Opera News
Perspectives of New Music
Popular Music and Society
The Schwann Catalogue

4. Scores and Recordings

Recordings of the following collections were released on Long Playing discs in the past, and may be available in libraries today.

Burkhart, Charles. *Anthology for Musical Analysis.* 5th ed. New York: Holt, Rinehart and Winston, 1993.

Davison, Archibald, and Willi Apel. *Historical Anthology of Music.* 2 vols. Cambridge: Harvard University Press, 1949.

Gleason, Harold, and Warren Becker. *Examples of Music Before 1400.* 2d ed. Van Nuys, Calif.: Alfred, 1987.

History of Music in Sound. 10 vols. London: Oxford, 1953. Recorded by RCA. (This anthology contains only partial scores, but the recordings are complete.)

Kamien, Roger. *The Norton Scores: An anthology for listening.* 2 vols. 5th ed. New York: W. W. Norton, 1990.

Morgan, Robert P. *Anthology of Twentieth Century Music.* New York: W. W. Norton, 1992.

Parrish, Carl. *Treasury of Early Music.* New York: W. W. Norton, 1964. (Available in paperback form.)

Parrish, Carl, and John F. Ohl. *Masterpieces of Music Before 1750.* New York: W. W. Norton, 1950.

Schering, Arnold. *Geschichte der Musik in Beispielen.* Leipzig, East Germany: Breitkopf and Härtel, 1931.

Starr, William J., and George F. Devine. *Omnibus.* Parts 1 and 2. Englewood Cliffs, N. J.: Prentice-Hall, Inc., 1964 and 1974.

5. Musical Anthologies

Cohen, Albert, and John D. White. *Anthology of Music for Analysis.* New York: Appleton Century Crofts, 1965.

Downs, Philip G., ed. *Anthology of Classical Music.* New York: W. W. Norton, 1992.

Fellerer, Karl Gustav, ed. *Anthology of Music.* 47 vols. Cologne, West Germany: Arno Volk Verlag, begun in 1959.

Hardy, Gordon, and Arnold Fish. *Music Literature.* 2 vols. New York: Dodd, Mead and Co., 1966.

Hoppin, Richard H. *Anthology of Medieval Music.* New York: W. W. Norton, 1978.

Kirby, F. E., ed. *Music in the Classic Period: An Anthology with Commentary.* New York: G. Schirmer, 1979.

———. *Music in the Romantic Period: An Anthology with Commentary.* New York: G. Schirmer, 1986.

Lang, Paul Henry. *The Concerto 1800–1900.* New York: W. W. Norton, 1969.

Lang, Paul Henry. *The Symphony 1800–1900.* New York: W. W. Norton, 1969.

The Norton Anthology of Western Music. 2d ed. 1988. Two volumes edited by Claude V. Palisca have been published by W. W. Norton to accompany the fourth edition of *A History of Western Music* by Grout and Palisca. The scores found in these two volumes are discussed briefly in the Grout text. A partial recording of *The Norton Anthology of Western Music* is also available.

Norton Critical Scores. New York: W. W. Norton. Various dates. Each volume contains an authoritative study-size score of a major musical work and a comprehensive body of materials for the study of the work.

Plantinga, Leon. *An Anthology of Romantic Music.* New York: W. W. Norton, 1984.

Stolba, K Marie. *The Development of Western Music: An Anthology.* 2 vols. 2d ed. Dubuque, Iowa: Wm. C. Brown-Benchmark, 1994. Recordings accompany this set.

Wennerstrom, Mary H. *Anthology of Twentieth Century Music.* New York: Appleton Century Crofts, 1988.

6. Readings by Chapter
Chapter 1:
Ancient Precursors of Western Music

Brandel, Rose. *The Music of Central Africa.* New York: Da Capo Press, 1983.

Comotti, Giovanni. *Music in Greek and Roman Culture.* Translated by Rosaria Munson. Cambridge: Cambridge University Press, 1989.

Idelsohn, Abraham. *Jewish Music: Its Historical Development.* New York: Dover, 1992.

Malm, Wm. P. *Music Cultures of the Pacific, The Near East, and Asia.* 2d ed. Englewood Cliffs, N. J.: Prentice-Hall, 1977.

May, Elizabeth, ed. *Music of Many Cultures— An Introduction* (20 Essays, 3 Recordings). Berkeley: University of California Press, 1980.

Merriam, Alan P. *The Anthropology of Music.* Evanston, Ill.: Northwestern University Press, 1964.

Michaelides, Solon. *The Music of Ancient Greece: An Encyclopedia.* London: Faber and Faber, 1978.

Myers, Helen, ed. *Ethnomusicology: Historical and Regional Studies.* New York: W. W. Norton, 1993.

Nettl, Bruno. *Folk and Traditional Music of the Western Continents.* 2d ed. New York: Prentice-Hall, 1973.

———. *Music in Primitive Culture.* Cambridge: Harvard University Press, 1956.

Prajnanananda, Swami. *A History of Indian Music.* Hollywood: Vedanta Press, 1963.

Sachs, Curt. *Rise of Music in the Ancient World, East and West.* New York: W. W. Norton, 1943.

Sachs, Curt. *The Wellsprings of Music.* ed. by Jaap Kunst. New York: Da Capo, 1977.

West, M. L. *Ancient Greek Music.* London: Oxford University Press, 1992.

Chapter 2:
Early Middle Ages (300–1100)

Apel, Willi. *Gregorian Chant.* Bloomington: University of Indiana Press, 1958.

Fenlon, Iain, ed. *Early Music History.* 14 vols. Cambridge: Cambridge University Press, 1981 and following.

Hoppin, Richard H. *Medieval Music.* Ch. I–VII. New York: W. W. Norton, 1978.

———. *Anthology of Medieval Music.* New York: W. W. Norton, 1978.

Phillips, Elizabeth V., and John-Paul Jackson. *Performing Medieval & Renaissance Music: An Introductory Guide.* New York: G. Schirmer, 1986.

Reese, Gustave. *Music in the Middle Ages.* New York: W. W. Norton, 1940.

Seay, Albert. *Music in the Medieval World.* 2d ed. Englewood Cliffs, N. J.: Prentice-Hall, 1975.

Chapter 3:
Late Middle Ages: Ars Antiqua–Ars Nova (1100–1400)

Apel, Willi. *The Notation of Polyphonic Music.* 5th ed. Cambridge, Mass.: Medieval Academy of America, 1961.

———. *French Secular Music of the Late Fourteenth Century.* Cambridge, Mass.: Medieval Academy of America, 1950.

Arnold, John. *Medieval Music.* New York: Oxford University Press, 1986.

Boorman, Stanley. *Studies in the Performance of Late Medieval Music.* New York: Cambridge University Press, 1983.

Cattin, Giulio. *Music of the Middle Ages I.* Translated by Steven Botterill. New York: Cambridge University Press, 1984.

Collins, Fletcher, Jr. *A Medieval Songbook: Troubadour and Trouvère* Charlottesville: University Press of Virginia, 1982.

Gallo, F. Alberto. *Music of the Middle Ages II.* Translated by Karen Eales. Cambridge: Cambridge University Press, 1985.

Hoppin, Richard H. *Medieval Music.* Ch. VIII–XX. New York: W. W. Norton, 1978.

———. *Anthology of Medieval Music.* New York: W. W. Norton, 1978.

Hughes, Andrew. *Medieval Music: The Sixth Liberal Art.* 2d ed. Toronto: University of Toronto Press, 1980.

McGee, Timothy J. *Medieval and Renaissance Music: A Performer's Guide.* Toronto: University of Toronto Press, 1988.

Marocco, W. Thomas, and Nicholas Sandon. *Medieval Music.* New York: Oxford University Press, 1977.

Reese, Gustave. *Music in the Middle Ages.* New York: W. W. Norton, 1940.

Roche, Jerome. *Dictionary of Early Music: From the Troubadours to Monteverdi.* New York: Oxford University Press, 1981.

Seay, Albert. *Music in the Medieval World.* 2d ed. Englewood Cliffs, N. J.: Prentice-Hall, 1991.

Stevens, John. *Words and Music in the Middle Ages: Song, Narrative, Dance and Drama.* New York: Cambridge University Press, 1986.

Chapter 4:
Renaissance (1400–1600)

Brown, Howard Mayer. *Music in the Renaissance.* Englewood Cliffs, N. J.: Prentice Hall, 1976.

Bukofzer, Manfred. *Studies in Medieval and Renaissance Music.* New York: W. W. Norton, 1947.

Carpenter, Nan Cooke. *Music in the Medieval and Renaissance Universities.* Norman, Okla.: University of Oklahoma Press, 1972.

Einstein, Alfred. *The Italian Madrigal.* 3 vols. Princeton, N. J.: Princeton University Press, 1949.

Fellowes, E. H. *The English Madrigal Composers.* London: Oxford University Press, 1977.

Fenlon, Iain. *The Italian Renaissance: From the 1470's to the End of the 16th Century.* Englewood Cliffs, N. J.: Prentice Hall, 1990.

Greenberg, Noah, and Paul Maynard, eds. *Anthology of Early Renaissance Music.* New York: W. W. Norton, 1975.

Harmon, Alec, ed. *Oxford Book of Italian Madrigals.* New York: Oxford University Press, 1983.

Ledger, Philip, ed. *Oxford Book of English Madrigals.* New York: Oxford University Press, 1978.

Lowinsky, Edward E. *Secret Chromatic Art in the Netherlands Motet.* New York: Columbia University Press, 1946.

Reese, Gustave. *Music in the Renaissance.* Rev. ed. New York: W. W. Norton, 1959.

Reese, Gustav. *New Grove High Renaissance Masters.* Edited by Stanley Sadie. New York: W. W. Norton, 1984.

Roche, Jerome. *The Madrigal.* 2d ed. New York: Oxford University Press, 1990.

Stevens, J. E., ed. *Music and Poetry in the Early Tudor Court.* New York: Cambridge University Press, 1979.

Walker, Ernest. *A History of Music in England.* 3d ed. London: Oxford University Press, 1978.

Chapter 5:
Baroque (1600–1750)

Anthony, James, et al. *New Grove French Baroque Masters.* New York: W. W. Norton, 1987.

Anthony, James R. *French Baroque Music.* New York: W. W. Norton, 1981.

Arnold, Denis. *New Grove Italian Baroque Masters.* New York: W. W. Norton, 1984.

Bianconi, Lorenzo. *Music in the Seventeenth Century.* Translated by David Bryant. New York: Cambridge University Press, 1987.

Bukofzer, Manfred E. *Music in the Baroque Era.* New York: W. W. Norton, 1947.

Celletti, Rodolfo. *Bel Canto.* New York: Oxford University Press, 1991.

David, Hans T., and Arthur Mendel. *The Bach Reader.* Rev. ed. New York: W. W. Norton, 1966.

Dean, Winton. *The New Grove Handel.* New York: W. W. Norton, 1983.

Dean, Winton, and J. M. Knapp. *Handel's Operas: 1904–1726.* 2 vols. New York: Oxford University Press, 1987.

Donington, Robert. *Baroque Music: Style and Performance.* New York: W. W. Norton, 1982.

Geiringer, Karl. *The Bach Family.* New York: Oxford University Press, 1981.

Grout, Donald J. *A Short History of Opera.* 3d ed. New York: Columbia University Press, 1988.

Hutchings, Arthur. *The Baroque Concerto.* 3d Rev. ed. New York: W. W. Norton, 1978.

Newman, William S. *The Sonata in the Baroque Era.* 4th ed. Chapel Hill: University of North Carolina Press, 1983.

Palisca, Claude V. *Baroque Music.* 2d ed. Englewood Cliffs, N. J.: Prentice-Hall, 1981.

Rifkin, Joshua, et al. *New Grove North European Baroque Masters.* New York: W. W. Norton, 1985.

Smither, Howard E. *A History of Oratorio.* 3 vols. Chapel Hill: University of North Carolina Press, 1977–87.

Chapter 6:
Classic (1750–1820)

Burney, Dr. Charles. *An Eighteenth Century Musical Tour in Central Europe and the Netherlands.* New York: Oxford University Press, 1959.
––––––. *An Eighteenth Century Music Journey in France and Italy.* New York: Oxford University Press, 1959.
Carse, Adam. *The Orchestra in the Eighteenth Century.* Cambridge, England: W. Heffer, 1940.
Dent, E. J. *Mozart's Operas.* 2d ed. New York: Oxford University Press, 1991.
Downs, Philip G. *Classical Music.* New York: W. W. Norton, 1992.
Geiringer, Karl. *Haydn, A Creative Life in Music.* New York: W. W. Norton, 1946.
––––––. *The Bach Family.* New York: Oxford University Press, 1981.
Grout, Donald J. *A Short History of Opera.* 3d ed. New York: Columbia University Press, 1988.
Heartz, Daniel. *Haydn, Mozart and the Viennese School.* New York: W. W. Norton, 1995.
Landon, H. C. Robbins. *Haydn's Chronicle and Works.* 5 vols. Bloomington: University of Indiana Press, 1995.
Newman, William S. *The Sonata in the Classic Era.* 3d ed. Chapel Hill: University of North Carolina Press, 1983.
Pauly, Reinhard G. *Music in the Classic Period.* 3d ed. Englewood Cliffs, N. J.: Prentice-Hall, 1987.
Pestelli, Giorgio. *Age of Mozart and Beethoven.* Translated by Eric Cross. New York: Cambridge University Press, 1984.
Rosen, Charles. *The Classical Style: Haydn, Mozart and Beethoven.* New York: Viking, 1971.
Solomon, Maynard. *Mozart: A life.* New York: Harper Collins, 1995.

Chapter 7:
Romantic (1820–1900)

Abraham, Gerald. *A Hundred Years of Music.* New York: Knopf, 1993.
Barzun, Jacques. *Berlioz and the Romantic Century.* 2 vols. New York: Little, Brown, 1982.
Campbell, Stuart, editor and translator. *Russians on Russian Music, 1830–1880.* New York: Cambridge University Press, 1994.

Chase, Gilbert. *America's Music.* 3d ed. Champaign: University of Illinois Press, 1987.
Cooper, Martin. *French Music from the Death of Berlioz to the Death of Fauré.* New York: Oxford University Press, 1951.
Dahlhaus, Carl. *Nineteenth-Century Music.* Translated by J. Bradford Robison. Berkeley: University of California Press, 1980.
Donnington, Robert. *The Opera.* New York: Harcourt, Brace, Jovanovich, 1978.
Einstein, Alfred. *Music in the Romantic Era.* New York: W. W. Norton, 1947.
Grout, D. J. *A Short History of Opera.* 3d ed. New York: Columbia University Press, 1973.
Kramer, Lawrence. *Music and Poetry: The Nineteenth Century and After.* Berkeley: University of California Press, 1984.
Landau, Annaliese. *Lied: The Unfolding of Its Style.* Lanham, Md.: University Press of America, 1980.
Longyear, Rey M. *Nineteenth-Century Romanticism in Music.* 3d ed. Englewood Cliffs, N. J.: Prentice-Hall, 1987.
Newman, Ernest. *The Wagner Operas.* New York: Knopf, 1991.
Plantinga, Leon. *Romantic Music.* New York: W. W. Norton, 1984.
Prawer, S. S. *Penguin Book of Lieder.* New York: Penguin, 1982.
Rosen, Charles. *The Romantic Generation.* Cambridge: Harvard University Press, 1995.
Solomon, Maynard. *Beethoven.* New York: Schirmer, 1979.
Zetlin, Mikhail O. *The Five, the Revolution of the Russian School of Music.* New York: International Universities Press, 1959.

Chapter 8:
Early Twentieth Century (1900–1945)

Austin, William W. *Music in the 20th Century.* New York: W. W. Norton, 1966.
Crawford, John C., and Dorothy L. Crawford. *Expressionism in Twentieth-Century Music.* Bloomington: Indiana University Press, 1993.
Eimert, Herbert, and Karlheinz Stockhausen. *Anton Webern.* Valley Forge, Pa. European-American Press, 1958.
Kislan, Richard. *The Musical: A Look at the American Musical.* Rev. ed. Englewood Cliffs, N. J.: Prentice-Hall, 1995.

Leibowitz, René. *Schoenberg and His School.* New York: Da Capo Press, 1975.

McVeagh, Diana, et al. *New Grove Twentieth Century English Masters.* New York: W. W. Norton, 1986.

Machlis, Joseph. *Introduction to Contemporary Music.* 2d ed. New York: W. W. Norton, 1979.

Martin, George. *The Companion to Twentieth Century Opera.* North Pomfret, Vt.: Trafalgar, 1992.

Martin, William R., and Julius Drossing. *Music of the 20th Century.* Englewood Cliffs, N. J.: Prentice-Hall, 1980.

Morgan, Robert. *Twentieth Century Music.* New York: W. W. Norton, 1991.

Prendergast, Roy M. *Film Music: A Neglected Art.* 2d ed. New York: W. W. Norton, 1992.

Salzman, Eric. *Twentieth-Century Music: An Introduction.* 3d ed. Englewood Cliffs, N. J.: Prentice-Hall, 1987.

Schwarz, Boris. *Music and Musical Life in Soviet Russia: 1917–1970.* New York: W. W. Norton, 1972.

Sessions, Roger. *The Musical Experience of Composer, Performer, Listener.* Princeton, N. J.: Princeton University Press, 1950.

Somfai, Laszlo, et al. *New Grove Modern Masters: Bartók, Stravinsky, Hindemith.* Edited by Stanley Sadie. New York: W. W. Norton, 1984.

Stuckenschmidt, H. H. *Twentieth Century Music.* Translated by Richard Deveson. New York: McGraw Hill, 1969.

———. *Schoenberg: His Life, World and Work.* New York: Schirmer Publications, 1978.

Chapter 9:
Music Since World War II

Cage, John. *Silence.* Middletown, Conn.: Wesleyan University Press, 1973.

Carlson, Effie B. *Bio-Bibliographical Dictionary of Twelve Tone and Serial Composers.* Ann Arbor, Mich.: UMI, n.d.

Cope, David. *Computers and Musical Style.* Madison, Wisc.: A-R Editions, 1991.

Cope, David. *New Directions in Music.* 6th ed. Dubuque, Iowa: Wm. C. Brown Company Publishers, 1993.

Darter, Tom, and Greg Arbruster. *The Art of Electronic Music.* New York: Morrow, 1985.

Ernst, David. *The Evolution of Electronic Music.* New York: G. Schirmer, 1977.

Ligeti, György. *Ligeti in Conversation.* Jersey City, N. J.: Da Capo Press, 1985.

Manning, Peter. *Electronic and Computer Music.* 2d ed. New York: Oxford University Press, 1994.

Meyer, Leonard B. *Music, The Arts and Ideas.* Chicago, Ill.: University of Chicago Press, 1994.

Nyman, Michael. *Experimental Music: Cage and Beyond.* New York: G. Schirmer, 1981.

Read, Gardner. *Music Notation: A Manual of Modern Practice.* New York: Taplinger, 1979.

Schwartz, Elliott, and Barney Childs, eds. *Contemporary Composers on Contemporary Music.* New York: Holt, Rinehart and Winston, 1967.

Stone, Kurt. *Music Notation in the Twentieth Century: A Practical Guidebook.* New York: W. W. Norton, 1980.

Strange, Allen. *Electronic Music Systems, Techniques and Controls.* 3d ed. Dubuque, Iowa: Wm. C. Brown Company Publishers, 1990.

Xenakis, Iannis. *Formalized Music: Thought and Mathematics in Composition.* Ann Arbor, Mich.: UMI, 1992.

Chapter 10:
Jazz and Popular Music
of the Twentieth Century

Balliett, Whitney, *American Musicians: Fifty-six Portraits in Jazz.* New York: Oxford University Press, 1986.

———. *American Singers: Twenty-seven Portraits in Song.* New York: Oxford University Press, 1988.

Berendt, Joachim. *The Jazz Book.* Westport, Conn.: Lawrence Hill, 1992.

Brown, Charles T. *The Art of Rock and Roll.* 3d ed. New York: Prentice-Hall, 1992.

Ewen, David. *All the Years of American Popular Music.* Englewood Cliffs, N. J.: Prentice-Hall, 1977.

Feather, Leonard. *The Encyclopedia of Jazz in the 60s.* New York: Da Capo Press, 1986.

Feather, Leonard, and Ira Gitler. *The Encyclopedia of Jazz in the 70s.* New York: Da Capo Press, 1987.

Friedwald, Will. *Jazz Singing: America's Great Voices from Bessie Smith to Bebop and Beyond.* New York: Chas. Scribner's Sons, 1992.

Gammond, Peter. *The Oxford Companion to Popular Music.* New York: Oxford University Press, 1991.

Haralambos, Michael. *Right On: From Blues to Soul in Black America.* New York: Da Capo Press, 1979.

————. *Soul Music: Birth of a Sound in Black America.* Jersey City, N. J.: Da Capo Press, 1985.

Hentoff, Nat. *Jazz Is.* New York: Limelight Editions, 1984.

Hodier, André. *Jazz, Its Evolution and Essence.* New York: Grove Press, 1986.

Jone, LeRoi. *Blues People: Negro Music in White America.* New York: Morrow, 1971.

Kaufman, Fredrick, and John P. Guckin. *The African Roots of Jazz.* Van Nuys, Calif.: Alfred, 1979.

Malone, Bill. *Classic Country Music.* Washington, D.C.: Smithsonian Institution, 1990.

————. *Dead Elvis.* New York: Doubleday, 1991.

Marcus, Greil. *The Aesthetics of Rock.* Jersey City, N. J.: Da Capo Press, 1987.

Oliver, Paul, et al. *New Grove Gospel, Blues and Jazz.* New York: W. W. Norton, 1987.

Pattison, Robert. *The Triumph of Vulgarity: Rock Music in the Mirror of Romanticism.* New York: Oxford University Press, 1987.

Pleasants, Henry. *The Great American Popular Singers.* New York: Simon and Schuster, 1974.

Schuller, Gunther. *Early Jazz: Its Roots and Musical Development.* New York: Oxford University Press, 1986.

Tanner, Paul O. W., et al. *A Study of Jazz.* 8th ed. Dubuque, Iowa: Wm. C. Brown Publishers, 1997.

Whitcomb, Ian. *After the Ball: Pop Music from Rag to Rock.* Rev. ed. New York: Limelight Ed., 1986.

Wilder, Alec. *American Popular Song: The Great Innovators, 1900–1950.* New York: Oxford University Press, 1972.

Williams, Martin, ed. *The Art of Jazz: Ragtime to Bebop.* Jersey City, N. J.: Da Capo Press, 1981.

Glossary

Absolute Music Without textual or programmatic associations.

A Cappella A term used to designate choral music without accompaniment.

Agréments A French term applied to small melodic ornaments.

Aleatoric Music A type of composition based on the element of chance in both the selection of sounds and their performance.

Ballet de Cour (Ballet of the Court) A dramatic presentation in dance at the seventeenth-century French Royal Court.

Basso Continuo The bass part in music of the Baroque period, usually performed by a harpsichord or organ together with viol, bassoon, or cello. It was normally read and played from a figured bass.

Binary Form A form consisting of two sections: A-B.

Cadence A melodic or harmonic ending of a phrase or movement. Authentic, plagal, and deceptive are terms used to describe degrees of repose.

Canon The musical term denoting strict imitation within a polyphonic texture.

Cantus Firmus A melody, either composed or taken from another source, upon which certain polyphonic works are constructed.

Chord A combination of three or more tones sounded simultaneously.

Chromatic Alteration Altering a tone of the diatonic scale by means of accidentals.

Clavecin The French term for harpsichord.

Coloratura Virtuoso ornamentation and embellishment on a melodic line, normally referring to the human voice.

Concertato Style A style of musical performance associated with the seventeenth century that commonly features a basso continuo with melodies shared among several voices in alternation.

Consonance In traditional harmony, an interval or chord that produces an effect of repose or agreeableness.

Contrapuntal *See* Counterpoint

Contrary Motion The movement of two voices in opposite directions.

Contratenor The third voice, added to the tenor and discant in fourteenth- and fifteenth-century vocal compositions.

Counterpoint The combination of two or more distinctive melodic lines into a single musical fabric. It is often used synonymously with polyphony.

Diatonic The scale made up of five whole tones and two semitones. The term is also used to describe melodic motion in scales without chromatic alterations.

Dissonance In traditional harmony, an interval or chord that produces an effect of harmonic tension.

Dominant The fifth degree of the diatonic scale or, in harmonic practice, a chord built upon the fifth degree.

Double-Stop The simultaneous playing on two strings of a bowed instrument.

Drone A sustained note or notes, usually in the bass, that is retained throughout a section or a whole piece. The principal note is usually the tonic, but it sometimes alternates between the tonic and dominant.

Dynamic Markings Signs, abbreviations, and words used to indicate degrees of loudness and volume of sound.

Empfindsamer Stil (Sensitive Style) A mid-eighteenth-century style that emphasized melodic simplicity and refined expression. *See* Galant Style

Episode A secondary passage or section that digresses from the main theme. Episodes are frequently found in rondos and fugues.

Equal Temperament A system of tuning in which the octave is divided into twelve equal semitones.

Expressionism A term borrowed from the visual arts. In music, often associated with atonalism and the music of Schoenberg.

Falsetto A style of singing by the male voice in which a very high head tone is produced.

Figuration Stereotyped chordal patterns used in the realization of a figured bass.

Figured Bass The numerical symbols placed beneath the staff from which continuo players realize the harmonic intent of the composer.

Galant Style An eighteenth-century style noted for its regularity of phrase, lightness of texture, inclination to ornamentation, and simple harmonies. The music of Louis Couperin is in this style.

Genre Style or type of music.

Harmony A simultaneous sounding of two or more tones; the theory and practice of chord construction and progressions.

Hocket A medieval musical device in which notes alternated rapidly between two (or among three) voices, resulting in an unusual, prominent rhythmic pattern.

Homophony Music in which one dominant melodic voice is supported by an accompaniment.

Imitation The repetition, exact or with minor variations, of a melodic, rhythmic, or harmonic entity in music.

Impressionism This term was borrowed from the visual arts. In music it refers to a style that emphasizes chromaticism, ambiguous tonalities, and rich timbres. It is most commonly associated with Debussy and Ravel.

Incipit The opening line of text or music, or both, from a composition.

Interval The distance in pitch between two tones played either successively (melodic interval) or simultaneously (harmonic interval).

Intonation The degree of accuracy of pitch.

Inversion (1) An interval is inverted by transferring its lowest tone to the octave above, or by transferring its highest tone to the octave below. (2) A chord is inverted by placing any other than its root or fundamental tone in the bass. (3) A melody is inverted by changing each descending interval to the same ascending interval.

Isorhythm A repetitive device used in medieval music. Its two parts are the *talea,* the repeated rhythmic element, and the *color,* the repeated melodic element. These need not be of the same duration.

Legato In a connected style.

Libretto Literally, little book. The text of an opera.

Lied, Lieder The German terms for Art Song.

Liturgy The official order of service in the Roman Catholic Church. The word also applies to authorized services in most Christian churches.

Melisma An elaborate, flowing ornament sung on one syllable in a melody. It normally refers to medieval music.

Melodrama A work or part of a work in which spoken parts are performed in alternation with instrumental passages, or in some cases together with such instrumental accompaniment. There are examples from the time of J. J. Rousseau to Stravinsky.

Meter The organization of time in music by means of more or less regularly accented and unaccented beats.

Modulation The process of moving from one tonal center to another in the course of a single composition.

Monochord An instrument consisting of a single string stretched over a resonating body.

Monophony A single melodic line without accompaniment.

Monothematic A composition based on a single melody or theme.

Motive A short melodic or rhythmic figure that is repeated to give design to a melodic or rhythmic phrase.

Musique Concrète Music in which natural sounds are recorded and manipulated electronically.

Mutation The transition used by a voice in moving from one hexachord to another in medieval music.

Ornamentation Added notes, such as trills or turns, to a melody.

Ostinato A short melodic figure that is repeated in one voice, usually the bass, throughout a section, movement, or composition. This is also known as ground bass. If the repeated pattern is confined to the rhythm, it is referred to as a rhythmic ostinato.

Parallel Motion Two or more voices moving in the same direction at a constant interval.

Pedal Point A sustained pitch, usually in the bass, originally from the pedal board of the organ.

Period A group of measures that makes a natural division of the melody, usually two phrases, analogous to a sentence in speech or writing.

Phrase A segment of melody that has a natural pause or ending. It is analogous to a phrase in speech or writing.

Pitch The aspect of a tone determined by the number of vibrations per second.

Pizzicato To pluck the string of a bowed instrument.

Polyphony A musical texture made of two or more simultaneous melodies sounded by independent voices or instruments.

Polyrhythms (cross-rhythms) The use of different rhythmic patterns simultaneously.

Polythematic A composition based on more than one melody or theme of equal importance.

Program Music Music of a descriptive character, especially but not exclusively of the nineteenth century, often designed to follow a specific pictorial narrative. It often employs imitative or evocative (representative) sounds.

Range The distance between the highest and lowest pitch of a melody, voice, or instrument.

Refrain One or two melodic phrases repeated at the end of each stanza.

Ritornello (1) An instrumental interlude before or after an aria or scene. (2) The tutti section of a concerto grosso. (3) The last two lines of the stanza in the fourteenth-century madrigal.

Rubato Elasticity of tempo in performance.

Scale A series of adjacent tones arranged according to whole and half steps, or any other regular increment of pitch.

Sequence The repetition of a melodic motive in the same part above or below the original.

Serial Composition The principles of composition set forth by Arnold Schoenberg that most frequently, but not exclusively, involve the twelve-tone system.

Song Cycle A series of art songs connected by a central poetic idea.

Stile Rappresentativo The style of presentation employed in the performance of the earliest operas and oratorios of the seventeenth century. It was characterized especially by free rhythmic declamation.

Strophic A song of which all stanzas are sung to the same music.

Syncopation A rhythmic device that displaces the accent from a strong beat to a weak beat or a weak portion of the beat.

Tablature Name for the various early systems of notation in which symbols, letters, or figures were used instead of notes on the staff.

Temperament A system of scalar tuning based on musical and mathematical considerations.

Tempo The rapidity with which beats succeed each other in a musical texture. Tempo marks are words and abbreviations used to indicate degrees of speed.

Tenor (1) Designation for a high male voice. (2) The melody upon which medieval masses and motets were constructed. *See* Cantus Firmus

Ternary Form A form consisting of three sections: A-B-A.

Tetrachord A scale-series of four tones, the highest and lowest of which form the interval of a perfect fourth.

Texture The density of melodic and harmonic elements designated by such terms as homophonic, polyphonic, chordal.

Theme A distinctive melody, or musical idea, that serves as a basis for musical composition. Also, a melodic gesture that is transformed variously, by the composer.

Through-Composed The opposite of strophic; a song that has different music throughout the composition.

Timbre Quality (color) of a tone as produced on a specific instrument or voice; also referred to as tone color.

Tonality The result of harmonic organization around a central tone, called the tonic or keynote.

Tone Color *See* Timbre

Tonic The first note of the scale, also called the keynote.

Transcription A composition originally written for one medium that has been transcribed for another.

Tremolo (1) The rapid repetition of a single note a number of times. (2) The rapid alternation between two different notes.

Triad A chord consisting of three tones.

Tritone The interval made up of three whole tones, also called the augmented fourth.

Tuning (temperament) A system of determining the intervals of the octave. Various methods are known as Pythagorean, just intonation, mean-tone, and equal-tempered.

Tutti Marking in a score that indicates entrance of all instruments or voices after a solo passage.

Twelve-Tone Music Music based on serial treatment of the twelve chromatic scale degrees. *See* Serial Composition

Vibrato A minute fluctuation of pitch both below and above the tone for the purpose of tonal coloring.

Virtuoso A performer with superior technical facility.

Index

late Middle Ages, 27
post-World War II era, 212–13
in Renaissance, 45
in Romantic period, 137–38
Function of Set Structure in the Twelve-tone System (Babbitt), 233
Furtwängler, Wilhelm, 184
Fux, Johann Joseph, **110**

Gabrieli, Andrea, **64**, 65
Gabrieli, Giovanni, 55, 64, **65–66**
Gaforio, Franchino, **68**
Galant style, 101
Gallican chant, 18
Galway, James, 216
Garden, Mary, 184
Gardiner, John Eliot, 218
Garfunkel, Art, 248
Gaspard de la nuit (Ravel), 194
Gavotte, 93
Gayle, Crystal, 250
Gazette Musicale (journal), 170, 171
gazza ladra, La (Rossini), 154
Gebrauchsmusik, 187
Gebrauchsmusik (Hindemith), 200, 206
Geistliche Konzerte, 86
Geminiani, Francesco, 75, **111**
General Booth Enters Heaven (Ives), 194
General History of Music, A (Burney), 132
General History of the Science and Practice of Music, A (Hawkins), 132
Genres, influence of, 210
Gentry, Bobbie, 250
Geographic location, influence of, 4
German opera, 89, 147, 154
German Protestant Chorales, 56–57
Gershwin, George, 178, **201**, *201, 202,* **203,** 246, 250
Gesamtkunstwerk (unified art work), 161
Gesang der Jünglinge (Stockhausen), 227
Geschichte der Musik (Ambros), 171–72
Gesualdo, Don Carlo, 57, **66**
Getz, Stan, 244, 250
Gianni Schicchi (Puccini), 167
Giant Steps (Coltrane), 248
Giasone (Cavalli), 99
Gigue, 93
Gilels, Emil, 216
Gillespie, "Dizzy," 248, 250
Giovanni Sammartini, **126**
Girl Crazy (Gershwin), 203
Giulio Cesare (Handel), *88,* 107
Give My Regards to Broadway (Cohan), 247
Glagolitic Mass (Janáček), 189
Glareanus, Henricus, **68**
Glass, Philip, 214, **230**
Glockenspiel, 255
Glogauer Liederbuch, 61, 69

Gloria tibi Trinitas (Taverner), 61
Gluck, Christoph Willibald, 103, 120, 121, **126,** 129, **131–32,** 206
Gnosiennes (Satie), 191
Goldberg Variations, The (Bach), 106
Goliards, 20
Gong, 255
Goodman, Benny, 243, 248, 250
Górecki, Henryk, **229**
Gorgia, 83
Gossett, Phillip, 234
Götterdämmerung (Wagner), 161
Gould, Glenn, 216
Gounod, Charles, 148, **162**
Gouts réunis, Les (Couperin), 101
Gradus ad Parnassum (Fux), 110
Graham, Martha, 213
Grainger, Percy Aldridge, 185
Grand opera, 146–47
Grand traité d'instrumentation et d'orchestration modernes (Berlioz), 157
Grateful Dead, 239, 250
Graupner, Johann, 176
Grave, 84
Gravicembalo. *See* Harpsichord
Greatest Jazz Concert Ever (Parker/Gillespie/Mingus/Powell/Roach), 248
Green, Bud, 247
Gregorian chant, 18
Gregorian Chant (Apel), 206
Gregory (Pope), *16,* 18
Grieg, Edvard, **166**
Ground, 101
Grove, George (Sir), **172**
Grundlage einer Ehren-Pforte (Mattheson), 111
Gubaïdulina, Sofia, **229**
Guerre, Elisabeth-Claude Jacquet de la, **101**
guerre, La (Janequin), 64
Guidonian Hand, 18, *19,* 22, *23*
Guillaume Tell (Rossini), 154
Guitar, 252
Gurre-Lieder (Schoenberg), 192
Gymnopédies (Satie), 191

Habá, Alois, 221
Haitink, Bernard, 217
Haley, Bill, 250
Halle, Adam de la, **39**
Hamilton, Nancy, 247
Hamlisch, Marvin, 248
Handel, George Frideric, 84, *88,* 101, **106–7,** *108,* 143, 148, 172
Handy, W. C., 241, 247, 249
Hanslick, Eduard, **172**
Hanson, Howard, 200, **233**
Harburg, E. Y., 247